Dream Projects

in Theatre, Novels and Films

Dream Projects

in Theatre, Novels and Films | *The Works of Paul Claudel, Jean Genet, and Federico Fellini*

YEHUDA MORALY

TRANSLATED BY MELANIE FLORENCE
EDITED BY DOV KAROLL

sussex
ACADEMIC
PRESS
Brighton • Chicago • Toronto

Copyright © Yehuda Moraly, 2021.

The right of Yehuda Moraly to be identified as Author of this work, Melanie Florence as Translator, and Dov Karoll as Editor, has been asserted in accordance with the Copyright, Designs and Patents Act 1988.

2 4 6 8 10 9 7 5 3 1

First published in 2021 in Great Britain by
SUSSEX ACADEMIC PRESS
PO Box 139
Eastbourne BN24 9BP

Distributed in North America by
SUSSEX ACADEMIC PRESS
Independent Publishers Group
814 N. Franklin Street
Chicago, IL 60610

All rights reserved. Except for the quotation of short passages for the purposes of criticism and review, no part of this publication may be reproduced, stored in a retrieval system, or transmitted, in any form or by any means, electronic, mechanical, photocopying, recording or otherwise, without the prior permission of the publisher.

British Library Cataloguing in Publication Data
A CIP catalogue record for this book is available from the British Library.

Library of Congress Cataloging-in-Publication Data
To be applied for.

Hardcover ISBN 978-1-78976-036-1
Paperback ISBN 978-1-78976-088-0

Typeset & designed by Sussex Academic Press, Brighton & Eastbourne.
Printed by TJ International, Padstow, Cornwall.

Contents

Foreword by Cyril Aslanov — vi
Acknowledgments — x
The Illustrations — xii

Introduction — 1

CHAPTER ONE
A Dialogue Long Dreamt Of — 8

CHAPTER TWO
A Triply Murderous Work — 34

CHAPTER THREE
A Metaphysical 'James Bond Film' — 62

Conclusion — 104

Notes — 127
Bibliography — 141
Filmography, Iconography and Unpublished Texts — 148
Index — 150

Foreword by Cyril Aslanov

The concept of *dream project* is ontologically connected with the very essence of novel writing, play writing and movie making. Indeed, until the book is printed, the play staged, and the movie produced, every draft, every play text and every scenario may be considered nothing more than a dream project, a sketch that the lunatic author could at any minute burn, or delete from the memory of his computer. Even in our age of digitalized literary production, there is still a moment when the text ceases to be a draft: either with the printing and diffusion of the printed matter or with the virtual publication as a PDF format.

For plays, the question of the boundary between the draft and the completion of the work, something that does not belong to dream anymore, is harder to define inasmuch as the history of drama is full of plays that were written but never really destined for the stage. Claudel himself, one of the three authors with whom Yehuda Moraly deals in his *Dream Projects,* did not manage to see the performance of the integral version of his *Soulier de satin (The Satin Slipper).* The first attempt to stage that monstrous drama in 1943 was a considerably reduced adaptation of the whole, so that from Claudel's perspective even *The Satin Slipper* can be considered a kind of dream project whose potential started to be actualized a long time after the author's death in 1955.[1]

What makes Moraly's study so fascinating is the fact that it bestows a semblance of existence on aborted works, leading the reader to the mental exercise of imagining what the fourth, ghost part of the envisaged *Coûfontaine* tetralogy would have looked like, if Claudel had written it and committed it to the stage. In a certain sense Moraly helps us share the dream of the playwright who aspired to transform his trilogy into a tetralogy. The subtle difference between a real trilogy and a dream tetralogy is found later in the book, not in the chapter dedicated to Claudel, but in the chapter on Genet. There Moraly reminds us that "the trilogies of the Greek dramatists are known to be in fact tetralogies". For someone like Claudel who translated Aeschylus's *Tetralogy* in 1894[2] and who was haunted by the grandiose Greek dramatist, it is clear that a trilogy could be completed only on the condition that it was followed by a satyric drama able to transform the trilogy into a tetralogy. However, this transformation never came about, perhaps because the intended fourth part of the projected tetralogy was far from being a satyric drama. Hence the necessity of leaving the fourth part of the tetralogy as a draft in a drawer or as a 'ghost' part.

The boundaries between real and dreamt work are so blurred that sometimes what is overtly considered an unrealised project is in fact much closer to the reality of the tangible work than the author himself would have been able to conceive. In the second chapter of *Dream projects*, Moraly reaches the conclusion that Jean Genet's dreamt framework *La Mort* (*La Mort* I as a prose work and *La Mort* II as a series of plays) was partially fulfilled, since the tetralogy consisting of *Les Bonnes, Le Balcon, Les Nègres, Les Paravents* is actually a significant part of the projected *La Mort* II. In other words, the phantasmatic quest for the fulfilling of a dreamt work may actually lead to the emergence of a concrete work as in the case of Proust whose *In Search of Lost Time* speaks about the impossibility of writing a book until the last words of the seventh and final volume of the whole heptalogy (– *dans le Temps*) reveal that this account of the allegedly failed attempts to write an impossible *magnum opus* is itself that *magnum opus*. Incidentally, in the second chapter of *Dream Projects*, Moraly stresses Genet's debt to Proust who might have inspired in him also the awareness that a dream project may prove to be less dreamt than one might have expected.

The third and last panel of the triptych is a fascinating study of Fellini's "phantom film" *Il viaggio di G. Mastorna, detto Fernet* (*The Journey of G. Mastorna*), a never filmed movie projected during the years 1965–66. As Moraly stresses, *Il viaggio di G. Mastorna* is comparable to a ghost in more than one way. First of all, it is the phantasmagory of a chaotic afterlife more similar to the 1969 *Fellini Satyricon* than to Dante's *Divine Comedy*. Secondly, as Moraly convincingly demonstrates, the "phantom film" continued to haunt Fellini's subsequent, completed productions as an everlasting source of inspiration. It is also quite obvious that the third chapter is the centre of gravity of *Dream Projects*, the peak in comparison to which the first chapter dedicated to Claudel's closure of the Coûfontaine cycle and the second one dealing with Jean Genet *La Mort* I and *La Mort* II are only warm-up exercises.

And indeed, a re-reading of the two first chapters in the light of the third reveals that beyond the issue of dreamt plays or ghost movies, there is another leading thematic in Moraly's book, namely the relationship between death and artistic creativity. This special connection between death and artistic creation is not only due to the fact that the deaths of Claudel, Genet and Fellini, respectively, interrupted their projects. In

Fellini's case, especially, it has also to do with the temporary death of inspiration that affected the maestro after the tremendous successes of *La Dolce vita, Le Notti di Cabiria* and *Otto e mezzo*. However, since the failure of *Il viaggio di G. Mastorna* was an everlasting store of motifs and ideas for other highly successful movies in Fellini's filmography, the apparent death of inspiration could be considered as a springboard toward another phase in the Maestro's career. In other words, what seems to be the death of inspiration was in fact the discovery of the potential of the idea of death as a source of living inspiration.

I would like to add a philological argument in order to reinforce the importance of the relationship between the macabre infatuation with the grotesque representation of the afterlife and the almost positive effect drawn for those gloomy phantasmagories. The key to this paradoxical reassessment of death is provided by the second name of the protagonist: *Mastorna*. This name that apparently sounds very Italian does not actually exist in the Italian onomasticon. However, it might sound familiar to anyone familiar with the Etruscan civilisation, or more precisely with the Etruscan substrate of archaic Rome. Indeed, *Mastorna* is a slight variation of *Mastarna*,[3] the Latinized form of Etruscan *macstarna/ macstrna*, a common name whose original meaning was "dictator" or maybe "magistrate". Whatever its signification might be, *Mastarna/ Macstarna/ Macstrna* was thought to be the Etruscan name for Servius Tullius, the sixth king of Rome who reigned from 575 BCE until his assassination in 535 BCE.

Thus, the protagonist of Fellini's grotesque afterlife fresco bears a slightly Italianized Etruscan name as if this onomastic twist were hinting at the legacy of the Tyrrhenian civilization that left a deep imprint on the origins of Rome in spite of the efforts of ancient Roman historiography to depict the Etruscans as alien enemies. Moreover, our knowledge of the Etruscan world has something to do with a certain aestheticization of death. Firstly, this civilization was annihilated by the expansion of Rome. Secondly, the scarce knowledge we have of the extinct Etruscan language, whose last speaker passed away around 20 CE, mainly consists of the obituary formulas engraved on funerary steles. Finally, Etruscan art familiarized us with a serene approach to death: as the dead couples represented on the two terracotta Sarcophagi of the Spouses found in Caere (Cerveteri) and dated to the end of the sixth century BCE have that inimitable Etruscan smile which gives the impression that in the Etruscan worldview, the afterlife was far from being sad or gloomy.[4] The Etruscan-like name Mastorna of the protagonist of *Il viaggio di G. Mastorna* suggests that Fellini relies on the Etruscan approach to death and afterlife. He even takes this state of mind further inasmuch as for him the afterlife is able to raise not only a mysterious Etruscan smile but also a farcical Italian laugh.

1   Antoinette Weber-Caflisch, "Claudel en son temps : *Le Soulier de satin*," in : Luc Fraisse (ed.), *L'histoire littéraire à l'aube du XXIe siècle. Controverses et consensus*, Presses Universitaires de France, Paris, 2015, pp. 293-315.
2   Raymond Trousson, "Paul Claudel traducteur de *L'Orestie*," *Bulletin de l'Association Guillaume Budé*, 4e série, no. 4 (décembre 1965) : 489-501.
3   Mauro Cristofani (ed.), *Dizionario della civiltà etrusca*, Giunti Martello, Florence, 1985, p. 169 (s.v.).
4   Larissa Bonfante, "Daily Life and Afterlife," in: Larissa Bonfante (ed.), *Etruscan Life and Afterlife: A Handbook of Etruscan Studies*, Wayne State University Press, Detroit, 1986, pp. 232–278.

Acknowledgements

I would like to begin by paying tribute to the memory of Anne Pétrof who, back in 1970, set me off on the path leading to this book. Anne was the partner of Bernard Frechtman, Jean Genet's agent and translator, and very kindly gave me access to the archives left by Frechtman after his death. I was thus able to read the letters, then unpublished, from Genet to Frechtman and to appreciate the importance for him of his great project, *La Mort* (*Death*). She later showed me manuscripts (still unpublished to this day), such as *Peur de mourir* or *Les Folles*, which are also linked to different stages of the dream project, unfinished but key to the entire work. The following year, Renée Nantet, the daughter of Paul Claudel, allowed me to consult the manuscript of *On répète Tête d'or* at the Société Paul Claudel; this was also unpublished at that time. I felt that this work served as a clear expression of the dialogue between Judaism and Christianity, so central in Claudel's work — and especially in the work through which I discovered Claudel, *La Sagesse ou la Parabole du Festin*, in the unforgettable production by Victor Garcia (1968–1969).

In 2000, in Rome, Umberto Rondi, the son of Brunello Rondi, one of Fellini's screenwriters, gave me the screenplay for *Il viaggio by G. Mastorna* with Fellini's handwritten corrections. Gianfranco Angelucci helped me with his valuable advice. Milo Manara gave me permission to reproduce some drawings from his comic strip. Maite Carpio sent me her film *Il misterioso viaggio di Federico Fellini*, Gilles Blanchard – his *Tête d'or*. Thanks as well to Antonis Daglidis, Vincent Pontet, Louise Quignon, Philippe Szpirglas, Jeanne and Marie Vitez, who granted me the rights to use their photographs. I would also like to acknowledge the Schoenberg family, and Belmont Music Publishers of Los Angeles, for approving my use of Schoenberg's blue self-portrait. Joel Klein of the Huntington Library (San Marino, CA), also deserves appreciation for sending me Newton manuscripts related to his Temple research.

Thanks are due also to Hava Aldouby, Rachel Azoulay-Shor, Dov Belz, Wendy Benhaïm, Nelly Ben-Israel, Gaby Bensimhon, Samuel Blumenfeld, Mimmo Cattarinich, Florence Colombani, Editions Sonatine, Michèle Fingher, Olivier Mergault, Marie-Victoire Nantet,

Acknowledgments

Françoise Ploquin, Maurizio Presutti, Marie Rémond, Charlotte Szlovak and Philippe Zard.

For the English version, I would like to thank Anthony Grahame, Editorial Director at Sussex Academic Press, for accepting the text for publication, Melanie Florence for her elegant translation, and Dov Karoll for his careful editing, as well as Yair Davidson, John London and David Maskell for their assistance

And, of course, thank you to everyone around me, my mother, my wife and my children without whom none of my work would be possible.

The Illustrations

The two cover illustrations are taken from a graphic roman published in 1992 by Fellini and Milo Manara based on the script *Il viaggio di G Mastorna*, a film dreamt but never accomplished, which is analyzed in this book. The front illustration shows Mastorna searching for his room in the land of the Dead, and the back represents a woman in the throes of giving birth. The search and the struggle of artistic creation are the main themes of this book, focusing on the labor pains of artists as they struggle with the creation of their ultimate work of art, a Dream Work that they will never complete.

The illustrations are placed within the chapers. Plates 1–7 relate to CHAPTER ONE; and likewise, TWO, 8–20; THREE, 21–31; and the CONCLUSION, 32–40.

The Author and Publisher have made every effort to identify, locate and contact all rightsholders for third-party illustrative material before publication. If we are notified of any omissions or mistakes, the Publisher will revise these at the earliest opportunity.

I will go further and say: **the** Book, convinced as I am that there is only one, attempted unwittingly by whoever has written, even the Geniuses. The Orphic explanation of the Earth, which is the sole duty of the poet and the literary *jeu* par excellence.
>
> Letter from Mallarmé to Verlaine on 16 November 1885,
> in Stéphane Mallarmé, *Correspondance (1871–1885)*,
> Gallimard, Paris, 1965, pp. 301–302.

There is your work – a voice said to me.
And I saw all I had not done.
And I knew ever more clearly that I was not he who had done what I have done – rather, I was he who had not done what I had not done.
>
> Paul Valéry, Cahiers/Notebooks. Translated and edited by
> Brian Stimpson, Paul Gifford, Robert Pickering et al.,
> Peter Lang, New York, 2000–2010, v. 5, p. 526.

Introduction

In his short story *Le Chef d'oeuvre inconnu* (*The Unknown Masterpiece*, 1832) Balzac depicts the young Nicolas Poussin, at the start of his career, coming to visit a famous painter, François Porbus. In the latter's studio he meets an enigmatic old man, Maître Frenhofer, a great expert on painting, who launches into a learned critique of one of Porbus's paintings. Maître Frenhofer is not only a great theoretician but also an outstanding artist who succeeds in bringing to life the painting he criticises with only a few touches of the paint brush.

Arriving at Maître Frenhofer's house, Nicolas Poussin discovers wonderful paintings which are nothing, says the mysterious artist, compared with his great work, *La Belle Noiseuse*, a picture he refuses to show anyone because he regards it as still unfinished:

> 'Show you my work?' exclaimed the old man, in consternation. 'No, no, I must still perfect it. Yesterday, towards evening, I thought that I had finished. Her eyes seemed moist, her flesh stirred. The locks of her hair waved freely. She was breathing! Although I managed to use a flat canvas to depict the relief of nature in the round, this morning by the light of day I discovered my error.[…] Just think, too much knowledge, like too much ignorance, leads to a dead end. I have such doubts about my work!' […] 'I've been working on this for ten years now, young man, but what are ten short years when the problem is a struggle with nature?'[1]

Three months later, *La Belle Noiseuse* is still not finished. Maître Frenhofer is going through a period of deep discouragement.

> The poor man was quite simply worn out from trying to finish his mysterious painting.[2]

When Porbus and Poussin are finally allowed to enter the studio they see masterpieces. However, the old man tells them, these are only sketches for *La Belle Noiseuse*, failures. When Maître Frenhofer eventually shows them the picture he has been working on day and night for ten years, all they can see is a jumble of lines.

'Do you see anything?' Poussin asked Porbus.

'No. And you?'

'Nothing. [...] All I can see in it is a confused mass of colours inside a multitude of weird lines, a wall of paint.'[3]

The story ends tragically. Unable to finish his painting, which he has 'perfected' to the point where it is only a confused mass of colours, Maître Frenhofer burns his entire works and kills himself.

Other fictional narratives, dramas and films depict an artist at the mercy of a work he is unable to complete; constantly deferred and failed attempts bring him to the verge of death or madness. The most famous is, of course, Proust's *À la recherche du temps perdu* (*In Search of Lost Time*). The whole series of volumes gives us a Narrator who dreams of writing a sublime work, which, however, he is always unable to create. Only at the end of the sequence, in the very last lines of *Le Temps retrouvé* (*Time Regained*), during the party given by Gilberte de Saint-Loup, does he find the way to write this work, which turns out to be the very one we have just read.

Federico Fellini – or, more accurately, his screenwriter Ennio Flaiano who had worked on a film adaptation of *À la recherche* – adopts this same formula for the celebrated *Otto e mezzo* (*Eight and a Half*, 1963). Throughout the film the director Guido Anselmi keeps striving unsuccessfully to write the screenplay for a film whose sets are already built and actors already under contract. Just as in *À la recherche*, we have to wait until the end for Guido to find a way of realising his work, which is of course the one we have just been watching.

In Louis Malle's *My Dinner with André* (1981) the theatre director André Gregory goes to the Sahara to create a stage production of *Le Petit Prince* (*The Little Prince*). He is unable to do so. The whole film relates the period of artistic and personal crisis which brings him to the edge of insanity.

In real life, too, artistic creation frequently, if not – at some point or another – inevitably, entails battling with a work dreamed of but which remains forever unrealised. My aim in this study is to demonstrate that this is a kind of law.

Oftentimes, an artist dreams of a project, starting and then abandoning it, taking it up again, only for this dream project to remain forever out of reach. In *Mallarmé et le mystère du "Livre"* (Mallarmé and the Mystery of the "Book") Éric Benoit traces the history of the versions of the 'livre total', the writing of which occupied Mallarmé from 1866 until 1892, before he destroyed all the drafts. At the outset in 1866 Mallarmé is clearly full of enthusiasm:

Introduction 3

I have laid down the foundations of a magnificent work. Every man has a Secret inside him, many die without finding it, and will never find it because once they are dead it will no longer exist any more than they will. I have died and been resuscitated with the jewelled key to my final spiritual casket. It is up to me now to open it in the absence of any borrowed impression. It will need twenty years during which I will cloister myself up inside myself, renouncing all publicity but reading it to my friends. I am working at everything at one time, or rather I mean that everything is so well ordered inside me that now as a sensation occurs it is transfigured and of its own accord places itself in such or such a book or poem. Once a poem is ripe it will come away. You will observe that I am imitating the law of nature.[4]

The first sketch of these 'three verse poems and four prose poems on the spiritual conception of *le néant*'[5] was finished the following year in 1867. Mallarmé appears extremely satisfied with it:

Yesterday I finished the first draft of the work, perfectly set out and imperishable, if I do not perish. I contemplated it with neither horror nor ecstasy and, closing my eyes, I saw that it was. The Venus de Milo [...], Leonardo's Mona Lisa seem to me, and are, the two great scintillating apparitions of Beauty on this earth – and this Work, such as I dream of it, the third. [....] Once the work is complete, I do not mind about dying; quite the contrary, I shall need so much rest.[6]

Mallarmé did not publish the text, however. Almost twenty years later he was to write to Verlaine:

I have always dreamed of and attempted something else, with the patience of the alchemist, prepared to sacrifice to it all vanity and all satisfaction, the way people used to burn their furniture and roof beams to feed the furnace of the Grand Oeuvre. What exactly? It is hard to say: a book, quite simply, in many volumes, a book which would be a book, architectural and premeditated, not a collection of chance inspirations, no matter how wonderful ... I will go further and say: **the** Book, convinced as I am that there is only one, attempted unwittingly by whoever has written, even the Geniuses. The Orphic explanation of the Earth, which is the sole duty of the poet and the literary *jeu* par excellence [...].
 I here confess my vice, laying it bare, dear friend, a vice which I have rejected a thousand times, my spirit weary and bruised. I am possessed by it, however, and perhaps I shall succeed, not in creating this work in its entirety (I do not know who one would have to be to do that) but in

> showing one fragment completed, in allowing its glorious authenticity to gleam in but one place, indicating all the rest for which one life would be insufficient. To prove by the completed segments that this book exists and that I have known that which I shall not have been able to complete.[7]

At a later date the project developed in the direction of 'lectures'.

> First of all, a word about the grand project mentioned for this year on my card. My dear fellow, I shall be appearing in public towards October, you understand, to perform a juggling act with the contents of a book: it would take infinitely too long to talk about this in ink.[8]

In the autumn of that year, 1888, the project was postponed to the following year. Paul Valéry recalls 'the room in the rue de Rome where behind an old tapestry there lay until his death, at which point they were to be destroyed, the packets of his notes, the secret material for his great unrealised work'.[9]

Ten years later, before his death, Mallarmé was indeed to ask that all the notes for his great unrealised work be destroyed. To Henri de Régnier he writes:

> You shall come to Valvins and we shall dig a hole in the middle of a field and bury all this sorrowful paper. We shall make a tomb for all this paper which contains so much of my life.[10]

The example of Mallarmé's book is famous but an examination of the artistic adventure of a creator (poet, dramatist, painter or film maker) often reveals the existence of a similar project, dreamed of for a long time and forever uncompleted. In the monologue of Trigorin, the writer in *The Seagull*, we can see traces of Chekhov's longing for the narrative work he always dreamed of but was never able to write. In order to realise this book, which was to have been his masterpiece, Chekhov would travel to the depths of human misery, the penal colony of Sakhalin. The outcome was disappointing but this descent into hell left its mark on his entire creative work. Are not his plays and short stories, like the book about the penal colony, an attempt to express absolute suffering? Similarly, on the morning of the day he died, Pirandello was still thinking about the décor for *The Mountain Giants*, the play he worked on over a long period from 1928 to 1936 without finishing it. To his favourite interpreter of his works, Marta Abba, he writes 'I truly believe I am in the process of writing [...] my masterpiece'.[11] And his son testifies to Pirandello's final artistic efforts, which went towards completing this play:

My father [...] was haunted by these phantoms for almost the entire second-last night of his life, so much so that the next morning he told me he had had to undergo the horrendous effort of composing the whole third act in his head and that, now all the difficulties were resolved, he hoped to be able to rest a little, particularly as he was now happy that immediately he was recovered he could write down in a few days all that he had conceived during these hours.[12]

It might well be then that an artist's dream project constitutes the centre, the key, to his oeuvre. The unfinished project of Mallarmé's *Livre* illuminates the poet's undertaking far better than his published poetry. First it is necessary to do what was done in the case of Mallarmé: reconstruct the projects and their evolution with the help of notes, drafts, interviews and letters. Then they must be considered alongside the rest of the published works to show how the unfinished project sheds light on the meaning of all the others.

In this study I shall make use of three drafts by three artists on whom I have already worked. Paul Claudel never succeeded in his intention to add a fourth part to his Coûfontaine trilogy which he considered incomplete: this would have been a dialogue between a blind Jewish mother and a daughter who had taken the veil. The *Journal* reveals him about to be able to write this dialogue, and his works contain many echoes of it, equally unfinished.

Jean Genet spent almost twenty years, 1948 to 1967, contemplating a project, *La Mort (Death)*, working on it non-stop, without publishing it. Sartre, at the conclusion of his 1952 *Saint Genet, comédien et martyr* (*Saint Genet, actor and martyr*), announces the new book.[13] Two years later, in 1954, Genet published *Fragments* of his great work in *Les Temps Modernes*, describing its principal aspects.[14] Correspondence with his agent and translator Bernard Frechtman reveals the evolution of the project, some drafts of which survive, in addition to the *Fragments*. Genet was not to finish the text but an understanding of the uncompleted project sheds light on his dramatic works as well as on his theoretical or political writings.

In Fellini's case, the twists and turns in the long-delayed shooting of the *Viaggio di G. Mastorna (The Journey of G. Mastorna)* have passed into legend. In *Otto e mezzo* (1963), Fellini depicted a film director who was unable to make a film whose actors were already signed up and huge sets already built. A few years later real life imitated fiction. Fellini collaborated with Dino Buzzati and Brunello Rondi on a screenplay about the realm of the dead (*Il viaggio di G. Mastorna*). Just as in the imaginary scenario in *Otto e mezzo*, the preparations for shooting are very well advanced. The enormous sets are ready. Thousands of costumes have been made. The actors' contracts are signed. And then to the despair of producer Dino De Laurentiis, Fellini abandoned the project.

The film maker was to return often to the *Viaggio di G. Mastorna* without ever succeeding in finishing it. He rewrote the screenplay with other screenwriters, Bernadino Zapponi and Tonino Guerra. The American film director Mike Nichols offered him a million dollars for the screen rights. Fellini refused because he still believed he would one day be able to make it himself. In his final months he even agreed to its becoming a graphic novel by Milo Manara, in which we see the start of the great work which meant so much to Fellini but which he never managed to complete.

There survive from the project the screenplay published after Fellini's death by his biographer, Tullio Kezich (*Il viaggio di G. Mastorna*, Bompiani, 1995), a lengthy letter-synopsis reproduced in a book by Dario Zanelli, *L'inferno immaginario di Federico Fellini*, an earlier version of the script – kindly shown to me by Brunello Rondi's son, Umberto Rondi – and a short film Fellini made for American television, *Fellini: a Director's notebook* (1969) in which he recounts his strange creative adventure. A film by Maite Carpio, *Il misterioso viaggio di Federico Fellini* (2003), brings together interviews with some of the collaborators on the unfinished project. In June 2013 Florence Colombani made a programme for France-Culture devoted to the *Voyage de G. Mastorna* in which she interviews French experts on Fellini and the artist Milo Manara. In September 2013 the publisher Sonatine brought out a slightly fictionalised version of the screenplay, with a preface by Aldo Tassone and an afterword by Ermanno Cavazzoni. The same year, *The Journey of G. Mastorna: The Film Fellini Didn't Make* was published in English with a preface by Peter Bondanella along with extensive commentary by the English translator, Marcus Perryman.

For each of the three projects my approach will be the same. First I will attempt to reconstruct the different stages of the unfinished work with the aid of drafts and testimony. The reconstruction allows us to witness the process of creation itself, from the birth of the idea through its ripening to the different versions of the project and then to its abandonment, or sometimes its abandonments since the author may come back to the project from a different angle before leaving it once more.

Next I will trace direct echoes of the project in the overall *oeuvre*, the recurrence of images and themes. Finally I will attempt the most difficult part: establishing a link between the abandoned project and the overall work, thereby shedding new light on this.

It may seem surprising that creative figures as different as Claudel, Genet and Fellini should appear alongside one another. However, I draw on the theatre, literature and cinema with the sole purpose of providing examples of the hypothesis I am trying to prove: namely that an artist's dream project, the one they long to produce and always abandon, is at the centre of a creative adventure which may well by its very nature be inexpressible.

CHAPTER
1
A Dialogue Long Dreamt Of

Israel is a unique people whose destiny and importance are unique in the eyes of God. I grasped that from the very day of my conversion when, on leaving Notre-Dame, I opened the Bible in two places: in the New Testament, the story of the pilgrims on the road to Emmaus taught me that the key to the Scriptures was to be found in the Old Testament. When I opened that, it gave me the marvellous chapter in Proverbs where I heard Wisdom calling me [...]. From the Old Testament I learned that it was the key to the New and that the key had been given into the hands of Israel.

Paul Claudel, "Entretiens avec André Chouraqui" (Conversations with André Chouraqui), *Cahiers Paul Claudel VII* (Gallimard, Paris, 1968, p. 175)

Architecture, painting, sculpture, literature and politics: the thousands of pages of Claudel's *Oeuvres complètes* cover every field. The ease with which he wrote is renowned. There is one work, however, by which he was haunted for a long period without ever being able to finish it. He wanted to add a fourth play to the Coûfontaine trilogy (*L'Otage, Le Pain dur, Le Père humilié* (*The Hostage, Crusts, The Humiliation of the Father*[1]) which would have depicted Pensée, a blind Jewish woman, conversing with Sarah, her daughter by Orian, the nephew of the Pope, representing Christianity. Claudel's *Journal* shows him ready to write it. During a stormy night in Guadeloupe the entire play came to him in a sort of vision.[2] However this vision did not result in the writing of this work, which was never realised.

This study will attempt to link this project to two others which appear similarly to express the impossible dialogue between Judaism and Christianity. Firstly the metaphysical drama with music, conceived between 1934 and 1938 for Ida Rubinstein and the Paris Opera, was not to be completed in spite of the best efforts of the eminent group working on it: Darius Milhaud, Arthur Honegger, Ida Rubinstein, Audrey Parr and Claudel himself. Later the planned revision of *Tête d'Or* conceived for Jean-Louis Barrault in 1949, *On répète Tête d'Or* (*Rehearsing Tête d'Or*), was finally abandoned as well.

The impossible fourth part of the Coûfontaine cycle

A central factor in the development of Claudel's ideas on theatre were his translation and production of the *Oresteia* of Aeschylus. In 1894, in Boston, he translated the *Agamemnon*, using a revolutionary approach which aimed to convey not only the meaning of the words but also their music. In 1913 for Wolf Dohrn and the Festival Theatre at Hellerau he resumed his *Oresteia* project and, with nothing but the title *Proteas* as a starting point, composed the fourth part of the translated tetralogy. This was to be a surrealist *bouffonnerie* in the spirit of Aristophanes and Offenbach, parodying the themes of the first three plays. On a trip to Brazil along with musician Darius Milhaud, he and Claudel conceived the music for the trilogy, a mix between speaking and singing. The *Incantations* from *Les Choéphores* (*Incantations* from *The Libation Bearers*), which Milhaud composed during this period to Claudel's dictation, are a fine example of music conceived for the theatre.

Alongside his translation of Aeschylus's cycle, Claudel had the idea of a contemporary trilogy. He applied the structure of the *Oresteia* to a closer historical reality: Restoration France. Like the ancient dramas, the Coûfontaine trilogy would depict the destiny of a family unfolding across several generations. In *L'Otage* (*The Hostage*, 1910) the Pope, held captive by Napoleon, is freed by an exiled noble, Georges de Coûfontaine, who hides him at the home of his cousin, Sygne, who has stayed behind on her own to take care of the family estate, now half ruined. Turelure, a peasant grown rich by the Revolution, learns what illustrious guest the seigneurial domain is harbouring. He proposes a deal to Sygne: if she marries him, he will keep quiet. Sygne who is secretly in love with Georges cannot bear Turelure. In order to save the endangered Pontiff, however, her confessor persuades her to make this immense sacrifice. To save the Pope she will marry Turelure. In the third act, the child she has by this despicable husband has just been born. Georges de Coûfontaine tries to kill Turelure but – making yet another sacrifice – Sygne throws herself between the two men and dies by the bullet intended for the husband she hates so much. In her death throes, with a supreme effort, she makes one last sacrifice, and manages to forgive him.

In the second play of the cycle, *Le Pain Dur (Crusts)*, written in 1913–1914, Turelure has a Jewish mistress, Sichel, formerly a renowned pianist and the daughter of a businessman, Ali Habenichts (which means 'I have nothing' in German). Beneath a likeable exterior she hides a cold and calculating personality. While mistress to the father, she is interested in his son, both as a man and as the bearer of a noble title. Through a cunning scheme she is able to set the son against the father, and mastermind the old man's murder. As is the case with most Jewish characters in French drama of this period, her surface generosity hides a consuming ambition, profound atheism and a complete lack of scruples:

> SICHEL: Oh, I know! I'm a Jewess and I've planned it all out, just how to snare you. Haven't I? You poor, innocent thing! You think I arranged each detail long ago – And suppose I did, what of it?
> Have I so many friends or resources or weapons on which I can count? No one but myself; just myself – and I'm a Jewess! And still that millstone hangs about our necks and still the curse of the world confronts us like a jaw set against us; a jaw we must pry open! Remember for how many centuries we have been cut off from humanity. Remember for how many hundreds of years we have been set apart as a miser sets his gold apart in one side of his purse. When the door is opened, so much the worse for those that let us loose! So much the worse for you, my handsome Captain! I love you, and I'll soon show you that I am the daughter of Hunger and of Thirst! Oh, but you're handsome, and we Jews are not spoiled! At last the door is open! I deny my race; I deny my blood; I loathe and curse the past; yes, I trample it under my feet, I dance on it, I spit at it! Thy people shall be my people and thy God shall be my God! To think that I shall be your wife, oh my beautiful Captain! Wait, and you'll see how useful I shall be to you![3]

After Turelure's death, for which she is partly responsible, Sichel contrives to marry his son, Louis. And the play ends on the terrible vision of the old bronze Crucifix sold by Louis to his Jewish future father-in-law, Habenichts, who scratches it with a key to test the quality of the metal. Sichel, now the Comtesse de Coûfontaine, has only one daughter by Louis de Coûfontaine, Pensée (Thought). Pensée is extremely beautiful but blind, just as the statue of Synagoga with bandaged eyes on Strasbourg Cathedral is blind. In *Le Père humilié (The Humiliation of the Father)*, Pensée follows her father to Rome, where he has been named ambassador, and falls in love with an Italian aristocrat, Orian, the Pope's nephew, by whom she has a child. Orian dies in the war. In an act of self-sacrifice, his twin brother, Orso, states that he is willing to give a name to the child that Pensée bears.

The sacrifice Sygne made in giving herself to the disgusting Turelure in order to save the Pope is not in vain. Two generations later, through

1. Paul Claudel (1868–1955). This poet, playwright and theoretician was also a diplomat who served as French Ambassador to the United States (1928–1933). (Photo: Underwood & Underwood).

2. *Le Pain dur* (*Crusts*) by Paul Claudel is the second part of Claudel's *Coûfontaine* trilogy. This is a set design by André Barsacq for his production, which was performed at Théâtre de L'Atelier (1949).

3. *Le Père humilié* (*The Humiliation of the Father*) is the third part of Claudel's *Coûfontaine* trilogy. The play was staged by Gilles Blanchard in 2020 at the Théâtre National de Bretagne. The poster expresses the link between the divine and the human through a unique version of Michelangelo's painting from the ceiling of the Sistine Chapel. (Photo: Gilles Blanchard).

4. Photo from Gilles Blanchard's production (2020) of *The Humiliation of the Father*, showing Pensée, the blind Jewish woman, who signifies Judaism, seducing Orian, the Pope's nephew. (Photo: Louise Quignon).

5. (left) *Tête d'Or* is a film by Gilles Blanchard. In 2007, Gilles Blanchard set Claudel's symbolist play (1889) in a French prison, with the roles divided between prisoners and professional actors.

6. Gilles Blanchard's *Tête d'Or* (2007). The Princess (Béatrice Dalle) is crucified by the former palace cook, a role played by a prisoner.

7. A page from *On répète Tête d'Or* (*Rehearsing Tête d'Or*). In 1949, Claudel rewrote *Tête d'Or*, a play he had originally created exactly sixty years earlier in 1889.

Orian, the Coûfontaines find themselves once more related to the Pope. This connection was to have been made concrete, shown on stage, in another play.[4] The dialogue between the two religions or, in Claudel's eyes, belief and unbelief, which was begun in *Le Père humilié* was in need of deeper exploration. For the performances of the Coûfontaine cycle at the Théâtre du Vieux Colombier Claudel was to write a preface describing the whole of the cycle and announcing its fourth part:

> This is how the Coûfontaine cycle currently ends but no doubt and as far as I can foresee will someday conclude with another play.[5]

In 1946 when *Le Père Humilié* was performed at the Théâtre des Champs-Elysées, Claudel recalled his intended fourth play:

> In my mind this play [Le Père Humilié] had not exhausted the destiny of a representative lineage. I was waiting for inspiration to bring me a fourth and last episode. The capricious powers which, across the generations, preside over the development of human action from its germ to its outcome, whether in reality or in fiction, refused me such a gift. Many times, and once in particular in Guadeloupe during a night of flooding following a terrible cyclone I believed I possessed an idea. With the dawn, it fled from me.[6]

In 1951 in his *Mémoires improvisés (Improvised Memoirs)* Claudel again mentions the impossible play:

> All I know is that this new drama would have centred on a very elderly Pensée, around 70 let's say, who would have played the role of a Pythia, bringing together in herself both the explanation of all these past upheavals and a view on to the future.[7]

The few indications in Claudel's *Journal* show that he was thinking of a lyric dialogue between two women: a mother, Pensée, who is about to die and her daughter, Sarah, who has become a nun. The dialogue between the mother and daughter is that between two religions or, for Claudel, that between Good (Christianity) and Evil (Judaism), believers and non-believing Christ-killers. But here the opposites are of equal worth. The believer is blessed, as is the non-believer:

> I who find it so hard to resist joy, how could I resist God? Pensée and her daughter (nun). Ah! Too fortunate woman! Those who sit on thrones and are dressed in double vestments, I have spent my life at their feet! Lepers.

And others, yet more fortunate in a paradise of delights [...] Pensée: grapes: reminder of those at his temples in the P[ère] H[umilié]. Do you think that I do not understand you, says Pensée. Y[ou] would be only too happy if y[ou] knew I am listening to y[ou]. Perhaps you would say less. I have spent these years or these centuries not listening to y[ou] so that I could hear [y]ou better. If my heart should forget you, Zion, these sweet words in the days of my childhood, *The Song of Songs*, King David's harp, the Temple of Solomon. End. Blessed be the ears which have heard God. Blessed be the ears which have not heard Him. B[lessed] be this breast. Blessed be this mouth which has received God. Blessed be this mouth which has not received Him. Blessed be this heart, etc. Death. Prayer. At the same time, flashback: Sygne. Le P[ère] H[umilié], the story of Israel, the Rhône region.

Whereupon a bell rings for the Angelus and I kneel naked in this broad bed among the four pillars underneath the mosquito net like Adam among the trees of Paradise. Complete darkness. Then I catch sight of the glass in my watch glinting in the darkness behind the mosquito net [...]. Then daylight comes amidst the wild crowing of the cockerels. Big drops of cold water on my body. The day begins.[8]

Claudel was never to write this dialogue glimpsed during a stormy night in Guadeloupe. Several years later, however, he was to work on other projects in which the dialogue between Judaism and Christianity, religious belief and atheism is simultaneously present and impossible to realise.

Dancing the Bible

For the five years from 1934 to 1938 Claudel was engaged in an ambitious enterprise of drama with music in which the Old and New Testament, Judaism and Christianity are in dialogue. How did this project, which deserves to be better known, come into being? In 1934 the Ohel Theatre, one of the theatrical companies in a renascent Palestine, directed by Moshe Halevy, undertook a tour to Paris with productions whose theatricality we can see in photographs. One of the first was devoted to the dramatic works of Isaac Leib Peretz (1852–1915), the great Yiddish author who wrote many theatrical works. The second was a play by the Russian author Nikolay Alexandrovich Krasheninnikov (1878–1941), *Jacob and Rachel*. There followed Stefan Zweig's *Jeremiah*, *The Book of Esther* by Yehuda Kaddish Silman and *The Good Hope* by Herman Heijermans.

Darius Milhaud spoke enthusiastically about these productions to the dancer and patron Ida Rubinstein. Who was Ida Rubinstein? Having come to Paris with the Ballets Russes – she danced Sheherezade alongside Nijinsky – she left Diaghilev in order to produce her own musical spectacles, in which she herself starred. D'Annunzio and Debussy wrote *Le Martyre de Saint-Sébastien* (*The Martyrdom of Saint Sebastian*) (1911) for her, and Ravel's celebrated *Boléro* (1928) was composed at her request. In the same year (1934) as she was to follow Darius Milhaud's advice and see the performances from young Palestine, she put on a theatrical evening at the Paris Opera, composed of *Sémiramis* (Paul Valéry, Arthur Honegger), *Perséphone* (André Gide, Stravinsky, directed by Jacques Copeau) and *Diane de Poitiers* (Elizabeth de Gramont, Jacques Ibert). After the performance by the Ohel Theatre she suggested to Darius Milhaud that he write a biblical work for her. For the libretto Milhaud immediately thought of Paul Claudel. After initially refusing, Claudel took only a few hours to write *La Sagesse ou la Parabole du Festin (Wisdom or The Parable of the Banquet)*, a new version of a little known text, *La Parabole du Festin*, written in Japan and influenced by Bunraku puppet theatre.

Several months later, in November 1934, Ida Rubinstein suggested that Claudel write another work for the same evening, one in which she would play Joan of Arc, thus displaying to the full, as usual, her talents as actor and dancer. She danced in *La Sagesse* while in *Jeanne d'Arc au bûcher* (*Joan of Arc at the Stake*) she was tied to the stake, reduced only to her voice. This time the music was to be entrusted to Arthur Honegger. In 1938, following the triumphant success of *Jeanne d'Arc au bûcher* in Basle, Ida Rubinstein proposed that Claudel collaborate, this time with Stravinsky, on a text inspired by an apocryphal book of the Bible, *Le Livre de Tobie* (*The Book of Tobit*). In addition Claudel gave Honegger the text of a *Danse des Morts* (*Dance of the Dead*) with words taken from the prophecies of Ezekiel.

This enormous project comprising biblical drama with music was intended for the stage of the Paris Opera. It links the Old and New Testaments. The role of Wisdom comes from *Proverbs* and *The Parable of the Banquet* illustrates a New Testament parable found in two versions, those of Luke and Matthew. A king has prepared a banquet but all the invited guests refuse to attend, even going so far as to kill the messengers. And so the king commands 'Invite anybody!' This parable is the basis for Christianity. Those invited to the great spiritual banquet (the Jews) do not wish to come. Therefore the king of the universe changes his mind. The whole of humanity will be invited (Christianity). And if they do not want to come they will be compelled to do so, using the whip (suffering as teacher). The parable shows the lame and the invalids whipped into taking their seats at the heavenly banquet:

> The Servants dressed entirely in black and wearing black masks who during the whole of the First Part had stayed lying face down on the stage, get up, each one carrying a whip in his hand. [...] Like ferrets in a burrow these servants leap into the cellars and soon we see a pitiful crowd of infirm and lame emerging, and as the Servants drive them on with violent blows from whips, tree branches, goads and bundles of ropes, they clamber on to the stage and join in a dance. [...] Everyone runs and whirls, unable to escape, whipped towards the Banquet Hall. Then gradually order is established. The room is packed full and all the guests neatly arranged on the tiers, leaving a large empty space in front of them. Silence falls.[9]

For Ida Rubinstein Claudel added a female dancing role to his stage tableau. He borrowed from the Old Testament the figure of Wisdom who, in *Proverbs*, invites people to her banquet:

> Wisdom has built her house, she has hewn her seven pillars. She has slaughtered her animals, she has mixed her wine, she has also set her table. She has sent out her servant-girls, she calls from the highest places in the town, 'You that are simple, turn in here!' To those without sense she says, 'Come, eat of my bread and drink of the wine I have mixed. Lay aside immaturity, and live, and walk in the way of insight.'[10]

Through the voice of the Chorus, Wisdom invites Humanity to the great heavenly banquet. But, as in the Gospel parable, no one wants to come. Then Wisdom decides to invite anybody at all. If no one wants to come she will use her whip to compel the guests to sit down to the banquet she has prepared.

The fourth part depicts the banquet itself, the Temple restored and Wisdom seated among the guests:

> The music begins.
> CHORUS. – Wisdom has built herself a house: she has carved the pillars of which there are seven.
> The whole earth had turned to liquid and I was the one who set her pillars firm. Their base is of silver. Their shaft is of pure marble, and on their capitals may be seen a mixture of fillets and pomegranates.

> The stage is completely overrun with craftsmen and –women, masons, carpenters, smiths, painters, sculptors, etc. and people of all races (among them women), all are carrying the tools of their trade.
> WISDOM. (She stands up) – You were slaves to the whip and I have made you servants of music!
> THE CRAFTSPEOPLE (CHORUS) – It is us, us, us, we ourselves who have done that! It is we who have rebuilt Jerusalem.[11]

Claudel's contract with Ida Rubinstein stipulated that he would also be responsible for directing the text. The diplomat had just retired and thus threw himself into his dream of musical sacred drama with great enthusiasm.[12] In June 1935 he had almost daily meetings with Audrey Parr and Ida Rubinstein about the project where the Old and New Testaments were in dialogue (*Proverbs* and *The Gospel*). It is notable that the group behind the project similarly constituted a dialogue between the two religions. Claudel, representing Christianity, and then three Jews, Darius Milhaud, Ida Rubinstein and Audrey Parr, who was of Jewish descent on her mother's side. The dramatist wanted to bring all his team together that summer in a chateau near his own in the Dauphiné:

> I have found a wonderful chateau where we can set up camp, very close to Morestel. It's called the Chateau de Marteray. It's idyllic![13]

This gathering was never to take place, however. Ida Rubinstein did not like the costumes and sets designed by Audrey Parr to Claudel's instructions. She was delighted on hearing *Jeanne d'Arc au bûcher*, but Darius Milhaud's music for *La Sagesse* seemed 'disastrous.'

Moreover, in order to immerse herself in the role of Jeanne, Ida followed Claudel's advice to spend periods at the Convent of Saulchoir. While there she decided to convert. Audrey Parr fell ill. So did Claudel. A doctor diagnosed "severe anaemia resulting from a form of poisoning." Performances of *La Sagesse* were repeatedly postponed and the war put paid to the project altogether. In 1940 Ida Rubinstein fled France in order to escape deportation. And while both during and after the war *Jeanne d'Arc au bûcher* with its Christian inspiration went on to be staged internationally, the biblical and Judaeo-Christian production as conceived by Claudel was never staged. Not only were these four works – *La Sagesse ou la Parabole du Festin, Jeanne d'Arc au bûcher, L'Histoire de Tobie et de Sara, La Danse des Morts* – written with the same person, Ida Rubinstein, in mind, but three of them at least were intended to feature in the same production, inspired both by Jewish sources (*Proverbs, The Book of Tobit*) and by Christian ones (The Gospels).

The failure of the project was due to more than just Ida Rubinstein's conversion and the coming of war. Something in the mixture of sources did not work and the result was less than a masterpiece. This failure which Claudel felt deeply was to lead to a radical change of aesthetic: no more total theatre (cinema, chorus, union of drama and dance etc.). In its place came the human, and only the human. However the notion of a Judeo-Christian dialogue lived on in another project, one which is barely known but extremely exciting, this time intended for Jean-Louis Barrault.

The Son of the Dove and "The Yid from the 127th"

Claudel wrote the first version of *Tête d'Or* (*Golden Head*) at the age of twenty, the second at twenty-six and the third when he was eighty-one. The reasons for the first rewriting were theatrical (tightening up the text, a surer sense of effects). The motivation for the second rewriting, which dates from 1949, was entirely different. His third version of *Tête d'Or* gave him an indirect way of responding to the Holocaust and Nazism. He tried once again to express the dialogue between Judaism and Christianity which he had succeeded in conveying intellectually with *L'Évangile d'Isaïe* (*The Gospel of Isaiah*) (published in 1951 but written earlier) but to which he had not yet managed to give dramatic form in a way he found satisfying.

What happens in *Tête d'Or*, a play both powerful and obscure, written in 1889 by a young man of twenty? It all starts with the sublime monologue by Cébès, declaring the absurdity of all things. Simon Agnel, a peasant, is possessed by a mysterious force. The second act shows him transformed into Tête d'Or, a famous general who has given back his exhausted country the strength to fight. Returning victorious from the war, he kills the old King David in order to take his place and drive out his daughter, the princess. In the third act Tête d'Or's armies have reached the highest point of the Caucasus. There they will be defeated. The wandering princess is hung on a tree by the Deserter, who used to be a cook at the palace. The dying Tête d'Or still has enough strength to rescue the princess and crown her.

From King Saul to Adolf Hitler
The character of Simon Agnel such as he appears in both the 1889 and the 1894 versions contains echoes of many previous literary figures, which have been identified by Pierre Brunel and Michel Lioure: Christopher Marlowe's Tamburlaine, Alexander the Great, Siegfried,

Dionysus, General Boulanger and even an Abyssinian ruler, Menelik, king of Shewa.[14] References to the Old Testament are less obvious. The Princess, in the second act, takes her speech from Wisdom in *Proverbs*. Her father, the King, is called David. And the character of Simon Agnel appears to be inspired by King Saul. This biblical figure has so many points in common with Simon Agnel that it cannot be mere coincidence. Consciously or not, Claudel has in mind the Old Testament which he had begun reading after his mystical revelation of 1886.

The story of Saul unfolds in three distinct places. First there is the field where the herdsman (taller than his companions) will suddenly receive royalty.[15] Then, after the mistake he makes in sparing Amalek, Saul is subject to fits of madness. Only the songs of the future King David are able to calm him. He wanders his palace, just as in the play David the king wanders his. Saul's destiny is to end on a battlefield where the king, having been defeated, throws himself on his sword, and his squire does likewise. These are the same settings and the same situations we find in the play, written at the height of Claudel's religious crisis. In the first act an ordinary man is suddenly chosen by a mysterious force to conquer the world. The prophetic trances to which he is subject in the first version recall those of Saul in the Book of Samuel. Just as Saul initially refuses to become king so Simon refuses to be chosen by the mysterious force. In the second act, Simon, now Tête d'Or, wins the war and David the king wants to give him his daughter, just as in the Bible Saul offers David his daughter Michal's hand in marriage. Saul wants to kill David and Tête d'Or kills the old king, David.

Above all, the deaths of the two kings resemble each other. Saul dies alone, defeated by his enemies, and his squire, seeing the king dead, kills himself.[16] In *Tête d'Or* the squire Cassius tells of the king's defeat before stabbing himself.

Equally, Tête d'Or's blond hair, his hatred of democracy, his violence, his misogyny and his fits, seem to prefigure the blond Nazi warrior. Significantly it was the rights to *Tête d'Or* which Claudel was asked for during the Occupation and he vehemently refused to grant them. He was certain that, in his writing, he had predicted Hitler. For Claudel the poet is a seer:

> The name for poet among the Latins was *vates*, meaning 'prophet'. However prophetic inspiration is only an intensified form of a general phenomenon. Everything happens as if there isn't a man alive, still less a woman, who does not have on his shoulder an invisible genius whispering ideas and impulses to him.[17]

We can see from the two following passages that Claudel in 1949 is fully aware of the parallel to be drawn between *Tête d'Or* – the text he published exactly sixty years previously – and Hitler whose career he had in some way foreseen in 1889. In the first version of the play, Tête d'Or's army has reached 'the edge of Europe,' the scene of the terrible battle which ends both the play and the military campaign of the blond conqueror. The second, 1894, version is more specific:

> The Caucasus. A natural terrace in an elevated position, open towards the North and the East and surrounded by massive trees.[18]

In the spring of 1942, on the borders of Europe, in Russia, in the Caucasus, the German armies suffered their first defeats. In a text written in 1949, for a new edition of *Tête d'Or*, Claudel alludes to the astonishing parallel between the imagined fate of the fictional dictator and real facts. He evokes the fates of conquerors – Alexander, Caesar, Napoleon – obsessed by a desire to own the world:

> The naïve and brutal undertaking always ends in failure. Alexander dies suddenly during a banquet. The Corsican creature is put in a cage where he can indulge his talent for mimicry to his heart's content in front of an audience who have had enough. Caesar was killed by an assassin. And as for the Caucasus ... yes, as for the Caucasus, for the moment it's better not to mention the Caucasus.[19]

The allusion is very obscure. Claudel makes himself clearer in the draft of *On répète Tête d'Or*. When Simon, who is putting on a production of *Tête d'Or* in the prisoner of war camp, reaches the passage in which the Caucasus is mentioned, he remarks:

> S(IMON). All these Pantagouriches and Boutonglozes of misfortune who have done nothing but imitate me without understanding anything at all! I became acquainted with their Caucasus a long time ago. A long time ago it climbed into my imagination, their Caucasus did, not the one from the newspaper but the real one, for real, above all these armed peoples.[20]

The resemblance between Hitler and Tête d'Or was extremely awkward for Claudel. Yet it is undeniable that Simon Agnel, the ordinary man impelled by a mysterious force, seems to prefigure Hitler's career. Appearing suddenly in a society in a state of deep crisis, Tête d'Or – blond like Wagner's Siegfried and the soldiers who were to invade Europe –

sweeps along a nation in decline and seizes power by the sheer assertion of his strength:

> *Tête d'Or.* I shall not fear! But I shall fare forth like the famine and the cyclone! Hate and Anger
> And Vengeance and the frenzied Image of Pain
> March before me, and Hope unveils its solemn face!
> Come! the time commands and the road will no longer be denied.
> I shall march! I shall fight! I shall crush the barrier beneath my conquering feet! I shall break the vain resistance like rotten wood![21]

These lines imagined in 1889 seem subsequently to have been overtaken by reality. If the play had been performed in 1943 as Barrault wished, Claudel would have appeared to have written a justification of Nazism in advance. The same faith in might, the same contempt for everything that the blond force could crush, the same hypnotic grip on a people whose shame was washed away by the warrior Messiahs, the same rejection of democracy. When Claudel refused to grant Barrault the rights to *Tête d'Or* he did not wish to be "laid bare" in this raw play, but it seems likely that his decision was also influenced by political considerations. And when, in 1949, he set his new *Tête d'Or* in a prison camp where there are two characters with Jewish names, he doubtless wished to neutralise the dangerous parallels.

The stages of the creative process

It is possible to reconstruct the different stages of this unfinished, third version with the aid of the information Michel Lioure gives in his edition of its draft.[22]

1. In his preface to the new edition of *Tête d'Or* Claudel puts forward an interpretation of the text which suggests the parallel with Hitler but simultaneously renders it harmless by integrating it into a larger scheme. The desire for invasion which all conquerors have is only the reflection of a higher reality, the desire for the absolute.[23] Only the Princess, who in Claudel's interpretative framework has become the Catholic Church, will be able to satisfy this desire:

> The sun, do you claim that I will be able to grasp it in my two hands? The voice says: You will be, if I give it to you.
> – Who are you?
> And the voice, that of the Princess who was accused in Act Two of the old drama, replies: I am the Catholic Church.[24]

2. The preface is dated 24 September 1949. The work Claudel was doing on *Les fourberies de Scapin* (*The Impostures of Scapin*) at the same time, June to October of that year, gave him the idea of applying the same dramatic scheme to his *Tête d'Or*. *Le Ravissement de Scapin* (*The Rapture of Scapin*) finished on 1 October, shows half-drunk actors performing *Les fourberies de Scapin* in a cabaret beside the Comédie-Française. The first level of theatre (the drunken actors) was to reveal the deeper meaning of the text: the carnivalesque trance from which Theatre springs. Using the same technique of theatre within theatre he would set *Tête d'Or* in a prison camp during the Second World War.

3. On 12 November 1949 Claudel met Barrault and explained his new conception of the play. The prisoners of German prison camp Stalag 27 are rehearsing *Tête d'Or*. The impetus for the performance comes from a strange character with an Aramaic name, Simon Bar Yona, a ward of the Public welfare, who is both director and main character. Barrault must have approved of the idea because the next day, 13 November, Claudel set to work. The stages of the composition may be seen in his *Journal*. In Jewish mysticism, which Claudel discovered through a book by Henri Serouya, *La Kabbale*,[25] he looked for material which would allow him to deepen the Jewishness of his protagonist, Simon Bar Yona. He copied out passages from Ibn Ezra and Nahmanides.

> Ibn Ezra says in his *Book of the Name* that the Whole knows the part by the way of the Whole and not the way of the Part.
> The Seal of Solomon
> 6 7 2
> 1 5 9
> 8 3 4
> 15 in every direction [...], 5 in the centre is the Logos. The other even numbers at the four corners are the four elements.[26]

4. A few days later (it is obvious how much this project meant to him) on 21 November he met Jacques Perret, the author of *Le Caporal épinglé* (*The Elusive Corporal*), who was to provide him with details about life in the prison camps where he had spent two years.

5. On 3 December, while copying out the text of *L'Évangile d'Isaïe*, the writing of which lasted from September 1948 until July 1949, he had an idea which made him resume the composition of *On répète Tête*

d'Or. In his article "*Tête d'Or 1949*" Pierre Brunel suggests that it might well have been the following sentence:

> Yes, who knows whether it didn't take the dreadful pressure of the camps and these people literally jammed, buried, kneaded one into another in order to crack the surface, the envelope separating them to give way, and the soul at last to become accessible to the soul.[27]

On 4 December he began work on Act II. Between Act I (rehearsal, in the camp, of Act I of *Tête d'Or*) and Act II some time has elapsed. Simon Bar Yona, the director and principal actor, has attempted to escape but has been arrested. We see him back in the stalag rehearsing *Tête d'Or*. Initially Claudel had intended to kill off Cébès in both levels of the drama, the production which the prisoners rehearse (play within a play) and in the real world of the camp. The allusions found throughout the draft to Simon's frailty and to his cough seem to suggest that it is not Cébès who will die in the second act but Simon in the third.

6. Claudel copied out the text but stopped in the middle of Act I. This is the sole fragment of text to have been reproduced in the Pléiade edition.

7. A year later on 2 September 1950 he wrote to Barrault explaining the "genesis of the monster"[28] and officially mark, as it were, that he had abandoned the project.

8. A few days later on 24 September 1950, he pasted into his Journal an article from *Paris Match* outlining the central idea of the third version of *Tête d'Or*. Captivity has shown the prisoners the collective meaning of humanity.[29]

Christ and the Synagogue

Who are the Jewish characters in this third version? Claudel is, in a way, returning to the dialogue between Judaism and Christianity which is present in the first version. Simon Bar Yona, the protagonist, has a Jewish name but its translation (son of the Dove) signifies that he represents Christ.

> X: And him as well, what way do they call him Bar Yona, Simon Bar Yona?
> X: Are you a Jew by any chance?
> X: Like the lad who's taken up wi' the role of the Princess. He thinks about nowt else.

X: 'E's not a Jew, 'e's a waiter.
S: Bar Yona, that means son of the Dove in Greek.
I'm no' anybody's son. So Mother Welfare, she thought that 'son of a Dove' was about right as a name for me.[30]

Dramas which make use of the 'play within a play' technique often establish connections between characters on the different levels. Here there are subtle links between Simon Agnel (play within a play) and Simon Bar Yona (play). In the play, Simon Agnel is a leader of men. In the real world of the camp Simon Bar Yona will be the director: he has 'humanity passionately in his fingers like a sculptor the clay or a farmer his animals'.[31] Equally, Simon Bar Yona may represent Claudel himself, justifying this text written exactly sixty years before.

O: Warrior! Tête d'Or.
S: Yes, Leader of gold! Why should I have been bothered by that? Warrior! Tête d'Or. I was seventeen years old.[32]

Above all, however, Simon Bar Yona evokes the figure of Christ. A tuberculosis sufferer with a shaven head, Christ? Claudel intended the comparison as he gives the character several attributes recalling the founder of Christianity. Firstly Simon Bar Yona, 'nobody's son', has never married:

SIMON: And I who was never with a woman. (He spits on the ground). No, I can't say that I've ever had a woman.[33]

The prisoners for whom he sacrifices himself wish to render him Evil for Good and 'get rid of him'.

X: There are some who're talking about a people's tribunal.
X: A sort of council of war where we'd all vote to get rid of him.[34]

And this shepherd of men, nobody's son, a bachelor, dies after a bloody martyrdom (the sufferings of tuberculosis and the blood he coughs) at Easter, like his model.

In particular the explanation Simon Bar Yona gives to the world is faithful to the Gospel message: it is necessary to accept suffering, the sign of atonement and redemption.

Opposite him, there are six actor apostles and "the yid of the 127th" who is to play the Princess of the old drama, the only female role in the play. In *Tête d'Or* the Princess only appears from Act II, in the palace of her father the king, who is facing a war he has little chance of winning. She quotes the speech of Wisdom, the character in *Proverbs* who invites people to the banquet of knowledge. This was the passage at which the eighteen-year-old Claudel opened the Bible after his revelation at Notre-Dame. In his *Mémoires improvisés* (*Improvised Memoirs*) he tells Jean Amrouche this:

> I was extremely struck by the whole magnificent *prosopopeaia* [personification] in *Proverbs* and all the female figures in my subsequent work resemble this discovery to a greater or lesser extent. There is hardly any female figure in my work without one of Wisdom's traits.[35]

In the first two versions of *Tête d'Or* the Princess addresses the sleeping watchers with the same words from *Proverbs*:

> I stand at the crossroads and even in the towns
> I stand in the marketplace and at the banquet's door saying:
> "Who will exchange hands full of blackberries for hands full of gold?
> And with his human heart weigh an eternal love?"[36]

As we have seen, Claudel reused this character for Ida Rubinstein in a work which had remained unproduced, *La Sagesse ou la Parabole du Festin*. When he began work on this third version he intended the Princess to have a role associated with Death, telling Arthur Honegger:

> This will take place in a concentration camp and the Princess will be Death who plays a bugle.[37]

In September 1949, just before he began writing this third version, Claudel had put the final touches to a very precise reading of the play. Tête d'Or's lust for conquest, like that of all conquerors, is merely the reflection of the desire for the infinite. The Princess is the Catholic Church which alone is able to open the gates to the World Beyond to man. She sounds the bugle, evoking the trumpet of the Last Judgement and the resurrection of the dead.

During the writing process everything changed. Who plays this mysterious role of the Princess in the prison camp? A Jewish café waiter. Is he chosen by Simon Bar Yona? Does he select himself? The text contradicts itself on this point. What is certain is that Simon-Claudel (the character and the author) have serious reservations about this waiter, "that other son of the Dove" and that this is very revealing:

X: You're the dove?
S: Yes, that would be me, the gate for you all, if it weren't for that other son of the dove, over there, behind the curtain, busy traversing me.
X: You mean the café waiter? He's really nice.
X: You were the one who chose him to be the Princess.
S(IMON): Then why's he not learning his role instead of cooking up goodness knows what? You can't get him to do any work![38]

Claudel found an elegant solution to the problem of how to show the Princess. Only her face was to be visible through a hole in a prison camp curtain, thus avoiding the cross-dressing which would be out of keeping with the context. Simon-Claudel's reservations about the Jewish waiter, however, were not primarily aesthetic but metaphysical. Between the two sons of the Dove, Christianity (Simon) and Judaism (the waiter) there exists a rivalry. There was no longer any mention of the Catholic Church which, in the initial stages of the rewriting, the Princess was to represent.

Let us return to the expression used by Simon Bar Yona, "Yes, that would be me, the gate for you all, if it weren't for that other son of the dove, over there, behind the curtain, busy traversing me."[39]

One need not be Sigmund Freud to appreciate the sexual connotation of the term 'traverse'. The rivalry is keen and later in his draft Claudel gives a different version of the facts. It is not Simon Bar-Yona who has chosen this dangerous actor to play the Princess. The Jewish waiter has foisted himself on them.

S: Who've you got to be the Princess while I was off somewhere else, busy with you?
X: It's that Yid, the bugler of the 127th.
X: We didn't pick 'im. 'E picked hisself.
X: As soon as 'e'd read the role, That's me, the Princess! 'S what he said. Impossible to take the role off him, 's done nothing but go over the part day and night, with his eyes rolling back in 'is head.
X: And sometimes when we woke, 'e was right there watching us, the bastard.
X: Yup, the gargoyle of Notre Dame.
X: You're not wrong, just like the gargoyle.
X: Haven't you seen the devil as is on the postcards, with 'is head between 'is legs looking at Paris?
S: Looking at Paris is interesting. And the reason he's blocking his ears is so he can't hear the angel behind him and he won't see him coming. You can't do two things at once!

THE VOICE *(behind the curtain)*. That's better.... I can see you better now. I see you all... No longer hid by shade or lighted lamp. It is I. What do you wish? Why have you called me?[40]

The Jewish waiter, the bugler of the 127th chosen by Simon, had been refusing to learn his part. Later on he puts himself forward and becomes obsessed by his role, going over it day and night. The writer, as Claudel knows, "is written" rather than writing. The characters of a play or novel appear to have a surprising independence and insist on going their own way. If, as Claudel states in the new preface of 1949, the Princess was to symbolise the Catholic Church, then why have the role taken by a Jewish café waiter, someone who plays the bugle, maybe the *shofar* or ram's horn? Before Claudel's horrified eyes, the Princess becomes not the Church but the Synagogue. And yet again Claudel tries – once more unsuccessfully – to stage the dialogue between the Old and New Testaments. When it comes to the waiter, Claudel-Simon Bar Yona's attitude is ambiguous. On the one hand, if he makes the Jewish waiter the bugler of the 127th this allows him to introduce the concluding image of the Princess in the bombed prison camp, both summoning the dead and blowing the trumpet (*shofar*) of the Last Judgement. However the waiter is also compared to the gargoyle of Notre-Dame which, like the Jewish people, stops his ears so as not to hear the Angel. The 'people of God killers' refuses to be converted.

The waiter (symbolising Judaism) stands up to the Son of the Dove (symbolising Christianity). Simon is frightened of answering him and loses his strength and confidence when he talks to him. Simon and Claudel wish both to dialogue with the waiter and to suppress his role:

S: Exactly, I'd like to cut out the Princess's role.
X: Good thing too.
THE VOICE *(behind the curtain)*: She's stronger than you are!
X: That bugler's not a fan of yours.
X: You'd think he'd taken the role just to play a trick on you.
X: He says you can whistle for it – he's took on the role and he's not giving it up.
X. That's between you and him.
X: Well then, let's have a little look at your snout.
THE VOICE: Patience.
S: It is I, dear Madam, who take the liberty of asking this of you.
THE VOICE: Soon! A glimpse of the young person will be revealed to you in just a moment, dear Sir.

But you do realise that it's not till Act III that we have our confrontation]?
S(IMON): And in the meantime we shall try to manage without you.[41]

Why does Simon-Claudel dread Act III in particular, where in both versions of the text the Princess has her crown restored after the death of Tête d'Or? If, in the text as it develops in 1949, Simon Agnel symbolizes Christ, and the Princess, played by the Jewish bugler of the 127th, is the synagogue, then Act III sees a reversal of the situation which is unacceptable to Claudel. The Princess (the Synagogue) whom Tête d'Or (Christ) had driven from the palace (the Temple) will, after a long period of wandering (the Diaspora) and great suffering, be crowned by the very one who had deposed her.

Claudel and the Jews: A surprising evolution

The ambivalent attitude of Simon Bar Yona with respect to the Jewish waiter is a reflection of Claudel's attitude towards the Jews. The early Claudel compounds Catholic antisemitism (the Jews are a race of deicides and thus accursed) with a more modern form (the moneyed Jew is destroying society). In 1886, when the young Claudel wrote *L'Endormie (The Sleeping Nymph)* his first play, *La France Juive (Jewish France)* by Drumont had great public success, making it the bestselling book of the nineteenth century. In 1900 Jules Renard evoked Claudel's visceral horror of the Jews "whom he cannot bear to see nor smell."

> Claudel is having lunch. He is talking about the damage the Dreyfus Affair has done to us abroad. This intelligent man, this poet, has an air of the rabid priest and bitter blood. "What about tolerance?" I say to him. "There are houses [i.e., houses of ill repute] for that," he replies. His sister has a portrait of Rochefort in her room and *La Libre Parole (The Free Word)* on the table [...]. He comes back to his horror of the Jews, whom he cannot bear to see nor smell.[42]

La Libre Parole was the newspaper of Drumont, spearhead of antisemitism in France, and the Marquis de Rochefort, whose portrait Camille Claudel had in her room, was an ardent anti-Semite and friend of Drumont.

One might suspect that, faced with Renard, Claudel was pretending to be on the Extreme Right but the letter he sent Péguy ten years later, after reading *Notre Jeunesse (Our Youth)*, was even more blatant:

> This whole part of the book, so beautiful and eloquent, where you talk of the Jews and of Bernard Lazare, could not but elicit my admiration although I am very little inclined towards the arguments and people you support. What a shame it is to find a true Frenchman, a soldier of Saint Louis [...] fighting alongside people not of his race, against his own, alongside wholly primitive people imbued with the divine curse [...]. And I struggle to understand your denial of the Jewish hand in this matter [the Dreyfus Affair]. I have lived in every country in the world and everywhere I have seen the newspapers and opinion in the control of Jews. I was in Jerusalem in 1899 and at the time of the second condemnation I saw the fury of those bugs with human faces who live in Palestine off the raids that others of their race carry out on Christians.[43]

For Claudel, as for Drumont, then, the world seemed to be in the hands of a vampiric race which was sucking the blood of Christians. Imagined at the same period, the vampire-like character of Sichel Habenichts in *Le Pain Dur* (1913) is fascinating but monstrous. The character of Sichel is one of a large family of manipulative Jewish women in literature. In 1898, Gyp's *Israël* depicts Jewesses exploiting aristocrats both financially and physically. In *Le Retour de Jerusalem* (*The Return from Jerusalem*) (1903) Maurice Donnay gives us the daughter of a Jewish banker, Judith Fushiani, who has climbed the social ladder by getting a count to marry her. She loses no time in rejecting him to throw herself into the arms of a married man, Michel. For her, Michel gives up all he has. She will take everything from him – family and honour – and then reject him, loyal only to those of her own race. Claudel's Sichel is no less dangerous. She betrays her elderly lover and then masterminds his murder. Her complete lack of scruples allows her to become the Comtesse de Coûfontaine. In *Le Père humilié* (1916) the blind heroine Pensée, symbolising the blind Synagogue, is pitiable but in *Au milieu des vitraux de l'Apocalypse* (*In the middle of the [stained glass] windows of the Apocalypse*) (1928) Claudel is able to deliver this aberrant interpretation of the star of David, thus reconnecting with his initial attitude towards Israel, a vampiric, satanic and cursed people:

> It is Lucifer's star made of two inextricably interlinked triangles, the dreadful combat with divine justice. It is impossible to contemplate without anguish this figure blocked in all directions, the ascension halted for all eternity by its own fall, this mineral and crystalline hexagon. Rather, when you study these two interpenetrating triangles you think of Isaiah's curse: "I will feed you with your own flesh and make you drink your own

blood as if it were wine." And also, "From the midst of you I will cause a fire to come out and devour you."[44]

Several factors appear to have given rise to Claudel's turning away from antisemitism in the 1930s. In 1931 he discovered the world of Hasidism and the Kabballah through a book by a Jewish convert to Christianity, Jean de Menasce (1902–1973), *Quand Israel aïme Dieu* (*When Israel loves God*). This book made a great impression on him. He recommended it to the Jewish composer Darius Milhaud as well as to 'the Jew of Antwerp', Joseph Schulsinger. Soon Claudel was to bury himself in the exegesis of Old Testament books. The idea of the large scale biblical drama with music he spent the four years from 1934 to 1938 working on may also have helped the rapprochement. Above all in Germany the persecution of the Jews was beginning. There is nothing like a common enemy to engender fellow-feeling. Claudel's protest letter written for the World Congress of Jews is a key text bringing together the Jews and the Catholics in the same persecution, faced with the same resurgence of paganism:

> The abominable and stupid legislation directed against those of your religion in Germany fills me with indignation and horror. Personally I have always counted the Jews as among my best friends and have experienced nothing but the utmost consideration from them.
>
> Furthermore my constant study of the Bible has profoundly convinced me of Israel's importance as regards Mankind. It is Israel who, with heroic courage and intellectual boldness, has always upheld against the power of Rome and the seductions of Greece the idea of a personal and transcendent divinity, superior to all the superstitions of paganism. And it is that very return of paganism in the lowest and most hideous form which is once more coming up against this unshakeable stone.[45]

Both Catholics and Jews were persecuted out of hatred for the divine. In annihilating the Jews the Nazis were trying to destroy Judeo-Christian morality. The Catholics hated the Jews because they had killed Christ. The Nazis hated them because they had created divine morality. Numerous passages from Claudel's *Journal* during the Occupation show him genuinely upset by the sufferings undergone by the Jews. In 1941 he wrote a letter to the Chief Rabbi of France which was given out to the prisoners in Drancy internment camp:

Château de Brangues, Morestel
December 24, 1941, Christmas Eve
Sir,
My good friend Wladimir d'Ormesson has just given me your address. I am keen to write to you to express the disgust, the horror, the indignation, which all good French people and especially Catholics feel towards the iniquities, spoliations and ill-treatment of all kinds, of which our fellow Israelites are currently victims. I have always found in the Israelites not only open minds but generous and delicate hearts. I am proud to have many friends among them. A Catholic cannot forget that Israel is still "the eldest son of the promise" as it is, today, the eldest son of pain. But "Blessed are those who suffer persecution for justice." May God protect Israel in this redemptive path. "I would not eternally be wrathful," said the Lord through the voice of His prophet.
Please accept the expression of my most distinguished feelings.
PAUL CLAUDEL
Ambassador of France

It should be noted that during this period most French intellectuals did not exhibit the same compassion, even in the privacy of their secret diaries.[46] After the war Claudel discovered the full magnitude of the disaster. He saw the creation of the State of Israel, the 'miraculous return', as the work of Providence, and in *L'Évangile d'Isaïe*, which he was writing at the time, expressed the wish to see Israel rebuild the Temple:

How beautiful it would be if the first use Israel made of its restored identity was to rebuild the new Temple at the crossing point of three continents and of three religions, or even simply to take the initiative, to call on the whole Universe to support it in this magnanimous undertaking.[47]

Further on in the same text he addresses the Christian who sulks over the supplanting of Christianity by the Jewish people.

As for you, Mr. Replaced, Mr. Supplanted, don't make that face, don't put on that expression, that vexed, disgusted and discontented air because your brother here was dead and has come back to life: he had perished and has been recovered.[48]

That 'vexed, disgusted and discontented' air is the same as Simon's when faced with the Jewish waiter in the third version of *Tête d'Or*. It may also, at a deeper level, be that of Claudel himself, still at the last ambivalent with respect to Israel. If he wishes Israel to become a sacred bank with the Virgin and her Son as its effigy, he appears nevertheless to remain very alien to the specific nature of Judaism. *L'Évangile d'Isaïe* is contemporary with the writing of *On répète Tête d'Or*. For an artist the true stage is that of the imagination. In order to understand the mystery of Israel better he stages the dialogue between Christ and the Synagogue. And once again, it is a failure.

> Israel is a unique people whose destiny and importance are unique in the eyes of God. I grasped that from the very day of my conversion when, on leaving Notre-Dame, I opened the Bible in two places: in the New Testament, the story of the pilgrims on the road to Emmaus taught me that the key to the Scriptures was to be found in the Old Testament. When I opened that, it gave me the marvellous chapter in *Proverbs* where I heard Wisdom calling me [...]. From the Old Testament I learned that it was the key to the New and that the key had been given into the hands of Israel.[49]

After Claudel's conversion in Notre-Dame in 1886, the year when, with *La France Juive*, France and then Europe embarked on a long process of hatred, he seems to have had a mission: to link the two Testaments, and find the key to the New Testament in the Old. The scrutiny of Old Testament texts appears absolutely central to his work. The little explored plethora of exegetical writings to which he devoted the latter part of his life is ample witness to his interest in biblical texts. Within his theatrical works too, however, the mystery of Israel is similarly key. From his first major play (*Tête d'Or*), written at the age of twenty-one, to his last draft (*On répète Tête d'Or*), written at the age of eighty-one, he presents the two Testaments in a dialogue.

Claudel is not put off by the severity of the Old Testament. In its sacrifices and its laws of almost unbearable harshness, the Old Testament appears very far from the spirit of love and gentleness which reigns in the Gospels. Yet in all his plays Claudel shows the positive part played by harshness, an evil which, as in the Old Testament, is only apparent.

The sufferings which Violaine endures transform her into a saint and mysteriously allow the advent of Joan of Arc to save France. Violaine's last words show the positive aspect of death:

VIOLAINE: How beautiful it is to live! (speaking low and with deep fervour) and how great is the glory of God!

JACQUES HURY: Live, then, and stay with us.
VIOLAINE: But how good it is to die too! When all is really ended, and over us spreads little by little The darkness, as of a deep shade.[50]

The sufferings of Rodrigue and Prouhèze raise them to the highest point at which Good and Evil are equivalent:

DON RODRIGUE: [...] What evil could happen to me on a night so lovely?
SECOND SOLDIER: It's a lovely night for you when they are either bringing you to jail or to sell you for a slave?
DON RODRIGUE: I have never seen anything so magnificent! You might say that I am seeing Heaven for the first time. Yes, a lovely night for me is this, when I celebrate at last my betrothal unto freedom.[51]

In *L'ours et la lune* (*The bear and the moon*), a little play written for a puppet theatre, Claudel demonstrates how useful Evil may be, how it creates connections. The Chorus refuses to return the diamond stolen from the orphans because the Evil that was done to them brought about important consequences:

THE CHORUS: [...] Here's your diamond, we've found it, what should we do with it?
THE PRISONER: You must give it back to the child.
THE CHORUS: But then he won't need Rhôdo any more, she will have nothing more to give him of her flesh and blood.
And your son in the sky will no longer need the woman on the earth, the one who took him for her star for ever, and who gave him all she had, body and soul.
And our friend Paul, if she no longer has this reason to work and build the big aeroplane factory.
Who will be the one who tests and drags these winged coursers, that she'll release in the sky, henceforth the only element for him?
And what use will your own captivity have been?
Is not a mother worth more than a diamond?[52]

Claudel's entire oeuvre was an attempt to express the dialogue between Pensée and Sarah, Judaism and Christianity, of which he dreamed but which he never succeeded in realising. He rehabilitates the principle of discipline, showing it to be merely another facet of divine benevolence.

X: What's it got to do with us, then, your play?
S: It's meant to explain something to you.
X: And what's that then?
S: The harsh, good, excellent reality. The present moment, the inestimable present. Reality. The bitter, bitter, bitter, bitter, bitter reality. In the end you have a reality so bitter it's the best thing there is.
X: We've got that taste in our mouths without you.
S: You have to love it, you have to say yes.[53]

In tracing the different avatars of the "dream project, ,the fourth part of the Coûfontaine cycle in which the Old and New Testaments, Judaism and Christianity would be in dialogue, we have looked at Claudel's life and work from 1889 to 1949. However it is necessary to go back even further and to make a connection with another project – this time partially completed – mentioned previously, on which Claudel worked until his final days: the translation and staging of Aeschylus's tetralogy, the *Oresteia*, only the first three parts of which survive. Around 1885 the adolescent Claudel read Paul de Saint Victor's *Les Deux Masques*[54] (*The Two Masks*), thereby discovering the double nature, tragic and satyric, of ceremonial Greek theatre. There he found Paul de Saint Victor already comparing Aeschylus to Ezekiel:

> Aeschylus [is] a brother of the Prophets. In and through him, the Greek genius and the Hebrew genius, so far apart and so different, touch brows and wings, like the cherubim of the Ark in the Bible, and bow down to the same God.[55]

In Aeschylus, his ultimate artistic model, Claudel would find an astonishing attitude towards Evil. At the end of *The Eumenides*, far from driving the wild Erinyes, the goddesses of revenge, away from Athens, Athena welcomes them into the city of reason, asking them to make their home at its centre to bless it, and changes their name to the 'Eumenides', the Benevolent ones. And if in 1893 Claudel resolved to translate the *Oresteia*, it was no doubt, as he said, to familiarise himself with the iambic metre, but perhaps also in order to gain a better understanding of the metamorphosis of Evil into Good which is found in the conclusion of so many of his plays. Translating and then staging the *Oresteia* occupied him until the very end of his life, when he wrote a new prologue to *Protée*, the fourth part of Aeschylus's trilogy which survived only as a title and which he therefore completely reinvented.[56]

His work on the Coûfontaine cycle followed Aeschylus's model, applying it to contemporary reality. The idea of following a family's destiny over several generations answers the cry of Cébès faced with the world's absurdity, with which Claudel's oeuvre opened:

> *Cébès.* – I stand here,
> Untaught, irresolute,
> A man new-born confronting things unknown.
> I turn my face towards the Future and the lowering arch of the sky.
> My soul is full of weariness!
> I know nothing. There is nothing I can do. What shall I say? What shall I do? How shall I use these hands that hang at my sides, these feet that bear me about as in a dream?[57]

The sacrifice made by Sygne in *L'Otage* appears pointless. However in the third generation, that of Sarah, Pensée's daughter, everything was to have reached its culmination in the fourth part where the two opposites, Judaism and Christianity, would have come together, having transcended their contrasts. For Claudel the poet was a seer. His lifelong hope was that the 'mysterious powers' inspiring his creations would grant him that dialogue. As has been shown, this dialogue between opposites which are to a certain extent equivalent is at the heart of a theatre of hope (exactly the opposite of a theatre of the absurd) with the aim of explaining the apparent absurdity of the world. A new metaphysical theatre, which both justifies Evil and unites opposites in a hymn of praise, prefiguring the song of the Elect in the World to Come.

CHAPTER
2

A Triply Murderous Work

You will know a bitter period – a sort of Hell- and it is after this passage through a dark forest that you will rise again, master of your art. One of the most moving mysteries is this: after a brilliant period, every artist will cross a desperate land risking losing his reason and his mastery. If he emerges victorious . . .
Jean Genet, The Tightrope Walker in The Criminal Child and other essays, translated by Charlotte Mandell and Jeffrey Zuckerman, New York Review Books (New York, 2020, p. 116)

In writing these words to his friend Abdallah in *Le Funambule* (*The Tightrope Walker*), Genet was simply evoking a personal experience and extending it to all artistic careers. After a 'brilliant period' he too had gone through the 'desperate land', the 'dark forest'. In the eight years from 1942 to 1949, Genet published five poems or poetry collections,[1] five narrative works,[2] two plays,[3] one ballet (*'adame Miroir/ 'adam Mirror*, 1949) and one text for radio (*L'enfant criminel / The Criminal Child*, 1949). After these years of extraordinary creativity, he was to publish almost nothing between *Journal du Voleur* (*Thief's Journal*) (1948) and *Le Balcon* (*The Balcony*) (1956). In a 1964 interview for *Playboy* he attributed these years of sterility to Sartre's book, *Saint Genet, comédien et martyr* (*Saint Genet, actor and martyr*) which made him famous the world over but, he said, plunged him into a deep crisis:

MADELEINE GOBEIL: What kind of impression did it make on you to read the book he [Sartre] devoted to you?
GENET: [...] My first reaction was to want to burn the book. Sartre had let me read the manuscript. I finally allowed him to publish it because my concern has always been to take responsibility for what I gave rise to. But it took me a while to recover. I was almost unable to continue writing. I could have continued to develop novels mechanically. I could have tried to write pornographic novels in a kind of automatism. Sartre's book

created a void that allowed a sort of psychological deterioration to set in. This deterioration allowed for the meditation which led to my plays.
MADELEINE GOBEIL: How long did you stay lost in this void?
GENET: For six years I lived in this miserable state, in this imbecility which lies at the shallow bottom of life: opening a door, lighting a cigarette ....There are only few shimmering moments in a man's life; all the rest is a dull gray.[4]

Genet's journey through the 'desperate land' ended well before the date he gave, 1958. In fact the period from 1955 to 1958 when he worked simultaneously on *Elle* (*She*), *Le Bagne* (*The Penal Colony*), *Le Balcon* (*The Balcony*), *Les Nègres* (*The Blacks*) and *Les Paravents* (*The Screens*) was an intensely creative one for him. Furthermore, his writer's block began far before Sartre's book was published. In 1952 he met Cocteau in Saint-Jean-Cap-Ferrat and told him he had burned 'five years' work':

> 18 August, 1952. Thought a lot about Genet's visit. A rigid, Jansenist Genet, accusing me of having sacrificed my morality to friendship for the past ten years – telling me he had nothing to say any more – that literature filled him with disgust – that he had burnt (torn up) his last five years' work.[5]

As we shall see, Genet's artistic crisis, which was to bring him to the verge of suicide, is linked to the writing of an 'impossible work', a huge project which he began, and abandoned, several times, and which in the end was never published.

The different metamorphoses of *La Mort* (Death)

In 1952, at the end of his *Saint Genet*, Sartre announces a new text Genet was working on:

> In short, if Genet writes, he will continue the adventure of *Igitur*; he will endeavour to attain the supreme state, that is, the highest degree of abstraction and reflection. He will see from on high the themes of the Flower, the Convict and Crime, but without believing in them: they will shrink beneath his gaze [...]
>
> I have the impression that he is trying to go as far as possible and that he is dreaming of a work in which each particular element would be *the* symbol and reflection of each of the others and of the whole, in which the whole would be at the same time the synthetic organization of all the

reflections and the symbol of each particular reflection, in which this symbolic whole would be at one and the same time the symbol of all the symbols and the symbol of Nothing [...] Is it a matter of writing three books, one on universal symbolism, another about his own case and a third on the ethics of art? A poem, an autobiography and a philosophical treatise? Of course not. Genet dreams of composing *a single work* with these three subjects, a work that will be a poem from one end to the other. Is that possible? In a sense, the undertaking is unparalleled; the work will have to be a mixture of Un coup de dés, The Seven Pillars of Wisdom and Eupalinos. But, on the other hand, Genet has always mingled the poem, the journal of the poem and a kind of infernal didacticism; if the work is ever written, it will be the completion of his art: not a revolution but a going to the limit.[6]

Genet dreamed of writing the ultimate work. Three books in one: a mirror of the world, enclosing all possible images (in the manner of Mallarmé's grand project), a treatise on Good, the values of which would come from his personal experience, and a mirror of the mirror, a treatise on Beauty which would reflect on creativity itself. Sartre evokes the notion of Mallarmé's Book, for which '*Un coup de dés jamais n'abolira le hasard*' (*A Throw of the Dice will Never Abolish Chance*) is only a sketch.

And what about Proust? The extent of Proust's influence on Genet, who discovered him in prison, is well known[7]. Proust's cycle was already that huge mirror of the world, a treatise on both the Good and the Beautiful whose values are aesthetic. Proust and Mallarmé would seem to hover on the edges of the ambitious project in which Genet, like his illustrious predecessors, wanted to immerse himself.

The two letters to Decimo

With Genet, everything was decided by writing. During his crisis the writer fell in love with a consumptive young man, embarking on a disastrous love affair, which Edmund White evokes thus:

Although Decimo C. is the man Genet loved the most in his life, almost nothing is known of him. Apparently he was a handsome Roman prostitute (some people said effeminate), the tenth child in a poor family ('decimo' means 'tenth'), a homosexual and utterly indifferent to Genet, to Genet's soul, money, fame and intelligence.[8]

Genet was to make his exit from this unrequited love affair through writing. On the train taking him away from Decimo he wrote him a letter which would become a text intended for publication, *La Lettre à Decimo* (*Letter to Decimo*).

This letter exists in two versions. The first begins with the words 'Caro Decimo' (Italian for Dear Decimo). In the second the words 'Cher Decimo' (French for Dear Decimo) have been added by hand. No doubt both these versions were typed by Genet's agent and translator, Bernard Frechtman, with an eye to their translation and publication in an American journal. On one level the letter is one of rupture. For three months Genet had shared Decimo with other lovers: the Baron, the Judge, the Englishman, the Professor and the Chilean. Genet had met those lovers and despised them. It appears that Decimo was impervious to Genet's genius, preferring these placid men to the turbulent poet of forty-two, who seems to have experienced the most violent and passionate love affair of his life with him. At a second level, besides the dimension of 'break-up' letter, the advice he gives to the young prostitute with tuberculosis expressed a new morality, the very one that he repeated in his play *Les Nègres*: the Other must accentuate his difference as much as possible.

At a third level Genet was trying to move beyond his own experience of the passion which was destroying him, and to define the nature of homosexual attraction.

The letter to Sartre

One thousand nine hundred fifty two, the year of Genet's passion for Decimo, was also the year in which *Saint Genet* was published. In this work Sartre developed an existentialist theory of homosexuality which Genet was to reject. That same year he sent a letter to Sartre, linking homosexuality and the death instinct:

> During childhood, a trauma shakes the soul. I think that what happens then is this: after some kind of shock, I reject life, but as I cannot conceive of my death in clear and rational terms, I live it symbolically by refusing to continue the world. Instinct then pushes me towards my own sex. Initially it refuses to leave childhood. Next it impels me toward my own sex. My pleasure will be without end. It will not contain the principle of continuity. It is an attitude of sulking. Little by little instinct will lead me towards virile attributes. But gradually my psyche will suggest funereal themes.[9]

We may assume that after receiving this letter, Sartre offered Genet the opportunity to develop his theories publicly in his journal, *Les Temps Modernes*. Genet takes the themes from his letter to Sartre and adds the text addressed to Decimo to serve as a lyric counterpoint.

Fragments

Fragments, a text published in *Les Temps modernes* in July 1954, is a first draft for the project on which Genet has resumed work:

> The pages which follow are not extracts of a poem: they ought to lead to one. This is a still-distant approach to one, since it is only one of several drafts of a text that will be a slow, measured progress towards the poem, justification of this text as the text will be of my life.[10]

Fragments (and the work of which the text is merely a 'fragment') is primarily a response to *Saint Genet, comédien et martyr*. For Sartre, Genet was only a pretext. Taking his case as a starting-point, the philosopher developed a new theory of homosexuality lived as a free choice rather than as a fate to be suffered.

Let us recall the main argument of *Saint Genet*. A childhood incident has set the course for Genet's whole life. This rupture is a metamorphosis. Caught stealing by his adoptive parents, Genet is transformed into a hooligan. He chooses the worst. He will be the wicked one, the thief which others see in him. The worst is neither in the being nor in the not-being which is nothing, but in the appearance whose function is to make apparent the nothingness. The dreamer, who lives by appearances, is wicked. He wishes to contaminate others and so brings the unreal into the light of day. He will be an aesthete, a poet. Thus Genet is not the plaything of a destiny, be this genetic, Marxist, or Freudian. He chooses freely to be homosexual and a poet in order to be wicked to the extreme.

Genet was never satisfied with the philosopher's theory. In the letter he wrote him he linked homosexuality with the death instinct. In *Fragments*, continuing the reflection sketched out in that letter, he took himself as an example from which to establish the general characteristics of homosexuality. From this Otherness, which he sought to establish as the ultimate value, he went on to attempt to found a new morality and a new aesthetic.

The text has three sections, 'Fragments d'un discours' (Fragments from a Discourse), 'Le Prétexte' (The Pretext), 'Fragments d'un second discours' (Fragments from a Second Discourse).

'Le Prétexte', which is the key to the other two texts, is placed second of the three. This is a technique often used by Genet, from the first sentence of the first letter he wrote to his former pupil, Ann Bloch,[11] in 1937, through to the *Captif amoureux* (*Prisoner of Love*). In *Les Bonnes, Le Balcon* and *Les Nègres,* the rituals also precede the exposition of the intrigue. Similarly, 'Le Prétexte', an autobiographical narrative, is a document essential to an understanding of the crisis of the years 1948–1954. In it Genet writes about his friend, the young Lucien Sénémaud:

> Strange mistake: a young lower-class boy had a face in which I thought I read the adventures we attribute to criminals. His beauty hooked me. I linked up to him, hoping to relive in him a passion outside the law. But he was solar, in harmony with the order of the world. When I saw this, it was too late, I loved him. Helping him to realize himself in himself and not in me little by little, subtly, the order of the world was to change my morality. Still, helping this child in his effort to live in the world harmoniously, I did not abandon the idea of a satanic morality that, no longer lived according to a passionate cynicism, became an artificial, antique notion. Lucid again, I knew myself in confusion and comfort. Resolving, through a calm insolence, through the calm assertion of myself, the social scandal provoked by pederasty, I thought I was free of it, with regard to the world and to myself. I was weary, even though the anxiety of eternity rose up, tormenting, an anxiety, incapable of being translated in my case through the sequence of generations, or by the idea of continuity filling my acts, an anxiety I expressed by my search for a rhythm – or a law within my system alone – or a Golden Section, eternal, that is to say capable of engendering, connecting and completing the finished poem, perfect obvious sign, untouchable and final in this human affair, my own.[12]

'Le Prétexte' makes the connection between Genet's encounter with Decimo, the 'pretext', and his inability to write the work he dreams of:

> The thought – not the summons – but the thought of suicide, appeared to me clearly around my fortieth year, brought, it seems to me, by the boredom of living, by an inner void that nothing, except an absolute decline, seemed able to abolish. Still no vertigo, no dramatic or violent impulse propelled me toward death. I calmly considered the idea, with a little horror, nauseous potion, and nothing more. At the time, after some wretched affairs undergone and then transformed into songs from which I tried to extract a particular morality. I no longer had the vigor (though I felt the innermost urgency) to undertake a work that came not from fact but from clear reason, a calculated work, that came paradoxically from number before having come from the word, from the word before the deed, undoing itself as it unfolded. This weird demand was then illustrated by this formula: to sculpt a stone into the form of a stone. For reasons I will give, hardly interested in the world's fate, having (or believing I had) accomplished my own, by my inner void condemned to silence – sculpting a stone in the form of a stone the same as being silent – logically and natu-

rally I contemplated suicide. That which exists, existing, the powers of poetry seemed vain to me: I had to disappear. Or exhaust myself in a long moment – until my natural death – in contemplation of the one I had become. Or mask my boredom beneath vanities.[13]

From 1948 to 1952, in the heart of the family he had just provided for Lucien, his protégé, in the house at Cannet, the building of which is related in Genet's correspondence with Frechtman, the pastoral idyll was complete. However Genet felt he was losing his creative powers. In 1949 in a radio broadcast – which was censored in the end – *L'Enfant criminel*, the 'poet enemy' expressed concern. If he was being invited to address the nation, what had he become? At the same period, in the ballet '*adame Miroir*, [M]adame Mirror (symbolising the playwright) is suddenly reflected in the mirrors of the labyrinth. As is everyone. Something had to happen in order for him to begin work again. His encounter with the 'pretext' came just at the right time to ruin the solar values of the Provencal villa. Enter Decimo:

In April 1952, in X..., I met a twenty-year old hoodlum. I fell in love with him. [...] Magnetized, he led me on by the effect of a force whose nature I can only poorly define [...] I persisted in my desire for him.[14]

Other sources mention the 'pretext', 'an Italian youth with the face of a girl and Mongol eyes'[15] who Genet wanted to feature in the film he wished to direct, *Le Bagne*. However the crisis occasioned by his relationship with Decimo was only a 'pretext', as he says at the top of the second passage of *Fragments*. He studied the love-hate relationship between them in order to understand the nature of homosexuality in general. It is a refusal to perpetuate oneself, a desire for sterility, that is to say a symbolic and imperfect death.

It isolates me, cuts me off both from the rest of the world and from every pederast. We hate each other, within ourselves and within each of us.[16]

Isolated, symbolically dead, the homosexual rejects the world of the living. He exists in another world, ruled by the aesthetic. His thought is discontinuous:

In the heart of a living and continuous system that contains us, that stumbles on reality and changes it, no pederast can be intelligent. Like their voice on certain words, their reasoning drifts or breaks. Now the notion of rupture appears.[17]

The logic of the homosexual is fairy tale-like: fairy tales, the stories of madmen and the daily lives of 'folles', 'drag queens' shows a reality in perpetual metamorphosis. That policeman wants to be a beautiful young girl. The artist, too, through metaphor, metamorphoses the world. Thus by his very existence the homosexual is like a poem:

> Wives and daughters of kings, Phaedra, Antigone, dead, then legendary, finally a gleaming collection of letters – and you – have won absolute prestige: death. Useful for saying nothing, now you are in the timeless.[18]

Funereal homosexuality? Fairy tale-like? Lovers' hatred? Pretentious waffle! Look at so and so, with their stereos, mixers and motorbikes. They've never even heard of Phèdre or Antigone. It would be better telling them about *The Perfect DIYer's Handbook* or *The Owner's Guide to the Law*. That may be so. But Genet goes to the limit of himself. That is his essential lesson for us. Seeing in homosexuality funereal structures and the vertiginous call of a fairyland which evades the world, Genet transforms these structures into values: the homosexual must be funereal to the extreme. In this way, the drag artist was heroically flinging his Otherness in the world's face. Genet wanted to be funereal, "dry, mineral, abstract".[19] The work to come, written according to this new aesthetic, would destroy its pretext (the lover), destroy itself, and destroy the author writing it:

> Get up! Go die! Not for a delicious widowhood and then another wedding, it is your absolute death that I am trying for, and my own. At my disposal I had the usual means: poisons, fear (you were dead of fear when you got tiny coffins containing your disfigured image), bullets, crushing you under my car, smashing you on the rocks! With a clean blow, to kill this handsome child would not have kept his ghost from hating me and going on to animate an even more handsome body and the irony of that would have finished me. A more subtle death is being prepared.[20]

By its very structure the work Genet dreamed of would go to the limit of homosexuality. The lover wished to kill the love object and then commit suicide, destroying everything, the world and any trace of him. Genet carries this desire for nothingness over on to the level of the writing. The book he aimed to write would realise in the aesthetic dimension the givens of homosexuality as they are experienced.

The work is to be discontinuous

The homosexual does not procreate. He is sterile. His very thought is discontinuous. To speak in a discontinuous way is to reject the 'normal' logic of cause and effect. Thinking becomes a series of quick intuitions on a given subject. In "Fragments d'un discours"("Fragments of a Discourse"), nine texts simultaneously celebrate and denigrate the Italian lover. These texts are separated by a space which will, in the later theoretical texts (*Le Funambule, L'Atelier d'Alberto Giacometti, L'Étrange mot d' . . . /The Tightrope Walker, The Studio of Alberto Giacometti, The strange word Urb)* become a star, an asterisk.

Thus the work towards which *Fragments* is making its way must in its final avatar inevitably be a confrontation of various genres, a work in prose reflected in a cycle of seven plays. This discontinuity is the intuition of a new logic which is multiple and contradictory.

The plural reading

Above all, in *Fragments* Genet, crazily, says two things at once. The text is discontinuous, intermingling with another text. The very first sentence features an apparently innocuous note:

The morose eyelid – where the chimera was broken, you were keeping watch.[1] [cited below]

We are conditioned to read the note as a commentary, an explanation. The note that appears on this phrase provides no explanation, however. Instead there are two other kinds of text, set against the first one. The first of the two, in quotation marks, is cited by the second, which continues its object, its reflection:

1. "Strange loves! A twilight smell isolates you. But it is less the dishevelled monster of your interlaced bodies than its image multiplied in the mirrors of a bordello – or your delicate brain? – that troubles you! Dripping with sweat you climb back up from those absurdly distant lands: you had capsized in yourself where flight is surest, your drunkenness swelling to the point of exploding – from your sole and reciprocal exhalation. Loves, name these games of reflections that are exhausted, shouted out endlessly on the walls of gilded rooms."
Thus speaks an oblique reason that, fascinated, watches death appear in each accident. Name, exhaust these games and come back to the air.[21]

Similarly, there is no (direct) connection between the second note and the text. The word 'nocturne' in the text refers us to a lamb which an

8. Jean Genet (1910–1986). In contrast to Genet's popular image as one who was unlettered and discovered literature in prison, research reveals that Genet was an extremely well educated artist, who focused on the fulfilment of his writing vocation. (Photo from Genet's interview with Bertrand Poirot-Delpech).

9. *The Maids* by Jean Genet, directed by Michael Almaz, performed at Habima Theatre, 1966, with Shoshana Douer and Tziporah Feld. (Photo: Ephraim Kidron).

10. *The Balcony* by Jean Genet, directed by Jacob Raz, set and costumes by Moshe Sternfeld, performed at the Khan Theatre, Jerusalem, 1982. In this production, the Chief of Police and the Head of the Revolutionaries were portrayed by the same actor (Aaron Almog). In the same way, Razia Izraeli performed two opposite roles: Carmen, the prostitute (pictured here), and Chantal, the symbol of the revolution. (Photo: Yaacov Agor).

11. Another photo from *The Balcony*: The Judge (Ouri Abrahami), or, more precisely, the client who acts as a judge in the house of illusions. (Photo: Yaacov Agor).

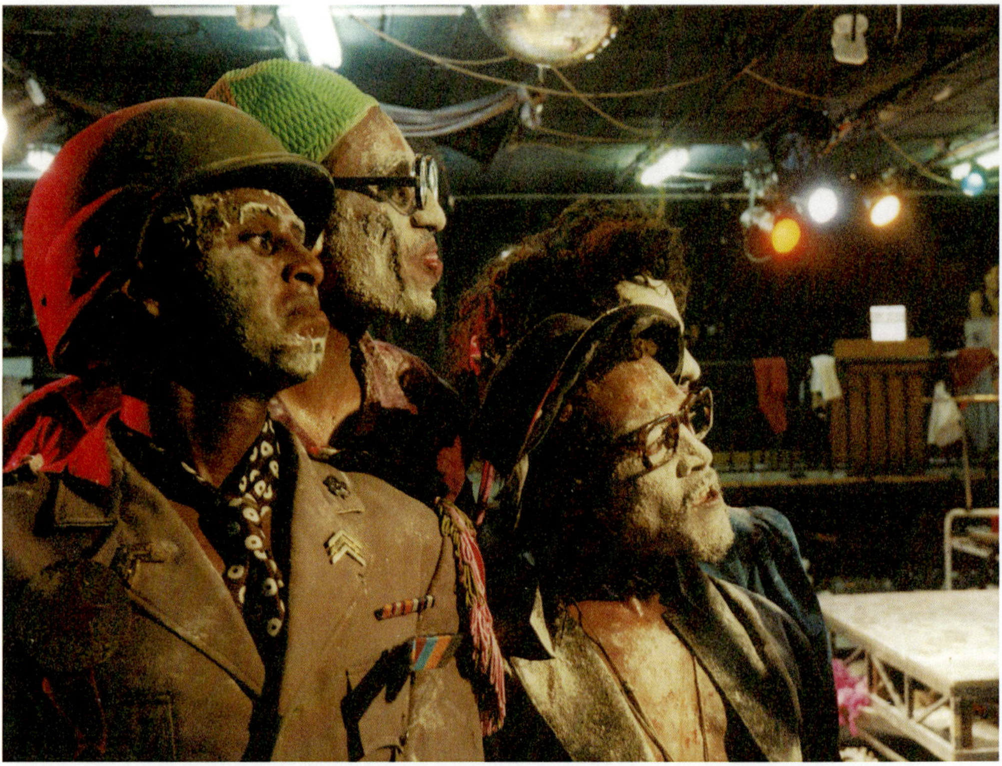

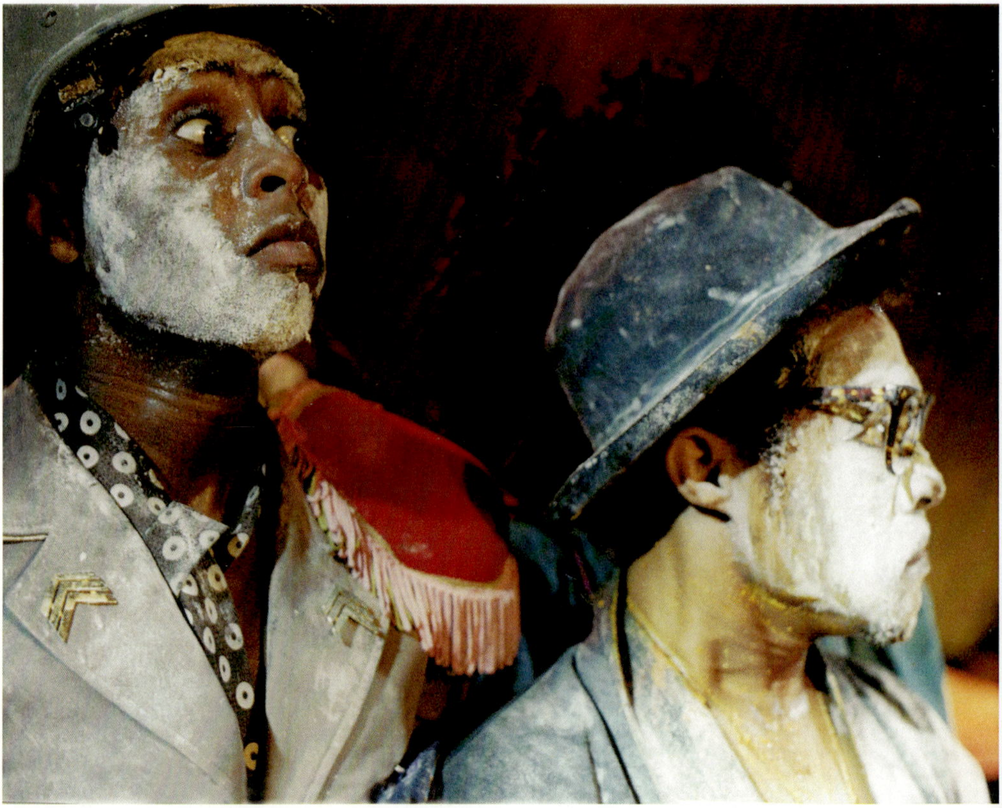

13–16. *The Blacks* by Jean Genet, directed by Moshe Malka (2012), from the Acco Festival. Moshe Malka and Yaffa Shuster led a group composed of artists of Ethiopian and Arab origin. They expressed their revolt against racism in the same way as Genet's blacks. (Photos: Philippe Szpirglas).

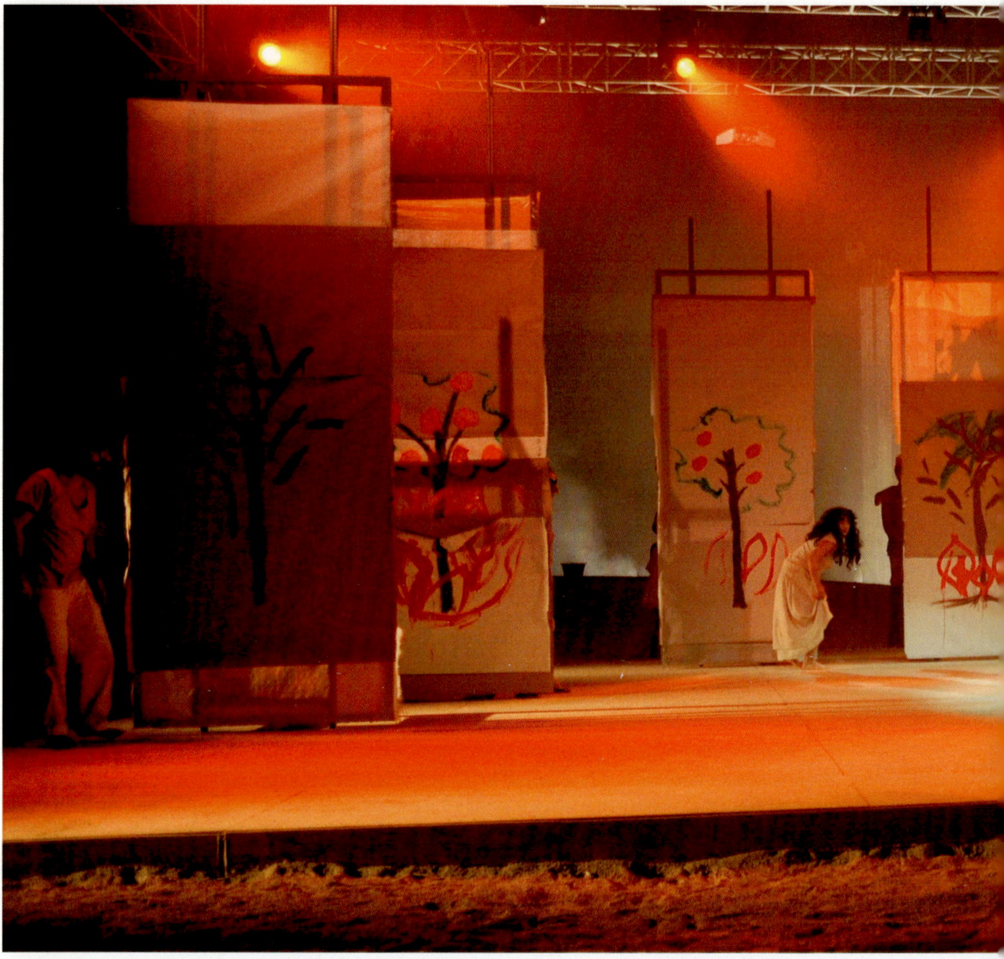

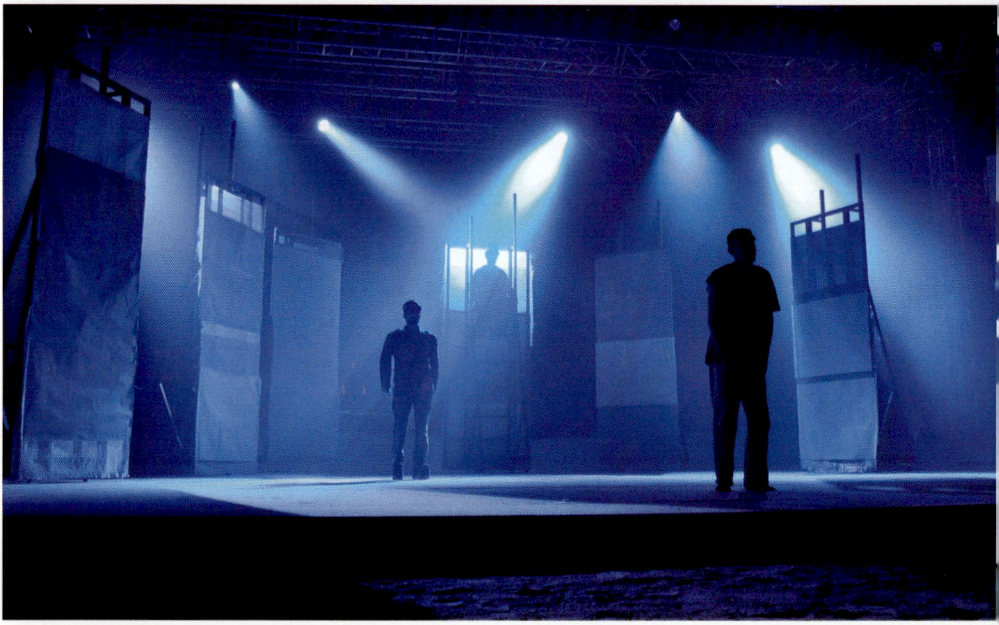

17–19. *The Screens* by Jean Genet, directed by Damianos Kostantinidis, scenography and costumes by Antonis Daglidis, lighting designer. Eleftheria Deco. (Photos: Antonis Daglidis).

20. This photo from *The Balcony* shows Aaron Almog, Shabtai Konorti, Avi Penini and Aliza Rozen. (Photo: Yaacov Agor).

eagle carries away, to Ganymede dying on a sheet embroidered with an eagle as per the Greek myth. There is no link between note and text, but the two notes follow each other. In *Fragments* Genet intermingles two texts, *La Lettre à Decimo* and a theoretical poem, in small print, fastened to the former by various numbers. It will be shown presently that Genet's oeuvre develops the idea that the plural reading, the fairy tale-like logic (that of madmen and of the dead) is the only possible reading of the world.

The work as tomb

Decimo was a prostitute suffering from tuberculosis. Throughout *Fragments* the dying heroine of the opera *La Traviata* is evoked. But we may also see traces of the opera *Norma*. Norma is dying of love for Pollione, the handsome Roman. But Pollione prefers Adalgisa. The only way to possess Pollione is to kill him. Norma denounces the Roman. Genet denounces and guns down, through writing. And without Pollione what is there to do except die? Norma climbs on to the pyre with him. Genet buries himself and his lover in his writing. This "Norma complex" (the lover wants to kill the beloved and then commit suicide) is transferred by Genet on to the structural level. The work he dreams of will kill Decimo and himself: 'A more subtle death is being prepared.'[22]

However it is also to be its own tomb. The book envisaged must destroy itself, and be equivalent to silence. Genet's writing must be similar to a sculptor sculpting 'a stone into the form of a stone'.[23]

It is 'a work [...] unmaking itself as it goes on.[24]

In *Fragments* this disappearance of the author, along with that of the pretext and of the mirror itself, is brought about by a kind of 'infinity mirror' effect. When two mirrors are placed opposite each other the person reflected grows smaller and disappears in the enchanted forest created by the infinity of reflections. This passage puts two texts opposite each other, the one apparently reflected in the other:

Beneath your glacial appearance, what shiver could move you?
What's wrong?
Nothing.   What steps, carved out of
Yes.   hard appearance, go down backwards,
Nothing.   Shades? What preparatory simulacrum
You're sad.   to start with? Under a clear, cold light, enter,
So I'm sad.   the rooms are ready: on the facing walls the
Why?   mirrors do not multiply the play of the event,

Because I'm sad. but are a prelude to its absence.
Why sad
Because.²⁵

The theatre within theatre effects in Genet's plays are the equivalent to these mirror effects. The empty rooms in which mirrors face each other anticipate *Le Balcon* and Genet's whole theatrical output. The theatre within theatre effects make possible an oeuvre which is criminal three times over: by destroying the pretext, the author who writes the work and the work itself.

As *Fragments* is not included in the five volumes of the *Oeuvres complètes* (*Complete Works*) Genet must have rejected it. And indeed alien voices, Sartre's and Mallarmé's, can be heard in this text. The brilliant analyses, the icy hieraticism, this is Mallarmé's *Hérodiade* and Sartre's *Saint Genet*, not Genet himself whose extravagance is less disdainful, whose literary excesses are always tinged with a humour which is quite absent from *Fragments*.

In response to Sartre's book, *Fragments* puts forward a new morality linked to the death instinct. If homosexuality is a break with the real, the homosexual goes to the limit of his self and wants to be funereal to the end, just as later, in Genet's drama, the Blacks want to be 'negroes' to the limit and the Arabs want to be 'treacherous' to the end. The standard-bearer of the revolution, says Ommu in *Les Paravents* (*The Screens*) will not be a hero of the Algerian uprising but rather Said, who betrays the revolt.

Genet's future work was to mirror the universe of homosexuality. The homosexual desires the death of the lover, his own death and the disappearance of the world. This triple crime is enacted by Genet's oeuvre. All his plays and his theoretical writings seem to consume themselves. And in *Le Balcon*, the tomb which the police chief wants built for himself in the middle of the town and where he wishes to watch himself dying for ever, is the ultimate work of art in which Genet would like to bury himself: all that is visible, however, is these few fragments buried in the sand.

Les Folles (The Drag Queens)

Cocteau came to hear about *Fragments* and wrote to Genet asking for a copy, only to receive this reply:

> Thank you for Les Temps modernes. I shan't send you the piece though. It's not worth it. It's shit. I submitted a poor draft, and then only because they paid me a lot for it. Don't read it. In four or five years' time you will have the real poem.[26]

Two years later, in 1956, Genet had still not published the work for which *Fragments* was a sketch, but was still working on it, telling Robert Poulet:

> This book will be of a most unexpected kind, printed on large pages with small pages in the middle of them, containing the commentary which is to be read at the same time as the narrative. At the end there will be a lyrical explosion entitled *La Mort* (Death).[27]

A draft survives with the title *Les Folles*, and can be considered in relation to the grand project. The text is similarly a reflection on homosexuality; the biographical basis, however, is no longer the tragic love affair with Decimo but a party arranged at the home of a 'Jewish lady covered in diamonds' where actors put on a performance in drag. Genet evokes public figures: the French social élite, generals, prefects, a French ambassador's wife, the head of the secret service, musicians and painters. He mentions the names of Marcel Jouhandeau and Jean Cocteau. He describes two actors in drag performing *La Dame aux Camélias (The Lady of the Camelias)* and the Fables of La Fontaine, specifically mentioning *La Cigale et la fourmi (The Ant and the Grasshopper)*.

In her 2003 book, *Cocteau: les années Francine (1950–1963) (Cocteau: the Francine Years (1950–1963)* Carole Weisweiller writes about the parties held by her mother, Francine Weisweiller, a friend of Jean Cocteau, at which Robert Hirsch, Jean Le Poulain and Marc Doelnitz would perform in drag for an audience of notable figures such as Cocteau, Genet and Roger Wibot, an old family friend and head of the Directorate of Territorial Security, an intelligence agency:

> Robert Hirsch, whom my mother had met when *La Machine à écrire* (The Typewriter) was staged at the Comédie-Française, would improvise sketches with some of his fellows from the Français and some non-actor friends. They had begun these improvisations, strictly reserved for an audience of friends, on the top floor of the restaurant La Régence, which no longer exists, called *Cour et jardin*, in Place du Théâtre-Français. Robert Hirsch was also fond of improvising sketches at the homes of friends such as Roger Hart and Michel Garmati, or at Sabine de Bonneval's chateau

where the family were guests. My mother was dazzled by so much wit and hilarity, and begged them to come and perform at her house. Some time later, Robert Hirsch and his companions commandeered Francine's wardrobes, draping themselves in her gowns and taking down the salon curtains to dress up as women . . . In front of an audience of friends including academicians, actors and members of high society, they put on little plays like Les Adieux d'une vieille sociétaire de la Comédie-Française (An elderly female member of the Comédie-Française makes her farewells), La Fuite à Varennes de Marie-Antoinette (Marie-Antoinette's flight to Varennes) and the parody of a recipe by Mapie de Toulouse-Lautrec, a famous culinary critic of the day: La tête de cheval à la famille (Horse head cooked in the family way.) recited by one Mme Monpelier Bonard alias Marc Doelnitz.

These performances were irresistibly amusing and never vulgar; they delighted people of all ages.[28]

Some of the photographs illustrating the text show several of the ten or so performances given by Robert Hirsch, Jean Le Poulain and other actors from the Comédie-Française: *La Chorale des grillons de Provence* (The Chorale of the Provencal crickets), the parody of a play by Anouilh, *Serpillettes ou le vent contraire* (Little cloths or an unfavourable wind). Among the audience are to be seen Jacques Chazot, Marie Daëms, Sabine de Bonneval and Jean Cocteau, this last in one of the rare photos where he is laughing uncontrollably. Twenty years later, in the 1970s, Gérard and Jeannine Worms, the brother and sister-in-law of Francine Weisweiller, still remembered Genet being at one of those remarkable evenings where the actors from the Comédie-Française succeeded in bringing tears of laughter to the eyes of a very select audience who were not easily impressed. There is no trace of *La Dame aux camélias* either in the photographs or in Carole Weisweiller's recollections. Yet in Genet's unpublished text, *Les Folles*, the scene which the actors parody is the concluding scene of Alexandre Dumas the Younger's play, depicting a young prostitute suffering, like Decimo, from tuberculosis.

It may be supposed that Genet wished to use the party given by 'les Folles' as a frame for presenting his memories of his love affair with Decimo, who was similarly a prostitute and had tuberculosis. In this new approach to the grand project he might, perhaps, have intertwined two levels: one describing the drag performance by the actors from the Comée-Française, in which homosexuality is given a parodic treatment, the other reflecting on homosexuality linked to the death instinct as in his letter to Sartre. The two spaces, Paris and Rome, would have been brought together. The argument he describes between the two 'actresses' calling on 'the great Sarah' for help – Sarah Bernhardt, one of whose greatest roles was la Dame aux Camélias – would have been set opposite Decimo, the Roman 'folle' dreaming of meeting the Pope, perhaps to seduce him.

For a time, therefore, Genet thought of using the evening as a pretext for a reflection on homosexuality. Once again he abandoned the idea, which would take on its most interesting shape some years later.

La Mort I, La Mort II (*Death I, Death II*)

The principal testimony to Genet's struggle with his ambitious work is his correspondence with his agent and translator, Bernard Frechtman. His reason for leaving France between 1957 and 1961 was so that he could complete the project in a hotel room in Greece or elsewhere. The letters reveal his enthusiasm, his hesitations and often his deep discouragement. At this stage *La Mort* was to be composed of two volumes. This was not a case of one work split into two, however, but of two different works facing each other like two mirrors: *La Nuit (La Mort I)* a work in prose and, opposite it, *La Mort II*, a cycle of seven plays:

> A series of seven plays forming a kind of cycle. A work at once open and closed, in which each play will be complete in itself while at the same time gaining its true value only in relation to the overall group, with characters reappearing from one play to another, responses, and entire fragments recurring wholesale here and there.[29]

The first piece in the cycle is *Les Paravents* (The Screens). At its premiere in Berlin in 1961 it was subtitled *La Mort I*, with the following explanation appearing in the programme:

> According to its author this play is the first in a series of seven works on the theme of death; the start, probably, of a cycle on the seven deadly sins.[30]

It seems likely that the German translator misunderstood the notes Genet gave Frechtman at this period:

> The definitive title will be *La Mère (La Mort II)* (The Mother (Death II)) Tell Rosica and Mayer. That's how it should be announced both in bookshops and in the theatre. Each of the plays will be composed in the same way.

For example:
Le Bagne (La Mort II) The Penal Colony (Death II)
Etc. The first volume, which is totally different but will complete these seven plays, will be entitled:
La Nuit (La Mort I) Night (Death I)
Is that clear? […]
I am going on with *Le Bagne* and another play *La Fée (La Mort II) (The Fairy* (Death II)). It's hard. I almost wish I were dead sometimes. It's so difficult. I fall asleep, exhausted, after writing one or two pages. Right in the first scene *the whole play absolutely must have already revealed itself* in the mind of the spectator. The spectator must proceed to encounter himself, and not external incidents. All the anecdotal coming and going is there to mask the poverty of the playwright.[31]

As a poem set opposite a cycle of dramas, the planned work is similar in its form to Mallarmé's own Great Work, in which he wanted to confront poetry and theatre:

I believe that Literature taken once more from its source which is Art and Learning will give us a Theatre whose performances will be the true religion of modern times; a Book, an explanation of Man which can satisfy our finest dreams.[32]

P*eur de mourir* (Fear of Dying)

There is another unpublished text which may be seen as linked to the great work, *La Mort*. Its title – *Peur de mourir* – appears in capital letters in Genet's handwriting. This amazing work was clearly written later than *Les Paravents* since it mentions that play as 'the culmination of his talent'. Genet begins with a picture of the closeness between sea and night, both monumental as death. Everything about the text reveals that Genet believes in life after death. Life and death, he says, are separated only by an invisible partition. This recalls the white screens passed through by the dead in *Les Paravents*. Genet appears to want to prove the existence of the divine by the desire for eternity common to everyone. He redefines the notions of heaven and hell. If all that one is given at birth is realised, the soul mingles with the mass of past lives and it is heaven. If the opposite occurs and the gifts received have not been used, this situation will be experienced as hell. It is necessary, therefore, that a man makes use of all the possibilities of his being.

Elsewhere Genet echoes the advice in his text on Rembrandt: the artist must shed all his human characteristics (pride, wickedness, desires) in order to be free from all which still ties him to life. In this way he will be able to write a limpid work which gives an unmediated reflection of the world.

It appears that Genet came back to the themes of *Peur de mourir* in the interview he granted Antoine Bourseiller in 1982, in which he returns almost verbatim to the text he had written twenty years earlier:

> One thing is sacred for me – and I knowingly use the word sacred– time is sacred. Space doesn't matter. A space can be reduced or enlarged enormously, it has little importance. But time – I have had the impression, and still do, that a certain amount of time was given to me at birth. Given by whom? That I don't know, of course. But it seems to be given by a god. But, in any case, don't imagine a god – even if it's not a question of a dancing god – don't imagine a god who moralizes the way you do, with a shadowy face, like the one you know. That's not it. It's a god who is cheerful enough to guide me and to make me win at chess, for example. And then, in the end, it's something like what I was saying to you yesterday, it's a god that I invent, as one invents rules. I refer to him, that's a given, but I invent him. That's all I can tell you. But he doesn't dance, like the one Nietzsche would like to believe in, he doesn't dance but he amuses himself. In any case he amuses himself with me; he doesn't leave me for a second.[33]

Genet was to complete neither the cycle of seven plays nor the great prose work. In 1964, after his friend Abdallah's suicide, for which he felt in large part responsible, he tore up his papers, presumably the drafts of this huge unfinished work, on various incarnations of which he had worked for over twelve years.

In the 1970s, Gallimard replaced Bernard Frechtman as the literary repository of the eternal wanderer. Genet entrusted the publishing house with two unfinished texts which were published in 2010 under the title of *La Sentence* (The Sentence). Their themes and form make it possible to see them as connected to the 'dream project': new attempts to give expression to the book out of which would come a new aesthetic and a new morality.

La Sentence

In *La Sentence* Genet sticks pages on to large leaves of paper. In the space around the pages are texts in smaller writing commenting on the central page. To make it easier to read, he plays with colours: sometimes the central text is in black and the commentary in red, sometimes the situation is reversed (folio 9).

The opening of the central text will be familiar to us because Genet returned to it in his last work, *Le Captif amoureux* (Prisoner of Love).[34] On a flight to Japan he experiences a kind of revelation as he is freed from oppressive Judaeo-Christian morality:

> As soon as that word was spoken [the 'Sayonara' pronounced by the air stewardess] I was aware of the way in which the dark and decidedly thick Judaeo-Christian morality was coming away in strips from my body, at the risk of leaving me white and naked. I was astonished by my passivity. The operation was happening without me, I witnessed it, I felt the wellbeing it brought me but I played no active part in it [...]. I had battled against that morality for so long that my struggle had become grotesque.[35]

Several passages in *Le Captif amoureux* show that Genet was acquainted with the characteristics of Jewish calligraphy. In the Talmud, several texts are juxtaposed on one page: in the centre the Mishnah (the oral law) followed by its commentary, the Gemara, surrounded by various commentaries written in different scripts. For his treatise on antimorality, then, Genet takes the calligraphy belonging to the defining text of the Jews and inverts it. Then the scene changes and we are back in the cell where the convicted prisoner devotes himself to writing. Genet ends the text by repeating the initial revelation: flee the God of the Jews:

> This sordid coupling – marginal, or if you prefer, insufficient – poses a delicate problem: before being born on my travels to the Far East, fleeing the West was the dream which led my plane to Japan where I could escape the God of the Jews, evade His vengeance or His justice and the sign which I trace endlessly around the place where sentence was pronounced.[36]

Genet's wish to found a new morality based on difference was limited to fleeing ancient morality, simultaneously dreaded and desired because it is the sign of a transcendence whose presence he never stopped sensing within him.

J'étais et je n'étais pas (I was and I was not)

This text develops a passage from *La Sentence* in which Genet asks himself questions about his existence prior to his birth:

Before – I don't mean before I came out of the c*** of some unknown woman – but long before – before, where was I? Shapeless and non-existent, I was, but how? Where? Pending the coupling of two lost beings, I was awaiting my day, but before that? Had I been for all eternity? Did I belong to all eternity? J'étais et je n'étais pas.[37]

In *Peur de mourir* Genet argued for the immortality of the soul by the feeling, which he could not explain, that he is responsible for his actions. In *J'étais et je n'étais pas* he shows a soul which is infinite before birth. Birth interrupts the soul's infinity and this time life is followed by death and nothingness.

It was not my soul which pre-existed my physical body, compelling it to appear: it was my identity which preceded me. Intuition, the result of a daydream, that trickster madness, I couldn't say precisely, while my certainty grows ever stronger, perhaps indestructible, and whereas I know that I was before being born and that I was since eternity, I also know that this identity of my body will come to an end.[38]

There is thus an inversion of the commonly held idea of an immortality of the soul which continues to exist after death. Identity finishes at death but prior to death it has been in existence for all time.

The tone of these drafts, whose publication Genet would never have allowed during his lifetime, anticipates that of *Le Captif amoureux* whose epigraph[39] shows clearly that it too is a work in progress.

Genet wished to flee the West and 'the God of the Jews'. In the Palestinian camps he found the leaven of a new humanity who shared his horror of Israel. Israel is the great negative value in the book, with, set against it, the dyad of the Mother and the Son, crucified yet again by the same diabolical enemy, 'a real alliance with the devil, Israel'[40].

In *Les Folles* Genet had the intention of using the drag performance in the salon of a 'diamond covered Jewish lady' as the pretext for an extended reflection leading to a new morality. In *Le Captif amoureux* he has a new setting, the Palestinian camps. But the Genet we know and love is absent, and in his place is the writer denounced by Éric Marty, the one who, at Yasser Arafat's suggestion, writes a pamphlet in which Israel, like the Jewish people of times past, becomes the receptacle for every vice, every ridicule, every dire threat.

Instead of having me being baptized, the orphanage, even though it didn't know whether my mother was Jewish, might have had my body marked with the "shallow slandered stream." If I'd been brought up in the Talmudic faith I'd be an elderly rabbi now, all prayers and tears, slipping damp notes between the stones of the Wailing Wall. My son would be a major spy in Mossad, working in the Israeli Embassy in Paris, and my grandson would be a Mirage pilot, smiling as he dropped his bombs on West Beirut.[41]

This is reminiscent of Voltaire who, on his death bed, wrote a text omitted from all modern editions, *Un Chrétien contre six Juifs* (One Christian against Six Jews), the anti-Judaism of which might (possibly) guarantee him a passport to the afterlife.

Echoes of the dream project in Genet's oeuvre

With the help of *Fragments* and the descriptions Genet gave of it to Jean-Paul Sartre, Robert Poulet, Jean Cau and Bernard Frechtman, it is possible to identify certain features of the great lost work. According to Sartre it was to be a universal system of symbols resembling the totality of images of the universe, a kind of 'great mirror of the world'. The cycle also aimed to be a Treatise on the Good. Faced with traditional morality it was concerned to identify other values based on the lived reality of the homosexual. In addition to a work on morality, Genet's summa was also to be a Treatise on the Beautiful expressing aesthetic principles with their basis in the homosexual experience defined as funereal and governed by the death instinct. The cycle's structure is odd: the work destroys itself at the same time as it comes into being. It is the fusion of opposites. Genet may not have written this work; consciously or not, however, he did reproduce its structure in the rest of his output.

Le Balcon (The Balcony)

Le Balcon, the first version of which was published in 1956, was written in 1955, just after *Fragments*, and thus in parallel with the great project. Of all Genet's plays, this is the one in which the aims he had adopted in writing *La Mort* are most clearly seen: mirror of the world, a work destroying both its pretext and itself. As for the tomb which the Chief of Police wants built for himself inside the brothel, Genet's intentions are obvious from the mention of the initial plan:

> Something like the interior of a tower, or of a well. The wall is circular; its stones are visible. At the rear, a staircase leading downwards. In the centre of the well there appears to be another well, with the first few steps of another staircase.[42]

This well inside a well, seeming to go on to infinity, is reminiscent of the mirror effects evoked in *Fragments*:

> Beneath a light frank and cold, enter, the chambers are ready: on opposite walls, the mirrors multiply not the games of the event, but are a prelude to its absence.[43]

Moreover the play, like the dream work, seems to destroy itself. Until scene 8 (the one with the balcony and Chantal's murder), the plot is clear. Around a house of illusions (le Grand Balcon) which everyone visits to realise his fantasies, a revolution breaks out, destroying all the 'pillars of power'. The Queen's envoy has a brilliant idea: since the real dignitaries are dead, the clients of the Grand Balcon and Madame Irma who runs it have only to appear before the people and order will be restored. What controls us, Genet is saying, is not a real force but an image.

From scene 8 onwards, however, and especially in scene 9, the text's writing defies the comprehension of the director or actors wishing to interpret it. In the first version of *Le Balcon* Genet overtly negated and destroyed everything which had been shown. All the characters whose deaths we had witnessed (Arthur, Chantal) jumped up with a smile to greet the audience. This was an obvious way of destroying the story which had been told, rather like Ionesco at the end of the anti-exposition in *La Cantatrice chauve* (The Bald Prima-Donna) negated all the details which had been related previously.

Genet came to find this technique too straightforward. He preferred a more subtle way of making the text destroy itself from the inside. The suppression and failure of the revolution are related like a sort of ballet. Chantal comes to greet the Queen. The Queen replies to her greeting. A shot is fired. Chantal collapses. Her body is carried off.

Is that the big scene of the attack on the palace and the suppression? Everything appears to be taking place in a world of mirrors where reality and fiction are not clearly distinguishable. Finally, in the ninth tableau, only very gradually does Genet make the play dissolve before our eyes. In just a few minutes, imperceptibly, Irma who has become the queen goes back to being Irma the owner, or perhaps only the manager, of the brothel. The brothel which had become a palace goes back to being a brothel. Imperceptibly the clients give up the roles they had in real life and become themselves once more. Thus the play ends as it began. Nothing has happened. It was all just an illusion:

> IRMA (starting to undress): Gentlemen, you are free!
> BISHOP: In the middle of the night?

IRMA: You can go by the little door that opens on to the alleyway. There's a car.
(The cast start to exit. A burst of machine gun fire)
IRMA: What's that? Our side . . . or the rebels . . . or what?
ENVOY: Someone dreaming, Ma'am . . .
(Carmen exits)
IRMA: Irma, call me Irma, and go home. Goodnight.
ENVOY: Goodnight, Madam Irma.[44]

The play seems to have cancelled itself out and destroyed its creator. The tomb where the Chief of Police watches himself dying appears to be the embodiment of the morbid desire for death expressed by Genet in his great funereal work, a work in which the creator would bury himself.

This same operation can be undertaken on each of Genet's four major plays: we see his labour subtly gnawing away at the written work. *Les Paravents* is also a mirror of the world which, in the way it layers all the levels of reality expressing themselves at the same time one on top of the other, culminates in a sort of apotheosis-chaos.

The theoretical texts

Genet's theoretical writings, little known in spite of their number and their beauty, are governed by the notion of 'discontinuity' which seems in *Fragments* to be a crucial principle of the homosexual manner of thinking:

> As their voice does at certain words, their reasoning drifts off or breaks. Here appears the notion of rupture.[45]

Almost all of them invite plural reading. In *Le Funambule* (The Tightrope Walker) which in a sense continues *La Lettre à Decimo*, two texts are combined: the letter to the tightrope walker and a text addressed to the reader. *Ce qui est resté d'un Rembrandt déchiré en petits carrés bien réguliers et jeté aux chiottes* (*What remained of a Rembrandt torn up into very even little pieces and chucked into the crapper*) juxtaposes, in common with a passage from *Fragments d'un second discours,* two texts: one recounting a biographical event, a train journey on which Genet has the blinding revelation that each man is worth as much as any other, and reflections on Rembrandt's art. *L'Étrange mot d' . . .* (*The strange word of Urb . . .*) similarly mixes two pieces of writing: one on theatre in the cemetery and one on language and the impossibility of expression. Plural reading and discontinuity are features which allow direct links to be made between the theoretical texts and the major work which Genet abandoned.[46] However my main aim is to consider the dream project in the context of Genet's oeuvre as a whole.

The dream project as a key to Jean Genet's oeuvre

It appears that the features Genet identified in discussing the work he dreamed of writing, or those which may be deduced from the fragments he created, may provide a way in to the works he published after his time in the dark forest, his plays and theoretical writings. His work was still intended to be a mirror of the world, attempting to reflect not any particular event but reality as a whole.

As mentioned earlier, Sartre wrote about Genet's future work, that he would try 'to attain the supreme state, that is the highest degree of abstraction and reflection.'[47]

A comparison of Genet's plays, in their multiple versions, with his novels demonstrates the process of abstraction Sartre talks of. The majority of the characters in his theatrical works come from his novels but in moving from page to stage they lose their features and become signs. If we consider Mme Decarnin in *Pompes Funèbres* (*Funeral Rites*) alongside Madame in *Les Bonnes*, for example, we see that the former uses words which are later echoed by Madame, or rather the tyrannical Madame acted by the maids in their ritual:

> 'Don't defend servants. They spit in the food.' [...] 'I can tell when she spits. I recognize the bitter taste, the taste of a maid's mouth, the bitter taste of all the bitterness accumulated in the bottom of the stomachs of all high-class servants...' [...] 'I hate...' [...] 'servants. Their bodies have no consistency. They pass. They are passed. They never laugh, they cry. Their whole life cries, and they soil ours by daring to mingle in it by way of what ought to be most secret, hence most unavowable.'[48]

On the stage, Mme Decarnin becomes a sign. "Madame" becomes the essence of the Master and of oppression. She has virtually no historical or biographical features. In the course of his different versions, Genet removes any passages which could pin her down, suppressing, for example, her short dialogue in front of her mirror which makes her age obvious.

Similarly Mme Irma, the brothel keeper in *Le Balcon*, is an abstract form of Mme Lysiane who has the same occupation in *Querelle de Brest* (*Querelle of Brest*). Genet uses the same character, a keeper of a brothel where strange rituals take place, but Madame Irma, an abstract figure, is also the great director, the artist, the enemy of the real, shut inside her creation, a role which could never be suggested by the very concrete figure of Madame Lysiane.

Likewise the lieutenant-sergeant pair in *Les Paravents* is a direct transposition of the Lieutenant Sablon-Querelle pairing in *Querelle de Brest*[49] but once again Genet transforms people and situations from the novels, where they are highly picturesque, into purely abstract figures. The themes of the dramas are taken from the world of the novels, but now they are regarded in the 'eternal light' which Genet speaks of in connection with Rembrandt:

> Rid the subject of its anecdotal qualities and place it beneath a light of eternity.[50]

In the same way, the biographical experience Genet evokes in *Lettre à Decimo*, that mixture of love and hate, becomes in *Fragments*, a universal reflection on the nature of homosexuality. This process of making things more abstract, something Genet did not succeed in doing completely with *La Mort*, would appear to be one of the characteristics of his theatrical works.

The 'Treatise on the Good'

For Cocteau, Genet was a moralist. Can Genet's oeuvre be seen as a 'treatise on the good' when all his works appear to be so immoral? That is just it. Taking the givens of homosexuality as a starting point, Genet aims to found a new morality. All his creative output, novels, theatre, theoretical and political writings, are an attempt to forge a morality of combat.

The heroic drag queen of the novels flaunts his difference before a world which rejects him. He is himself to the limits. Genet transposes the lesson of the drag queen to the outcasts of his theatre. Across the only four plays he opted to keep in his *Oeuvres complètes,* the tetralogy of the revolution, he develops one story, the values of which gradually become clear. The servitude of the outcast is cultural. The Maids die because they want to be Madame. In *Le Balcon* the revolution, begun in *Les Bonnes*, is destined to fail because Roger, the leader of the revolutionaries, secretly wishes he were Georges, the Police Chief. The revolutionaries have been unable to invent new values. Only with *Les Nègres* (The Blacks), considered by Genet to be his most perfect play, does the outcast live his difference to the utmost. The *'Nègres'* want to be absolutely *nègres*. They want to eradicate every trace of identification with the Whites. *Les Paravents,* written shortly after *Les Nègres* continues this 'revolution of values' described by Genet in *Fragments*. Pontecorvo's film *La Bataille d'Alger* (*The Battle of Algiers*) which, in common with *Les Paravents*, describes the Algerian War, begins with the purging of the kasbah by virtuous revolutionaries, eliminating amoral elements of the population, the very ones which Genet will, paradoxically, make the standard bearers of *the* revolution. Those drunkards, and pimps executed in the name of universal morality are familiar. They are the heroes Genet holds up as models. Saïd the hero of *Les Paravents* betrays those fighting for independence. At the end of the play, Ommu makes him the flagbearer for the revolution, preaching values opposite to those of Western society.

> Ommu: Blessed be Saïd [...]
> The Soldier (severely): [...] And to speak of a traitor the way you do is wrong. And what else? A thief, a bastard, a beggar...
> Ommu: (she is flabbergasted for a moment, then looks at THE SOLDIER ironically)
> Aha!... That was to be expected! Because you boys have already reached the stage of uniforms, discipline, jaunty marches and bare arms, parade and a heroic death, while singing "Madelon" and the "Marseillaise" and martial beauty...[51]

In the work he dreamed of creating, Genet wanted to establish a reverse morality whose values would be those of homosexuality taken to their limits. In making the traitor Saïd the – paradoxical – flagbearer of the Revolution he betrayed, Ommu puts forward the opposite of Western morality.

A Treatise on the Beautiful

In addition to a Treatise on the Good, Genet's work was intended also to be a Treatise on the Beautiful. His novels always depicted the writer at work, writing or abandoning the very text we are reading. At its deepest level Genet's theatre is a reflection on the process of writing itself. All the characters in his four major plays are 'poet figures', each in a different way showing the creator at work. Claire and Solange are victims of their mirror images. Through their rituals and role playing, they want to free themselves from Madame but succeed only in identifying with her even more. Irma in *Le Balcon* is the artist who buries him/herself in a work to help him/her distance themselves from a world they loathe. And the tomb where the Police Chief watches himself dying depicts art as a refuge, a substitute world. The 'black' clowns have learned to beware of the reflections which make them servile and to turn them back against their White oppressors. They are 'assassin clowns', models of an Art which is the enemy of society. *Les Paravents* shows us several 'poet figures'. Warda, like Irma, is an enemy of the real, which she negates through her ostentation and ceremonies. Ommu represents another function of Art. The wild prophetess – inspired by the dead whose words she conveys – prefigures Genet as the political writer he became after 1968 (from the article entitled "*Les maîtresses de Lénine*" (Lenin's Mistresses) to *Le Captif Amoureux*). Thus, in addition to their various psychological and sociological readings, these texts may be seen as an attempt to understand the creative process, a kind of Treatise on the Beautiful. What does it mean to write? What is it to play a role? In what does the enchantment of the theatrical process consist? In contrast to Warda who is protected by the splendour of her heavy golden skirts, the prophetess Ommu is a link between the world of the living and the world of the dead. In the space of the four major plays the dreamer as victim (Claire and Solange in *Les Bonnes*) has become both Tiresias and Angela Davis.

A work which kills three times over

As has been mentioned, the dream project, whose principles embody the sterility of homosexuality, must kill its pretext and the author writing it, before destroying itself. This triple crime connects with a revelation experienced by Genet shortly before he published *Fragments*. In 1955, on the advice of Annette Michelson, the companion of his agent and translator Bernard Frechtman, he went to see an ethnological film by Jean Rouch, *Les Maîtres fous* (*The Mad Masters*). In it Jean Rouch films a sect in Ghana, at that time a British colony, and its strange ceremonies. Once a year its followers gather in the depths of the forest. They go into a trance. They are possessed by the gods of white modernity: the general, the engine driver, the doctor's wife and so on. In just a few moments the whole of colonial society appears, evoked by convulsed followers. These then proceed to commit a horrendous act. They sacrifice a dog before boiling and eating it.

In his analysis of the film, Jean Duvignaud puts forward the following hypothesis. For the sect's followers, who are still Muslims, eating the dog, a forbidden meat, is a transgressive act. They are identifying themselves with the white gods who oppress them, and then causing them to commit a grave sin. In this way they are degrading the white gods and freeing themselves from the weight of their oppression. Jean Rouch does indeed state that after the ceremony the followers appear purged, cured, freed from the negative forces restricting them.

Genet saw this parodic and bloodthirsty ritual as containing mechanisms profoundly similar to those of his theatre, which celebrates

Western values only in order the better to destroy them. To Bernard Frechtman he writes:

> You said you might write an introduction to my play for *Preuves*. If that is still your plan, I'd be happy if you could draw as close parallels as possible between my theatre and *Les Maîtres fous*. There are lots of developments, connections, analogies to be made. Demonstrate them.[52]

However, surely this dual movement of exaltation and degradation is also that of Greek classical drama. This is what Genet seems to have realised during a trip to Greece in 1956, immediately after writing *Le Balcon*, *Les Nègres*, and an initial version of *Les Paravents*. Greek drama had itself the same sort of twofold and contradictory dynamic as the one to be seen in the behaviour of the *maîtres fous*.

The trilogies of the Greek dramatists are known to be in fact tetralogies. In the first three parts of the tetralogy the dramatists tell a story. The gods come off best. The third part often concludes with an 'apotheosis' in which the god appears in person to resolve everything. In *The Eumenides*, for example, the third play in Aeschylus's *Oresteia*, Apollo and Athena appear in human form in order to save wretched Orestes from the fury of the Eumenides, the goddesses of revenge, madness and death. However the drama festival was held in honour of the god of drunkenness, Dionysus, born twice, combining male and female in one body: god of duality, madness and excess. The first three parts of the tetralogy are followed by a fourth which parodies the other three. Aristophanes's texts are a good illustration of how once a year the Greeks made fun of their beliefs.

> I loved Greece for yet another reason, which I'll tell you about. It was, and is, the only country in the world where people were able to venerate, to honor their gods, and also not to give a damn about them. What the Greek people did in relation to Olympus, the Jews would never have dared, and would still never dare, to do for Yahweh, no Christian would dare do for the Crucified, no Muslim for Allah. The Greeks were able at the same time to mock themselves and to mock their gods. That to me is astounding.[53]

This twofold movement of exaltation and ridicule – found both in the mechanism of Greek drama and in the rituals observed in twentieth-century Africa (like those of the Haoukas) – might well correspond to an essential function of theatre and of art. At all events it brings to mind the elaborate construction-destruction dynamic which Genet wished for his grand project and which he regarded as the sign of every great work of art.

> It seems to me, after this reading [of *The Brothers Karamazov*], that every novel or poem or painting or piece of music is an imposture if it does not destroy itself, I mean does not construct itself as a carnival duck shoot where it is one of the heads we aim at. [...] Frans Hals must have laughed a lot with *The Women Regents* [of the Haarlem Almshouse] and *The Regents* [of the Old Men's Almshouse]. Rembrandt, too, with the sleeve of *The Jewish Bride*, Mozart composing his *Requiem* and even *Don Giovanni*. Everything was allowed them. They were free. Shakespeare, too, with *King Lear*. After having had talent and genius they know something rarer: they know how to laugh at their genius.[54]

As for the author's destruction of himself, Genet's theatre truly is the playwright's tomb. From the process of writing his dramatic works Genet emerges a completely different person. The Genet who wrote *Les Bonnes* was a poet hostile to the real, like Irma or Warda. The Genet who would, several years later, write *Les Paravents* was prepared to be the opposite of Warda, a writer whose desire is to alter reality and dictate its values. Like the mad masters in the African ceremony he emerged from his writing purged of himself, purified and ready to take on new things (political action and writings, screenplays, *Le Captif amoureux*.)

Thus even if Genet's attempts to produce his great work proved unsuccessful, they nevertheless gave rise to a process which made all the rest of his oeuvre possible. In piecing together the various stages of the project and analysing the 'fragments' which have survived, one cannot but be struck by the similarity between the aims Genet adopted for *La Mort* and those which he ultimately realised in his work as a whole.

The dual work of which he dreamed, the dramatic cycle opposite a prose text, is actually his overall oeuvre. The tetralogy of the Revolution – *Les Bonnes, Le Balcon, Les Nègres, Les Paravents* – is set opposite his theoretical, aesthetic or political texts, from *Le Funambule* to *Le Captif amoureux*, in which a new morality and a new conception of the Beautiful take shape.

In order to do Genet justice, it would be necessary to put on his entire works, Bayreuth Festival-style. The mise en scène of *L'étrange mot d'* . . . might serve as a starting point, putting the theatre in the middle of the cemetery. Everything would thus take place in a scene of ruins, the Western world whose end Genet foresees and whose death knell – to quote Derrida – he sounds. As an overture, certain theoretical texts could be read (or danced): *L'Enfant criminel* or *'adame Miroir*. Then the theatrical works would be performed at the rate of one per evening. It would be necessary to attain to that state of luminous madness which Genet analysed so well. Through the act of writing Genet raises his own personal characteristics (homosexuality) towards a new and different understanding of the world. The world he shows us is a 'double' world which can be apprehended only by the poetic trance.

CHAPTER
3

A Metaphysical 'James Bond Film'

It is a story which has been with me for some thirty years and as I have told it so many times, it has, by its unique influence, brought something to all the films I have made instead. A stimulating, bewitching presence which I was unable to do without, perhaps. A pilot boat which was guiding me to the way out of the harbour, compelling me to undertake other journeys, face up to unexpected adventures. In short, to make other films. So, Signor Fellini, how could you reconcile yourself to giving up this story for ever if it was this precious radioactive source?

Federico Fellini (July 1992) preface to the graphic novel derived from
Il viaggio di G. Mastorna (Le Voyage de G. Mastorna), (Éditions
Casterman, Tournai, 1996, p. 5)

Claudel, Genet, Fellini: three artists who worked tirelessly, almost always in the grip of the creative process. For them, not finishing a project was a relatively rare occurrence. Claudel wrote his first masterpiece at the age of twenty-one and continued until he was eighty-six, writing so much and on so many different subjects that even to read his entire works is a huge task. To the thousands of pages of his collected theatrical works (68 plays!) may be added countless prose texts or exegetical essays. Genet's case is more complex. However the five plays, five novels and the political writings he published are only the tip of the iceberg: his entire work is far bigger and only now beginning, piece by piece, to appear. Similarly, when Fellini's cinematographic output is considered, the intense rate at which he worked cannot fail to impress. In the first phase of his work, from 1951 to 1965, one film followed hard on another, with a masterpiece conceived, written, made and released to huge acclaim almost every year: *Luci del varietà* (*Variety Lights*) (1951), *Lo sceicco bianco* (*The White Sheik*) (1952), *I Vitelonni* (1953), *Agenze matrimoniale* (*Matrimonial Agency*) (1953), *La Strada* (1954), *Il Bidone* (*The Swindle*)

(1955), *Notti di Cabiria* (Nights of Cabiria) (1957), *La Dolce Vita* (1960), *Le Tentazioni del dottore Antonio* (*The Temptations of Dr Antonio*) (1962), *Otto e mezzo* (*8 ½*) (1963), *Giulietta degli spiriti* (*Juliet of the Spirits*) (1965).

Even this untiring artist, however, experienced a serious creative crisis, foreshadowed in *La Dolce Vita* (Marcello's inability to create), depicted in *Otto e mezzo* (the film which Guido is unable to make until the very end) and eventually lived out in the legendary making of *Il viaggio di G. Mastorna* (*The Journey of G. Mastorna*), the film Fellini began, abandoned, began again, abandoned a second time and which he never entirely gave up on even in his final days.

There are four published accounts of the ins and outs of the abortive attempts to make this film. Firstly, in English, *Fellini* by Liliana Betti[1], the director's secretary and the only person he would allow near him during these very fraught years. She was witness to the events she relates (the director's break with the producer, the sale of jewellery when the director's bank accounts were frozen by a furious producer), and quotes first-hand documents (Fellini's letter to the producer, De Laurentiis, trying to explain his behaviour). She also makes use of extracts from the diary Fellini kept while preparing *Il viaggio di G. Mastorna*. Her book is intended for the general reader, however, and does not go into the details of the failure of the creative endeavour. It is possible, indeed, that she was unaware of them, despite having been at close quarters.

Tullio Kezich devotes a chapter of his Fellini biography to *Il viaggio di G. Mastorna*[2]. He also wrote the introduction to the screenplay published by Bompiani in 1994, immediately after the director's death. Kezich is not entirely reliable however. For instance only Fellini's name appears on the edition of the screenplay, whereas rights to the work are owned by three groups: Fellini's heirs and those of his two co-writers, Dino Buzzati and Brunello Rondi. Neither the biography nor Kezich's introduction makes any mention of the role of Brunello Rondi who was Fellini's principal collaborator on the screenplay. Most importantly, the crucial fact that the screenplay derives from a short story by Dino Buzzati, *Il Sacrilegio* (*The Sacrilege*) goes unmentioned.

Another book, devoted in its entirety to *Il viaggio di G. Mastorna*, partially fills these gaps: *L'inferno immaginario di Federico Fellini* (The Imaginary Hell of Federico Fellini) (Guaraldi, 1995) by Dario Zanelli. Like Kezich, the author was both a journalist and a close friend of Fellini's.[3] He was also a man of the cinema, President of AGIS, the Associazione Generale Italiana dello Spettacolo, for the diffusion of art film and culture.

Director of the journal *Cinecittà*, he published several books on Fellini, including *Fellini's Satyricon* (Capelli, 1969) and *Nel mundo di Federico* (The World of Federico) (Nuova Eri, 1987). His book completes the information given by Kezich, especially concerning Fellini's relations with Brunello Rondi. Zanelli also provides the precious texts of an early version of the screenplay – presumably supplied by Rondi (who edited it) – and gives detailed accounts of conversations with Fellini. These are very personal conversations: interviews given between 1965 and 1967 but also conversations tape recorded or written down in minute detail with a view to subsequent publication.

When Fellini granted a journalist an interview he knew how to tell all without actually telling very much. The interview has become an artistic genre in its own right, and the great director was a master of it. In the conversations with Zanelli, however, events off-set are starkly revealed, notably where financial details of the preparation for the film are concerned. Did Fellini want the general public made privy to the banking acrobatics he was contemplating to deceive his detested producer? At the time he was very undecided as to whether he should continue with the film or abandon it. Fellini appears to have chosen the fellow cinema professional to confide in, and asked his advice in desperation. The book reveals the innermost thoughts of the distraught artist. It has a tone of utter sincerity to it, and contains unpublishable financial details, both being the mark of conversation between two fellow professionals who are also friends. Furthermore, these details reveal a little discussed aspect of artistic endeavour (the financial underbelly) and an underestimated facet of the great director: the businessman[4]. Might these have been interviews or telephone conversations recorded unbeknownst to Fellini in order to publish them after his death?

In 1995 Ermanno Cavazzoni produced a novelized edition of the screenplay. Separate French and English translations of this novelized screenplay were published by Éditions Sonatine and Berghahn Books respectively in 2013[5]. Cavazzoni, a poet and man of letters teaching at the University of Bologna, was also the author of *Il poema dei lunatici* (The Poem of the Lunatics) which inspired Fellini's last film, *La voce della luna* (*Voice of the Moon*, 1990). Under Cavazzoni's pen the screenplay (this time attributed to Fellini and his two co-screenwriters Buzzati and Rondi)[6] became an exciting text, able to hold its own against the most suspenseful adventure stories. The text has a preface by Aldo Tassone, an expert on Fellini, who also instigated the publication. His text "*La vie . . . est aussi la mort*", *le chef d'oeuvre inachevé de Fellini* ("Life . . . is also death", Fellini's unrealized masterpiece) takes its title from a dream

Fellini had in 1977 in which he is making a film with Pasolini, who had by then been dead for two years:

> "It's life and also death", sang someone along to a beautiful tune that they told me was from *Il Trovatore* (*The Troubadour*). "It's life and also death." I wake up with the echo of this festive, happy song in my head. Who was singing? Maybe Pier Paolo Pasolini, who in my dream had a small part in my movie. It was the final scene [...] Then I was in the car with him. [...] Pier Paolo watched the ancient Roman walls pass by on the left, which appeared framed by modern marble. "How will anyone ever describe those marvelous ruins!" sighed Pier Paolo, smiling and melancholy. "It's life and also death ... ". I can still hear that song, that night, and the mysterious yet crystal clear meaning of that verse. Was that the end of the film?[7]

Aldo Tassone sees this 'final scene' as a reference to *Mastorna* with whose final scene Fellini was never truly satisfied:

> The reference to Mastorna is quite obvious, it's strange that no one has ever noticed it. The author seems virtually to suggest that life and death hold hands, 'joking with a tender affection' like the two directors and friends in the dream ... And this *Journey* which is totally amazing and yet 'imbued with a deep nostalgia for life' does indeed leave us with a profound feeling of serenity, like the 'intoxicating' music played by the orchestra at the final concert.[8]

In Aldo Tassone's view the screenplay is therapeutic:

> ... it invites us to free ourselves from the terror of death, to rediscover our place in the great universal orchestra of life. Death is part of life's great mystery, neither would have meaning without the other, so let us accept them with serenity and stoicism: this appears to be the director's secret message to us.[9]

The scenario is followed by a very long letter from Federico Fellini to the producer, Dino De Laurentiis. This first letter-treatment appears to precede the writing of the screenplay and thus also the second letter-treatment cited in Dario Zanelli's book, which postdates not only the writing of the screenplay but also the corrections made to it. The book ends with Ermanno Cavazzoni's essay "Les Purgatoires du XXe siècle" (Twentieth-century purgatories) in which he writes that the notion of the world beyond is now part of reality:

> Since Immanuel Kant we have been able to dispense with the world beyond and its landscapes, for so long imagined, visited and described (…) Each of us drags his own pocket-sized hell around with him, and feels it quivering inside him like an acute gastroduodenal ulcer (…) Paradise, it's better to anticipate it here on earth, if one can, for example on a coral island in the South Pacific during a fortnight's holiday.[10]

It is this world, not the world beyond, which the screenplay evokes:

> Each of us is seeking the solution for his own case, settling down or leaving, but each path is an illusion. This is how one passes one's time on earth.[11]

This body of information is completed by two documentary films. The first, *Fellini: a director's notebook* (1969) is a documentary made by Fellini himself during the shooting of *Satyricon*, in which he talks about giving up the project *Il viaggio di G. Mastorna*. He films the enormous abandoned sets (the cathedral, the aeroplane), the unused costume stores, and does a few trial shoots for the phantom film with Marcello Mastroianni.

In 2003 Maite Carpio made a seminal documentary entitled *Il misterioso viaggio di Federico Fellini* (The mysterious journey of Federico Fellini). She traced several of those who collaborated on the film – Dino De Laurentiis, Pier Luigi Pizzi, Giuseppe Rotunno and so on – and in the documentary interviews them, intercalating passages from *Fellini : a director's notebook*. A France-Culture radio programme made by Florence Colombani in June 2013 gives us interviews with Jean-Paul Manganaro, author of *Fellini romance*,[12] Jean Gili, Italian cinema historian, Romain Brethes, a journalist who writes on graphic novels, Sam Stourdzé, curator of the exhibition *Fellini, la Grande Parade,* at the Jeu de Paume in Paris in September 2010, and comic book artist Milo Manara.

With the aid of these sources, therefore (Liliana Betti, Tullio Kezich, Dario Zanelli, Maite Carpio, Florence Colombani, Aldo Tassone) it is possible to attempt a chronological account of this crisis period in Fellini's life.

A mysterious failure

Dario Zanelli traces the *Mastorna* project back to Fellini's schooldays. Ercole Sega, a fellow pupil,[13] recalls the young Fellini was dreaming of a work which would be a response to Dante's *Divine Comedy*. Dante's

21. (Top left) Federico Fellini (1920–1996). The photo was taken during the filming of *Toby Dammit* (1968) by Mimmo Cattarinich.

22. Frame from the graphic novel by Federico Fellini and Milo Manara (1995), *Il viaggio di G. Mastorna ditto Fernet* (*The Journey of G. Mastorna called Fernet*). At the beginning of the story, Mastorna stares out the aeroplane window, gazing at the threatening storm.

23. Another frame from *Il viaggio di G. Mastorna ditto Fernet*. The dancer in the nightclub of the dead is giving birth to a child. In the realm of the dead, the theatricality of the birth process replaces death itself.

24. Mastorna, shown from behind, played by Marcello Mastroianni. From *Il misterioso viaggio di Federico Fellini* (*The mysterious journey of Federico Fellini*), by Maite Carpio (2003). Mastorna is standing in front of the abandoned, huge set of stairs built for the impossible film in the Dinocittà Studios.

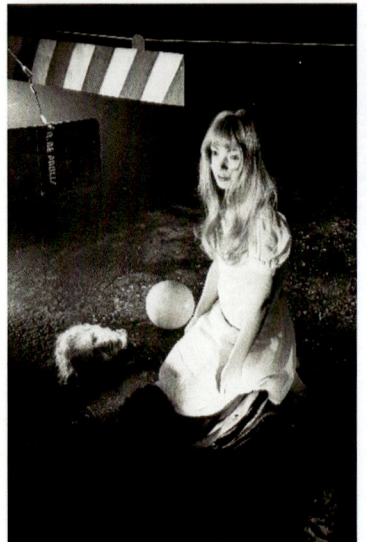

25. (Left) Photo from *Toby Dammit* (1968) of the girl near the severed head of the hero. Photo taken during the filming by Mimmo Cattarinich.

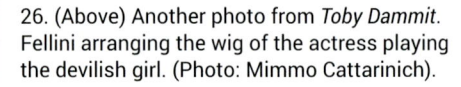

26. (Above) Another photo from *Toby Dammit*. Fellini arranging the wig of the actress playing the devilish girl. (Photo: Mimmo Cattarinich).

27. Photo from the set of *Toby Dammit* of Fellini directing two actresses. (Photo: Mimmo Cattarinich).

28, 29 and 30 (over page). In 2018, *Il viaggio di G. Mastorna* became a play, directed by Marie Remond at the Comédie-Française. (Photos: Vincent Pontet).

31. Fellini's self-portrait as Mastorna, drawn in hospital a few days before his death, taken from *Il misterioso viaggio di Federico Fellini*, a film by Maite Carpio (2003).

work depicts a logical afterlife working in accordance with a perfect order. Sins are punished and virtue rewarded. The adolescent Fellini was already dreaming of a film which would show the opposite: an afterlife subject to disorder and absurdity, a world of the dead as fraught and bewildering as the world of the living. Fellini began work for the film in 1965, immediately after shooting *Giulietta degli spiriti* and the death of his therapist Ernst Bernhard. At that point, after the successive triumphs of *La Strada* (1954), *Notti di Cabiria* (1957), *La Dolce Vita* (1960), *Otto e mezzo* (1963) and the failure of *Giulietta degli spiriti*, Fellini was undergoing two crises. One was artistic in nature: the wonderful team which Fellini had succeeded in assembling fell apart. From this point on he no longer saw eye to eye with Ennio Flaiano and Tullio Pinelli, the two screenwriters who had worked with him since the beginning of his career.[14] The incident of the flight from Rome to Moscow is well known. Ennio Flaiano who, as the writer of the film *Otto e mezzo*, was due a large part of the credit for the award the film was to receive at the Moscow International Film Festival, found himself seated in economy class while Fellini and his collaborators on the shooting travelled first class. This anecdotal incident is, however, symbolic. Ennio Flaiano was himself a hugely talented writer but Fellini used him without according him the recognition he deserved[15]. In any case, the failure of *Giulietta degli spiriti* made the Maestro realise that it repeated *Otto e mezzo*. He needed a new team in order to find new inspiration.[16] He therefore chose the renowned Dino Buzzati over Flaiano and Pinelli, while retaining another longstanding collaborator, Brunello Rondi.

He also parted company with two other collaborators. Firstly his producer, Angelo Rizzoli, who had just suffered the commercial failure of the very costly *Giulietta degli spiriti,* and secondly his artistic director, Piero Gherardi who had won two Oscars, one for *La Dolce Vita* and the other for *Otto e mezzo.*

Hats, outlandish costumes, wigs, over-the-top sets, the visual excesses of *Giulietta* arguably made it as much Gherardi's film as Fellini's. The work – so eagerly awaited by both critics and public – was a disappointment. Did Fellini blame Gherardi for the failure? He confides in Zanelli:

> Gherardi has a deep-seated tendency to make everything gigantic, as you saw from *Giulietta degli spiriti* [...]. There are good and bad sides to long-standing collaborations, as you know. Among the bad ones: laziness. Everything slows up, stagnates. In the end Gherardi himself recognised that our relationship was at an end and he seized on Monicelli's offer to go and make a film in Bangkok.[17]

To Rizzoli, Fellini preferred the most celebrated producer of the times,

Dino De Laurentiis. He was then at the very height of his fame: he had just built massive, luxurious studios (Dinocittà) which specialised in blockbusters adapted from famous texts. Piero Gherardi was replaced by a very well-known theatre designer, Pier Luigi Pizzi. It is obvious that the sweeping changes made by Fellini are moves towards the grandiose. Following the series of triumphs culminating in *Otto e mezzo* he was without doubt the world's most famous film director. Was he seeking to work with people more worthy of his new status? The phenomenon is not unknown. An artist, after becoming famous with a small team of faithful collaborators, replaces those with a real involvement by more renowned partners as soon as he is successful. And often pays a high price for his lack of loyalty. As for his director of photography, Gianni di Venanzo, he was to succumb to a shocking bout of viral hepatitis in 1966 during preparations for the macabre *Mastorna*. Fellini replaced him with Giuseppe Rotunno, Visconti's cinematographer.

The crisis in Fellini's artistic life coincided with a spiritual crisis. *La Dolce Vita* (1960), *Otto e mezzo* (1963) and *Giulietta degli spiriti* (1965) portray men in crisis, artists in crisis in a society in crisis. That nostalgia for Christ and a return to faith which imbue *La Strada* (1954), *Notti di Cabiria* (1957) and *La Dolce Vita* (the young girl with the face of the Madonna with which the film ends) give way to salvation through art in the closing sequence of *Otto e mezzo*. The director retreats into artistic creation, the only act of importance. In *Giulietta degli spiriti* Fellini goes further. The heroine severs her remaining ties to Christianity. The deliberate refusal to observe religious law saves Giulietta. At that point the spirits assailing her flee away. She is greeted by benevolent spirits and, delivered from religious morality, she is finally able to welcome in the natural forces which fill the world. The film ends: a happy Giulietta hears the voices of the earth. In other words: Fellini abandons the Christianity for which he has been nostalgic for so long, and returns to the spiritual forces of the material world: paganism.

The fictional solution corresponds to Fellini's own experience. He had a profound interest in the mystical and frequented clairvoyants. His library was full of books on spiritualism.

> I believe there is more to life than we yet know or will ever know. The religious; the mystical, the psychic, the miraculous; fate, destiny, coincidence. The land called the Unknown. I know I have been laughed at and ridiculed sometimes for my openness to everything from A to Z, astrology to Zen, from Jung to Ouija boards and crystal balls, but the promise of marvels fascinates me. I am not stopped by snickerers or scoffers. Let them

live planted in the mundane, those who believe everything has to have a pragmatic, scientific explanation.[18]

When Dino Buzzati, who was also a journalist, came to interview Fellini for the *Corriere della Sera,* the conversation soon focused on the supernatural and clairvoyance. Buzzati was preparing a series of newspaper articles (*In search of mysterious Italy*) and asked Fellini to act as his guide. In Turin, the film director introduced him to Gustavo Rol, a master of the paranormal to whom he was very close, and in Civitanova Marche, to a clairvoyant, Pasqualina Pezzola. During this period Fellini was engaged in an intense spiritual quest, triggered by the death, in 1965, of his Jungian psychoanalyst, Ernst Bernhard, which left him deeply disturbed.[19]

It was in this psychological turmoil that Fellini signed a contract with Dino De Laurentiis, who had just finished the epic *The Bible* (1965).

The great producer felt guilt towards the great director. Twelve years earlier, in 1953, De Laurentiis had turned down the project of the young director who was then just starting out. In *La Strada* the producer had wanted Silvana Mangano as leading lady rather than Fellini's almost unknown wife, for whom the role had been conceived. With Giulietta Masina, though, *La Strada* would prove an international success. Some years later, Dino De Laurentiis had refused to produce *La Dolce Vita*, disliking the screenplay. Another mistake: another international triumph. This time De Laurentiis was determined not to be wrong! The first project Fellini suggested to him was a science fiction film based on a story by Fredric Brown, *What mad universe* (1949). Here a science fiction writer is transported into a new space-time dimension. The Earth, under the dictatorship of an adventurer called Doppelle, is engaged in a war against the monstrous inhabitants of another planet. Gradually the hero of the text realises that he is not in the real world but inside the mind of a child, Joe Doppelberg, who believes he is Doppelle and wants to rule the world.

Dino De Laurentiis took on the project and acquired the rights to Brown's story. Fellini, however, changed his mind, perhaps thinking the theme too superficial.[20]

The producer may himself have been responsible for the new direction the plan took at this point. Films made at Dinocittà (*The Bible*) or the list of those the producer suggested to the director (*The Decameron, Orlando Furioso, Satyricon, Don Quixote*) appear to indicate that Dino De Laurentiis wanted to embark on a new kind of mass market film. No more historical epics or spaghetti westerns but, rather, great classics filmed in lavish conditions. The idea of filming *The Divine Comedy*, another iconic work, won out and was entirely in keeping with the purpose of the enormous Dinocittà studios.

It is not clear whether Dino Buzzati became involved at this point, or earlier. In 1938 the great Italian writer had written a short story, *Il sacrilegio* (The Sacrilege) which inspired the screenplay. In the story, an extremely pious child says during Confession that he has committed a sin. He is superstitious. The priest grants him absolution, but the sin – which to the reader seems quite venial – becomes much greater in the view of this solitary child. He falls ill and soon arrives in the land of the dead, place of judgement where the fate of souls is to be decided: they will go either to heaven or to hell. The child is judged extremely harshly: for this very minor sin his soul is damned. An old family servant intervenes and after an outraged plea in which he criticises the incomprehensible severity of the sentence, saves the little boy by offering his own life in place of the child's. The child returns to life and the old servant dies.

Fellini sent the producer a letter-synopsis – the one which appears in the book published by Éditions Sonatine – describing the new idea for the film: a journey to the realm of the dead.

The De Laurentiis business was a family concern. Dino was helped by his two brothers, Luigi and Alfredo. Luigi in particular, who had an enthusiasm for the occult, liked the project a lot and pushed the initially reluctant Dino to take it on. Work on writing the screenplay (synopsis and dialogue) began. Dino Buzzati was tasked with developing his story, *Il sacrilegio*. A long-standing collaborator of Fellini's, Brunello Rondi, would help him write the film. The three men set to work.

Reading that the screenplays for *La Dolce Vita* or *Otto e mezzo* were written by Federico Fellini, Ennio Flaiano and Tullio Pinelli, people might well imagine merry get-togethers with the three men indulging in virtuoso displays of wit which give rise to masterpieces. Fellini's method of working was quite different, however. Ennio Flaiano, Tullio Pinelli and Brunello Rondi never met and Fellini worked with each of them separately. Each independently wrote a text inspired by the same subject proposed by Fellini, who then created a montage of the different versions. Brunello Rondi's valuable account, reproduced in Zanelli's book, does not specify the part played by Buzzati. However the very fact that Rondi hardly ever met Buzzati confirms that Fellini continued to use his old method. Having obtained the producer's agreement, he set to work with both screenwriters, but working separately with each. He would go to Milan to meet Buzzati who would come to work with the director in his house in Fregene.

More is known from this point onwards about the different stages of

A Metaphysical 'James Bond Film'

his collaboration with Brunello Rondi. It all began in September 1965, after the Venice Biennale and a few months after Ernst Bernhard's death in June 1965. The two men worked together at Fregene. "The first treatment was born during walks in the woods"[21]. Then for the next two months they worked in a less structured way. Rondi assembled the elements and typed two hundred pages of the screenplay, half of the whole. After Fregene, Fellini and Rondi worked in an inn with no telephone by the Lake of Bracciano, Villa Giulia, at Manziana. The location was not chosen at random: it has links with the *Divine Comedy*; Manziana is situated not far from the forest where Dante begins his journey. The two men were trying to create a 'metaphysical James Bond film', to give an unfamiliar appearance to real surroundings. As Fellini wrote in his first letter-treatment to De Laurentiis, the film is an adventure story:

> I cannot overemphasise the term "packed with incident", the 007 stories will seem lacking in suspense and short on twists in comparison with ours.[22]

No doubt the idea was in vogue because the previous year, in *Alphaville* (1965), Godard had filmed Paris as if it were a far off planet. Here is Rondi describing the end of the working process:

> Buzzati and I gave Fellini loads of episodes, after each of us had worked on our own (following the rule imposed by the director who always kept me away from Flaiano and Pinelli). Fellini rewrote everything, for the first time in his life, I think. Then he gave the definitive version to his secretary. Next he gave it to us to read. We made our observations. Before he went to Milan looking for locations (the station, the airports) we met up again in Manziana to put the finishing touches to it. Overall, though, the text remained the same one as the producer was given.[23]

De Laurentiis was given the text of the screenplay in April 1966. He was not happy with it. Could this have been the point at which he began offering Fellini huge amounts of money to change his mind and devote himself to a new project, *Orlando Furioso*, *Don Quixote*, or *The Chronicle of the Merovingians*? For his part, Fellini was disappointed by the collaboration with the renowned Buzzati, from whom he had hoped for more.

> Buzzati had accepted my proposal enthusiastically. It was affirming for me to find in him an interlocutor who really liked my story, who had no

objections nor misgivings; quite the reverse, he respected me. He wrote a huge amount and put in all the commas which I tend to miss out. But to be honest, from an author like him I was hoping for a more personal contribution. Maybe it was my fault. I think my way of working threw him. He remained an outsider to the film.[24]

Buzzati was disappointed by the definitive version of the screenplay. He found the dialogue which Fellini had kept "scant and bewildering." To which Fellini had this to say:

In the cinema, dialogue is secondary. Besides, my dialogues are always done again at the dubbing stage, because my actors are foreign. They speak in their own language. One reply gets longer, another shorter. In the end, everything has to be changed [...] The dialogue is really not important. A close-up of a cup of coffee expresses the separation of two lovers better than any number of sentences.[25]

Fellini and Buzzati were unable to work with each other. Note the remarkable parallel which may be drawn between the 1963 fiction (*Otto e mezzo*) and the reality of the years 1965–1966. In *Otto e mezzo,* Guido, the renowned director, employs the famous writer Daumier to help him write his film. However the writer remains a hostile outsider with respect to the project, in which he is participating only reluctantly. One might also wonder how Buzzati viewed his role as co-screenwriter with Brunello Rondi, perhaps a humiliating part for an internationally renowned writer.[26] In *Otto e mezzo,* Fellini depicts a director who has lost all desire to make his film but is committed to directing a team who have already begun work. That is just what was to happen two years later with *Mastorna*. Everything happened as if reality (the shooting of *Mastorna*) was an extension of fiction (*Otto e mezzo*).[27]

The gigantic sets were already under construction: Cologne Cathedral, the motel, the aeroplane, the multi-decker train for the station sequence. Pier Luigi Pizzi was making the hundreds of costumes needed for the blockbuster. This was a world apart from the brightly coloured festivities of *Giulietta*. Fellini wanted grey, sad tones, costumes which looked as though they had been dipped in ashes. With Giuseppe Rotunno, his new director of photography, he was exploring a black and white broken by only rare touches of colour.

Fellini did not care for the Dinocittà studios. He rented a small office in town in which he saw actors for his film. He was looking for extras of Slavic origin so that the setting would be vague, and actors of very diverse nationalities to give the film an indefinable tone. He had already chosen actors for the supporting roles. Wanda Osiris and Vittorio De Sica were to play the presenters at the tribunal where the dead would receive their prizes, Toto the clown would be the undertaker and the singer Mina the air stewardess (the Beatrice figure of this anti-*Divine Comedy*).

One big problem remained, however – who should play the main character? Fellini was loathe to cast Marcello Mastroianni, lest he appear to be repeating himself after *Otto e mezzo*. For a time he considered Laurence Olivier, even travelling to London to meet him.

> Laurence Olivier has a stupendous face, but he would not be credible as Mastorna. His face has a peaceful spirituality, a deep, calm intelligence, the detachment of a man who has comprehended everything, and grown familiar with the thought of death, overcoming it or merely giving it a suitable place inside himself. By the end of the film, G. Mastorna could have Laurence Olivier's face, not earlier.[28]

What about Steve MacQueen? Fellini was unfamiliar with him. He hesitated. Gregory Peck? Eli Wallach? Paul Newman came to Rome to discuss the part with Fellini but the latter could not make up his mind. Oscar Werner? Omar Sharif? Danny Kaye? Peter O'Toole? Vittorio Gassman? Enrico Maria Salerno? At one point he was even thinking of taking on a clown. Two clowns were already going to be playing Mastorna's two doubles: the philosophy teacher De Cercis, and the dead Neapolitan man, Armandino. Fellini then had the idea of having one clown play the three roles, which are all aspects of one character.[29] The variety of possibilities entertained by Fellini is evidence of the artistic turmoil in which he found himself. He spoke of feeling helpless where the film was concerned. In the notebook of dreams he kept, on the advice of his late therapist, Ernst Bernhard, his dreams during this period were menacing ones. He confided in Dario Zanelli:

> My uncertainties and doubts about *Otto e mezzo* were all beneficial: I was making a film about uncertainty and doubt. This is not the case here. *Mastorna* needs as much vitality and energy as possible from the one relating it.[30]

In the end Fellini chose Marcello Mastroianni. He was playing the role of Rudolph Valentino in the musical comedy *Ciao Rudy*! In order to make a new film with Fellini he was prepared to pay the financial penalty to break his contract. However Fellini could no longer begin the shoot. The sudden death of his photographic director Gianni Di Venanzo during the preparations for the film could not have failed to affect him. Legend has it that Rol, the Turin clairvoyant in whom he put all his trust, advised him not to make the film.[31]

There was a further bad omen: at the station, Mastorna was to see a friend greeting him from the top of a multi-decker train, a friend who had been dead for decades. It was this which would show him that he was dead. The multi-decker train was a very important part of the set. Its accidental collapse must also have made a deep impression on Fellini. Liliana Betti quotes an extract from the diary Fellini kept during the shoot:

> Try to give up the fight halfway through the film, as though the very idea of the story Mastorna's voyage had the ill-omened and reasonable power to paralyze its author's creativity. Everything is blocked […]. Death is something so unknown that the sheer notion of speculating about it is senseless and wildly presumptuous. The wall of the eight-story railroad car collapses on the platform of the station built in the studio. HALT! ADJOURNED! TILL WHEN?[32]

The reasons Fellini gave Dario Zanelli were more prosaic:

> I am in a period of turmoil. Psychological turmoil, in particular. Dino De Laurentiis wore my patience out. Not only did he make 1500 million [lire] from the Americans (I've never had that much money in my life, the maximum was 900 million with *Giulietta*), not only did he pocket 300 million from renting his studios, but then he wanted to reduce costs – or else ask the Americans for more money. In reality he doesn't believe in the film. He has done, and continues to do, all he can to prevent me making it. He offers me fabulous sums to make *Orlando Furioso* or for an episode of *The Witches* whereas he does nothing but put obstacles in *Mastorna*'s path.
>
> I'm going to apply directly to United Artists! If they're willing to finance my film I shan't need that De Laurentiis any longer. I'll gain from that, I'll have the 1500 million at my disposal. If I manage to spend less, then I'll be the one who profits, not De Laurentiis.[33]

And so he announced to his secretary, Liliana Betti, and his artistic director, Pier Luigi Pizzi, that he wanted to postpone the filming. In September 1966 he wrote to Dino De Laurentiis to release himself:

> Dear Dino, I have to tell you about my internal struggle, which has been going on for some time now and which has finally come to a conclusion.
> This is a serious decision, which I do not wish to dramatize, but it is the

only honest reply to my mind, which is worn out with useless and repeated efforts [...] I cannot begin the film because after all the things that have happened, I will not be able to complete it. Do not misunderstand me: I have no doubts as to the film itself. But there have been so many contradictory, disturbing incidents, which have nothing to do with the film, but which have surrounded the birth and course of the preparations with an atmosphere of resistance and stagnation. All this has alienated and exhausted me, and there is no way I can make my film in such conditions [....]

Moreover, I really need a little peace and solitude. Therefore, I ask you, in all friendship, to deal with Giorgio De Michele[34] whom I have entrusted with everything.[35]

Imagine Dino De Laurentiis's fury on receiving this news, after he had already invested hundreds of millions of lire in preparations for the film. The producer immediately began legal proceedings against the director, demanding the sequestration of his goods and freezing of his bank accounts. In exactly the same way, the producer in *Otto e mezzo* threatens to ruin Guido when he realises the latter no longer wants to make his film. And throughout the film Guido, the fictional film director, fears what was to happen three years later in reality. On 25 September 1966 the bailiffs came to put seals on property belonging to Fellini, who no longer had access to his frozen bank account.

> I recall that one morning he came from Fregene with a package containing two or three gold brooches and a small medallion. This incredible nest egg was sold to a jeweler on Via del Tritone and the cash allowed Fellini to take a friend out to lunch: Hans Richter, the famous painter and Dadaist.[36]

He spent several months looking for a producer to replace De Laurentiis, in order to attract American capital. Then, in accordance with the scheme suggested to Zanelli, he founded his own production company, Fulgor. Next he applied to an official body, the Italnoliggio. However all his attempts to resurrect *Mastorna* from the ruins failed. Fellini had only one solution left to him: a reconciliation with his producer. Their meeting is reminiscent of one between two members of the Mafia. Early one morning the director met with the producer in a car driving around the side streets by the Villa Borghese. That car was followed by another containing the lawyers for both parties. Eventually Fellini and De Laurentiis got out of the car and embraced. Everything was sorted. For the time being.

Fellini resumed preparations for the film but something inside him seemed to have broken. He spoke of retiring from the cinema and opening a shop. Then came a new (smart?) move by Dino De Laurentiis. For the role of Mastorna, Fellini had finally settled on Enrico Mario Salerno. The producer, however, wanted a bigger name. Forced to make a quick decision, Fellini chose Ugo Tognazzi. The actor signed the contract on 16 March 1967 but suddenly Fellini appeared to lose all interest in the film. Detecting some uncertainty on the part of his future director, the actor, possibly wishing to amuse him, turned up at Fregene one Sunday afternoon dressed as a peasant, with a hen in each hand.

> The incredible masquerade and its inscrutable reasons amused, confused, and touched Fellini. The flashing vision of a peasant Mastorna was an unbearable hallucination, a presage.
> Fellini got sick.[37]

On 10 April 1967, ten days before shooting was to resume, *La Strada* was shown on television. His wife, Giulietta Masina, went to watch the film at her sister's house. Fellini was on his own at home when he was suddenly gripped by terrible pains and was rushed to hospital. Dino De Laurentiis naturally thought this was an act, and sent specially chosen doctors to examine the artist. Their diagnosis was gloomy: Fellini was ill, seriously ill even. Was it pleurisy? Or Sanarelli-Schwartzman Syndrome? This was the opinion of Ercole Sega, an old school friend of Fellini's, now a doctor, the person to whom the young Fellini had confided his ambition to write a reverse *Divine Comedy*. Yet again shooting was postponed.

> Luckily, Fellini recovered from his pleurisy and anaphylaxis. Not only that, but he also recovered from *Mastorna*. The violent trauma of the illness and its long course seemed to pulverize three years of conflicts, hostilities, difficulties, tensions. Fellini emerged detoxified, reconciled with everybody and everything, full of new energies, perhaps with fewer illusions, fewer childlike enchantments, yet enriched by a more fertile, more severe contact with reality.[38]

Fellini had been reborn after making his way through that 'desperate land' which, according to Genet, every artist experiences.

> One of the most moving mysteries is this: after a brilliant period, every artist will cross a desperate land, risking losing his reason and his mastery. If he emerges victorious . . .[39]

Once he was restored to health, Fellini severed his ties with Dino De Laurentiis. Liliana Betti gives a detailed account of this scene which she probably witnessed at first hand:

> It was late at night. In Dino De Laurentiis's immense, incredibly luxurious office at Castel Romano, you could hear only the humming of the air-conditioner. The lawyers for both parties gathered in a corner of the room to put the final touches on the dissolution. Fellini sat absentmindedly at the large table where the meeting was taking place. Dino De Laurentiis nervously pretended to be leafing through some magazines. He had a bitter and angry expression on his face. Luigi De Laurentiis, his brother, was pacing up and down the room, constantly gazing at Fellini with inquiring, almost astonished eyes, as though he didn't quite understand what and whom it was all about.
>
> Every so often, some difficult, incomprehensible legal term would rebound from the group of lawyers:, reciprocal usucapion, via compulsiva [...] With the generosity of a prisoner about to regain his freedom, Fellini said gently to Dino: "You see, Dino, you and I were stuck in a hole". [...] De Laurentiis gazed at Fellini uncertainly for a moment, then said with restrained irritation: "You sure get over things fast."[40]

But the saga of *Mastorna* was not yet at an end. It was to continue for another thirty years and only the broad outlines will be given here. While Fellini was recuperating, a new producer came into his life. Antonio Grimaldi had made a mint with Sergio Leone's spaghetti westerns and now announced he was prepared to buy back the screen rights to *Mastorna* in order to become producer for the renowned Fellini. He was the one who put up the 435 million lire which De Laurentiis claimed in return for releasing Fellini. But, once freed, the director had for the moment no interest in *Mastorna*. Instead he suggested other fascinating subjects to Grimaldi: *Orlando Furioso*, *The Satyricon*, *The Merovingian Chronicles* or *The Decameron*, all originally put forward by De Laurentiis. And so shooting on the *Satyricon* began.

In 1971 Fellini bought back the rights from Grimaldi and began working on it again with his new co-writer Bernardino Zapponi and later with Tonino Guerra, but could never produce something with which he was satisfied. Towards the end of his life, in 1990, the project took on its umpteenth shape. The artist Milo Manara was asked by the director of the revue *Il Grifo* to collaborate with Fellini on a graphic novel inspired by *The Journey of G. Mastorna*. The two men had in mind a version which would appear in three issues under a title slightly revised to include a touch of clownery: *Il viaggio di G. Mastorna, ditto Fernet*

(The Journey of G. Mastorna, known as Fernet).[41] In the graphic version Mastorna would now be not a cellist but a clown musician. However a new and disturbing coincidence scuppered the project. Manara published the first part of the graphic work in the July-August 1992 issue of *Il Grifo*: twenty pages culminating in the scene of the night club and the dancer's giving birth – applauded madly by the dead – followed by the television announcement of the plane crash. At the end of the page, however, instead of 'To be continued', the words 'The End' appeared by mistake. Fellini interpreted this error as a sign from fate and refused to go on with the project. He had no time in any case, setting off on his own journey to Mastorna's country a few months later. Just as Rol had predicted, *Mastorna* was to be his final work. Only a few days before his death in September 1993, Fellini was still drawing Mastorna's mysterious outline. It was his last self-portrait.[42]

The different versions of the work

The many vicissitudes linked to the writing of *Mastorna* explain the large number of versions of the screenplay.

A. First there is the letter-synopsis Fellini sent Dino De Laurentiis in the late summer of 1965. Substantial extracts from it are reproduced in the chapter on *Mastorna* in Tullio Kezich's Fellini biography. The letter was also published in French in the Éditions Sonatine translation of the screenplay (2013). It is of great interest as it includes extremely theatrical passages, such as the fight with the eagle and the suit fitting in the hotel room, which are absent from the more developed text, which is much more restrained. In certain places Fellini also explains his intentions:

> Supposing that it must have one, the meaning of the film should be as follows. We project on to a dimension we normally call the world beyond, all our hopes, our rigorous education and our ignorance, without realizing that this other world, invented, imbued with mystery, fantasy or morality, inevitably conditions our life in this world, which is, consequently, in its turn invented and made mysterious, in other words caught up in false schemas. The joyous disorder which I want to translate into the film should objectivise the other world in the same way as the protagonist (and most of us along with him) imagines it, and suggest the character's liberation.[43]

B. An English text was deposited with the Italian Society of Authors.

Presumably this is a translation of the text sent to De Laurentiis, which the director wished to protect immediately.

C. The screenplay, which was typed in March 1966, is a synthesis of the respective texts by Dino Buzzati and Brunello Rondi. Umberto Rondi, the screenwriter's son, was kind enough to give me access to it. This was the text on which preparations for shooting were to be based. It is full of crossings out. Entire sequences disappear.

D. Fellini's second letter to Dino De Laurentiis postdates not only the work carried out with Rondi and Buzzati but also the cuts made to the screenplay. The letter – which was published in Dario Zanelli's book, after Fellini's death – takes account of the cuts made to the typescript by hand, and the handwritten alterations For example, the episode of La Cicciona's kitchen, which he cut on the typescript, is thus not mentioned in the letter. The night club where Mastorna meets the clairvoyant is replaced in the typescript by public lavatories; the letter then describes lavatories, not a night club. The car in which Mastorna travels to the station is replaced in the typescript by a bus; the letter then has a bus not a car, and so on.

E. Lastly there is the text published by Kezich after Fellini's death. This version, while taking account of the work done on the project with two other co-writers, Bernadino Zapponi and Tonino Guerra, shows only minor differences from the 1966 text. In the unpublished screenplay typed in 1966 the protagonist's name is Mastorna. In the revised text published by Kezich the name is initially Mastorna. Then Fellini seems to have changed his mind as Mastorna becomes Guido Zeta. The name of the director in *Otto e mezzo* is Guido. There may have been an intention to present the new film as a sequel to *Otto e mezzo*: already in the earliest versions Giuseppe's wife is called Luisa, as is Guido's wife. The performance in the nightclub at the beginning of the film is of a dancer giving birth: the audience witnesses her labour pains and the baby's birth. In the text of the screenplay this page is crossed out with the words 'rewrite this scene' on it. In the text published by Kezich the birth scene has disappeared and is replaced by a scene, about an evil action Guido Zeta has done in the past (the artist has destroyed the domestic relationship of one of his admirers). The episode of the stolen case and fight with the hotel watchman (who is actually the actor from the night club in disguise) has been added. However it appears that the screenplay had been revised only as far as this scene. The protagonist's name reverts to Mastorna and thereafter the text in Kezich's book is identical to the 1966 typescript.

F. Milo Manara's graphic version published in 1992 contains only the first sequences from the screenplay.[44]

G. Ermanno Cavazzoni's text, which appeared in an English

translation in 2013, is a slightly novelized version. The details added are entirely in keeping with the spirit of the text and help to transform the screenplay into an adventure story, which was Fellini's intention.

H. It would appear that the end of the first letter-treatment, published in 2013, contains evidence of yet another reworking of the text.

> What is still valid and what am I still pleased with in *Mastorna*?
> 1. The fundamental idea: that is "it's life ... and also death", as someone sang in my dream with Pasolini.
> 2. The idea of the great adventure.
> 3. The photographic style as the expression of death, of everything which no longer exists and is fixed lifelessly in an eternal immobility.[45]

This text cannot date from 1965 since it refers to a dream of 6 June 1977. Nor can it be addressed to Dino De Laurentiis, as was the letter, since the producer would not be familiar with Fellini's dreams ("My dream with Pasolini"). The tone of this passage is that of an artist reappraising his work. It is possible that this piece of paper, filed with the 1965 letter, was written long after 1977, at the point when Fellini had bought back the rights and intended to resume work.

The following account of the screenplay is therefore based on the typescript from 1966, the two letter-treatments and Ermanno Cavazzoni's narrative, and indicates the cuts made to the manuscript, and certain variants to the text published in 1994 after Fellini's death.

1. The accident

An aeroplane on a long-haul flight is buffeted by a tremendous storm. On board a film is being screened in which Laurel and Hardy can be seen getting out of a large bathtub. Mastorna is a man of around forty-six, with a face drenched in sweat. There is a sudden long silence. The plane seems to have come out of that realm of time. The gentle voice of the air stewardess informs the passengers that the captain is going to attempt an emergency landing because of the bad weather.

The plane then lands in a square in an unknown city, perhaps the cathedral square in Cologne. The snow and wind prevent Mastorna from recognizing the city where he has landed, however.[46]

2. The motel

Mastorna wants to make a phone call to his family but this is not possible as the lines are down. Furthermore there is a power cut in the hotel. He wants to send a telegram. The office is shut, the employees on a meal break.

A Metaphysical 'James Bond Film'

3. The nightclub

In the motel nightclub, Mastorna watches a cabaret act in a language he cannot understand. A half-naked woman appears. Her belly dance develops into writhing. Finally on the stage a man displays a baby which has just been born. Mad applause greets this spectacular birth.[47]

4. Mastorna's room

In his hotel room, Mastorna has put down his cello case. He opens it and sounds the strings with his bow. The phone rings. On the other end, someone speaks in a familiar tone. Mastorna cannot recall this Tubino, who seems to know him so well. He watches television.[48] The first letter-treatment includes a Kafkaesque comic sequence which Fellini did not retain. The doorman wishes to give Mastorna a present, in the name of the hotel management. A tailor enters with his two assistants:

> "... It is a custom of this establishment to honour our guests by making them the gift of a new item of clothing. You may choose a uniform, or a suit, and many of our guests just opt for a plain coat" [...] The peculiar honour that this strange motel shows its guests may be viewed kindly, but M. does not want anyone to take his measurements.

The three characters are unyielding though, and an absurd scene ensues. A real physical tussle.[49]

There's a knock at the door. It's a member of the hotel staff who has come to announce that the bus which will take him to the airport to continue his journey is about to leave.

In the 1966 screenplay, from his window Mastorna sees an excited crowd, a brightly lit street, in a festive atmosphere (whereas the previous night the motel stood alone on a dark plain). In the text published in 1995 the hotel employee leaves through the window and the sight greeting Mastorna is the sea, a calm, grey sea. The text continues with Mastorna chasing after his luggage and cello with which the hotel employee has run off. He turns out to be the actor in drag from the nightclub, the German admirer Mastorna betrayed.

In the 1966 screenplay, a cosmopolitan crowd – with which Mastorna mingles – pours into numerous places of worship standing next to one another: churches, synagogues, mosques.

5. Someone offers to accompany him to the station[50]

This exposition scene occurs, like in crime novels, after a shocking violent start. We will learn that Mastorna is a cellist who was on tour in Hamburg. Because of a hurried sexual encounter he has missed his train back to Italy where he is to appear in a concert. At the last moment he was able to get a flight. He is in a great rush. The concert is taking place in Florence tomorrow and he absolutely has to find a train to get there. The city he is crossing reminds him of the one where he spent his childhood. The man accompanying him also seems familiar but Mastorna is too tired to try to remember.

6. The station

Now he is in an enormous railway station. The names of the destinations written on huge signboards cannot be made out. When he asks for a ticket to Florence the employees seem not to understand. Amid the bustle of passengers looking for their trains an amazing procession arrives: a Pope, surrounded by cardinals and choirboys. In the next sequences we will witness the decline of this dead pope. He will lose the procession and his fine vestments and gradually become dead like the other people. From the top deck of a four-decker carriage[51] someone gestures to Mastorna through the window. The train departs but something horrendous suddenly occurs to Mastorna. The face belongs to a childhood friend who died forty years ago. Mastorna cannot accept the obvious truth: he isn't dead, he feels alive, he has a body. Jumping on a passing stewardess who smiles and lets him do as he wishes, he tries to have sex with her just to prove he is alive. However, in the stewardess's eyes he sees his plane which has crashed in the mountains, the scattered bodies of the passengers and his own corpse.

> The woman has long eyelashes that hide the depth of her imperturbable, slightly ironic eyes and it is in those blue eyes which slowly dilate, until they disappear, that he sees, as if on a screen, a horrifying scene.
> **Exterior. Mountain range. (Plane wreck.)**
> The peak of a snow-covered mountain. Close-up of crevices in a glacier; between one crevice and another, a peculiar black stain: the wreck of a large aeroplane. Helicopters hang over the disaster scene, like buzzards in a funereal merry-go-round.
> Next to the wreck, torn, charred, twisted bodies. Now a man lying on his back, head thrown back, his forehead crushed. but the face is intact, the mouth and eyes half-open: it is him, Mastorna. All that remains of his poor body. The long eyelashes of the hostess lower slightly, the atrocious scene sinks and dissolves in the blue of her eyes.[52]

Mastorna really is dead and in the land of the dead. He faints.

7. The station master's office

Mastorna comes round in the station master's office. He is surrounded by people from his former life: his catechism teacher and a colonel, his superior officer during his military service. They are all comforting him. Despite their gentle words of comfort Mastorna is devastated. A little person is gesturing to him through the window, enjoining him not to heed the words of these solemn figures.

8. The pariahs of the city of the dead

Armandino is a Neapolitan[53] living on the fringes of the city. He gives Mastorna telephone tokens so he can phone his wife. Mastorna makes the call. The new tenant explains that, following the terrible accident, Luisa Mastorna has moved to a new apartment and that she does not know her new number.

Suddenly male nurses appear, wanting to vaccinate him. If he wishes to stay in the city then he must comply, otherwise no hotel will accept him. Armandino advises him to refuse and, as he has not succeeded in reaching his wife by phone, takes him to a medium who puts the dead in contact with the living.

In the 1966 screenplay, after a long journey by metro (scored out), the scene with the medium takes place in a night club, but a handwritten note by Fellini has been added: "This scene takes place in public lavatories". The letter-synopsis sent to De Laurentiis does indeed describe the scene as set in enormous municipal lavatories with dim neon lighting.

The medium, who looks like Oscar Wilde, is crouching in a very dark corner. He pulls a little machine and tells Mastorna to concentrate on a 'very pure, linear' feeling". In the 1966 version Mastorna's cry of "I love you, Luisa" is taken up by Armandino, the medium and all the people in the nightclub who cry "I love you, Luisa" while performing a collective striptease.

> Everyone else in the night-club has climbed onto the stage, and to the orders of a powerful looking striptease artist with a mournful face, they are doing a collective striptease. An acrid smell of sweaty, grimy naked bodies is given off from the infernal exhibition.[54]

In the letter for De Laurentiis (and the American backers reputed to be prudish) there is no mention of this collective striptease.

9. The orgy of the dead

The scene which follows, in quotation, is almost intolerable:

Laughing madly, the young man throws himself over a balcony and falls head first eight floors to the ground, shouting with joy. He hits the paving with terrible thud, like a walnut being smashed open.

He has fallen onto the tarmac of the road below. The body is motionless, atrociously twisted out of shape, lying in a pool of blood and spilt brains. He stays like that for a few moments, then jumps up, like the coiling of a spring, alive, young, good-looking, healthier than ever.

You, too, go on, throw yourself down! You can't die any more!

A terrible noise begins. The people from the night-club have come out onto the terrace and are now throwing themselves over the balconies, in comic poses, and – with sinister thuds – are smashing onto the road below. A few seconds later, they get to their feet, unharmed, happy.[55]

10. La Cicciona's kitchen

In the 1966 typescript, this long sequence is crossed out with the word "Suppressed". It is not included in the list of sequences in the synopsis sent to De Laurentiis. It is published by Kezich, however. It is all set in a huge kitchen containing a Neapolitan family who have died in a car crash. The mother (La Cicciona), grandfather, daughter and granddaughter all died together and are still together. In the bed is an enormous snake which is petted by the child. Another sister, long dead already, killed herself for love.

This kitchen turns out to be a brothel. Soldiers and passers-by arrive. La Cicciona's daughters take the lift downstairs to show themselves to clients. Suddenly a very important client arrives, probably a man of the cloth. It is vital that Mastorna does not see him. And the kind-hearted La Cicciona will ask for a reward from another ecclesiastic, a prize for Mastorna.

11. Make-up

A team of make-up artists, hairdressers and manicurists get hold of Mastorna and prepare him for the awards ceremony.

12. The awards ceremony

The master of ceremonies, over there, on a stage which seems infinitely far away, is being witty and announcing the prizes, one by one, handing out statuettes and medals. Armandino, who has brought Mastorna here, assures him he merits a prize.

> Imagine the Césars ceremony in Los Angeles, that same atmosphere like a circus horse act crossed with a graveyard. The high-pitched shrieks of fans and teenagers at the arrival of the prize winners. Among them is

also the pope whom Mastorna saw at the station. Now he is alone, however, dressed in rags, his white silk slippers dirtied, his diadem squint and a bitter, anguished look on his face, nothing left of his former self-assurance.[56]

Mastorna, dressed and made up, is thrust on to the stage. The image they put up is not his. The text about his life is written in an absurd way and read out badly by a clumsy presenter who drops pages. And the prize he is awarded is a small gold medal. Mastorna is horribly disappointed. In front of everyone he declares his profound disillusion with this pathetic and ridiculous prize giving.

> He looks at the trophy in silence, with a look of mockery and then, with a little tap of his hand, he knocks the box out of the hands of the lady who looks at him stonily, jaw-dropped, eyes wide opened. In the sudden silence that has descended on the entire hall, Mastorna begins to speak with a wavering voice:
> Eternal happiness? Here? With you? In this circus? In this noise and vulgarity? In this cretinism? I can do without your eternal happiness! (...)
> This is your afterlife? Authentic life? This is what we were supposed to be struggling for, after so many years of fear, anxiety, solitude, suffering? A stinting, bitter life all just to get to this bitter ceremony? This is the kingdom of Heaven? . . .
> Men have built enormous cathedrals . . . have suffered, hoped, been killed . . . for what? For this charade?[57]

13. The immortality of the body

De Cercis, his old philosophy teacher, comes to congratulate him on daring to voice his protest. A lengthy scene in a provincial café follows, in which De Cercis expounds his theory of the immortality of the body rather than that of the soul.

> We don't believe in the immortality of the soul, there is no actual proof, so I do without it, am not interested in it. On the other hand, I do believe in the immortality of the body; what we call death, the decomposition of the body, is but a change of state, a metamorphosis, in which the body becomes something else, by an observable — albeit aesthetically far from pleasing — biochemical process.[58]

This scene was typed and then crossed out by hand. The long, strange scene in which the passionately atheist philosopher and his companion, the barmaid, suddenly become very tired and fall asleep in the street, to be picked up by a group of police nurses who will take them to dormitories where they may one day wake again (the death of the dead) does not feature in the letter-synopsis.

In the screenplay the whole scene is cut as far as the nurse's cry "Who can do something for Mastorna?"

14. The cemetery

An undertaker appears.[59] Mastorna follows him over to his own grave. The undertaker and Mastorna travel through a dark city which recalls parts of Rome, New York, London and Amsterdam. A former mistress appears in his path, in tears, drawing him close and then pushing him away. Here they are in the cemetery, an 'architectural folly' jumbling together all styles and eras. The dead emerge from their tombs and sit outside to receive visits from their relatives.

The only person who comes to visit Mastorna is Iole, the nanny who took care of him when he was small.

15. The ancestors

Iole leads him to his predecessors' house, where his parents, grandparents, uncles and aunts are waiting for him. Mastorna finds all his childhood memories:

> It's a sort of hidden trove where all the things from his childhood are jumbled together in a heap, a sort of archive or museum of memory [...]
>
> To ward off their burdensome presence and escape the vacuum filled with his memories, Mastorna throws a flaming brand and sets everything alight. The flames leap ever higher, consuming toys, clothes, the entire construction where Mastorna has taken refuge and become a devastating fire which spreads to the house and garden.[60]

Mastorna is saved from the fire just in time. Here he is, unconscious in the ambulance; at his side is the beautiful stewardess whom he has already encountered several times on his journey and who will become his faithful companion, like Beatrice for Dante in the *Divine Comedy*.

16. The identity photo

Mastorna finds himself in some sort of clinic. He is congratulated on having been able to get rid of his memories. Now, in order to continue his journey, he needs identity documents. The passport photo will be of a moment in his life when he showed himself completely sincere. The jury tasked with identifying a moment of authenticity in his life consists of people he has known in the past.

A film retracing Mastorna's existence appears on a screen. A pianist plays a tinkling musical accompaniment like in the days of silent films. The judges have trouble finding an occasion for the passport photo: even in the most private moments, Mastorna is playing a role.

A cry of genuine disgust and revolt does, however, reverse the situation. At a given moment, Mastorna – tormented by this exhibition of his private life – cries out "Watch it without me, it has nothing to do with me." The jury members give a sigh of relief: if he is indifferent to everything, he is on the right track and can continue his journey. And they hurry to find a moment at which he was genuinely himself to use for the photo on his dead man's passport. In a traffic jam he finds himself alongside a car with a big dog in it, and puts his tongue out at it. There it is: on his ID photo for the land of the dead he will be the man "who sticks his tongue out at dogs when he has nothing better to do".

> "Now, if anyone stops you and asks you who you are, show him this [the ID photo for the land of the dead] and tell him: 'I'm someone who, when he doesn't know what to do, sticks his tongue out at dogs in the back of a car'. And if you like, you could also add that beautiful, highly religious phrase you pronounced a few moments ago: 'It has nothing to do with me'. Well done, indeed, all the best, dear Mastorna, have a good journey. May I hug you?"[61]

17. Farewell to parents

The stewardess guides Mastorna into a car where his parents are waiting for him.

> The man and wife, calm and polite, begin speaking to Mastorna, saying it was entirely a matter of chance that they had been his parents for a while. Things might have been different. For example, you might well think they were his children or his brother, or his sister, and they gradually hypothesize ever freer and unprejudiced relationships.[62]

In the letter-synopsis, these discreet words are aimed at the American backers with their reputation for prudishness. The text of the screenplay is more explicit. It includes a kiss with the mother, and more than affectionate glances between those who were father and son. All of them, freed from all constraints and absurd prejudices, feel that they can now have any kind of relationship they want.

18. The airport

The parents leave. Armandino appears in the crowd of passengers looking for their destination. He does not remember Mastorna however. A voice is heard: "The only passenger on flight number 52 should board at gate . . . " but the gate number is inaudible and Mastorna, with the stewardess, will have to search for a long time before a tiny plane arrives. He climbs aboard using a rope ladder.

19. The little Chinese girl pilot

The cabin of the toy plane is scarcely bigger than a trunk. Mastorna crawls towards the cabin while the plane continues its crazy path. He is thrown against the walls of the plane and injured. Finally he finds the pilot, an elderly Chinese man, asleep on the floor of the toy plane. A five-year-old girl is at the controls; she is laughing as she flies the plane, making it execute all sorts of unexpected movements. Her answer to Mastorna's questions ("Where are we going?") is to laugh and pull faces. Only when he gives up and says "I'm stupid, go wherever you like, I don't want to think any more" does the little girl announce "We've arrived."

20. The valley in the mountains

In a valley surrounded by high mountains Mastorna eventually comes to a wooden hut. The stewardess greets him, and shows him the way, a narrow mountain path.

21. The night in the customs officers' hut

Mastorna spends the night with the stewardess in the customs officers' hut.

22. Departure

Mastorna wakes suddenly in the middle of the night. He looks at the face of the stewardess asleep next to him and then murmurs a silent goodbye to her.

> I imagine M. and the final apparition of "Beatrice" [the stewardess] on a little mountain path going ever upwards. After an unexpected bend in the path, the vision of a calm and boundless sky. Even the final frontier has been crossed. The companion cannot continue the journey with him. M. must go on alone. He has passed through all the trials, freeing himself from his preconceptions, abandoning his mistaken ideas about life, ridding himself of nostalgia for sensations and the 'manipulations of emotions'. His heart is strong and at peace, he may continue the journey on his own. Beyond the bend in the road, whatever adventures and encounters he has will be nobody's business but his own.[63]

23. Finale

Mastorna arrives at the door of a theatre. He comes on to the stage out of breath and joins his colleagues already in position in the orchestra pit. His wife, silent and patient, is attending the concert.

> Another member of the orchestra looks at him [Mastorna] in surprise, with curiosity and whispers:
> What kept you until now?
> Mastorna opens his mouth as if to reply but just then there are three sharp sounds from the conductor's stand.
> The orchestra settles into silence and picks up the instruments. The trumpet, pipe, and flute players bring these instruments to their lips.
> Mastorna has raised the bow of his cello, ready for the first note.
> The raised hand of the conductor holds the baton still, then it suddenly falls and the whole orchestra begins to play a solemn tune, grandiose, desperate, infinitely sweet, intoxicating.
> Up in the roof, where the skylight is open onto the spring day, swallows fly in and swirl, chasing one another in the rays of the sun and the specks of dust, tinged with gold.[64]

From antiquity onwards, numerous texts, plays and films have tried to depict the world beyond. For example, 'dialogues in hell' put together in the next world characters who have lived in different epochs. In Lucian Samostrata's *Dialogues of the Dead* various conditions of men figure: philosophers, heroes, kings of legend. After Fontenelle (1663), Fénelon wrote the *Dialogues of the Dead* (1712) for the Duke of Burgundy, in which Plato, Aristotle, Confucius, Socrates and others converse with one another. In *La descente de l'âme de Molière dans les Champs-Elysées* (*Molière's soul comes down into the Champs-Elysées*) of 1674, Molière answers criticisms made of his works. *Les dialogues aux enfers de Machiavel et de Montesquieu* (*The dialogues between Machievelli and Montesquieu in hell*) written by Maurice Joly in 1864 were reworked by Mathieu Golovinski around 1901, giving rise to the notorious fake *Protocols of the Elders of Zion*.

The realm of the dead is also the subject of the Orpheus myth and numerous variations on it: Monteverdi's *Orfeo* (1607), Gluck's *Orphée* (1764), Cocteau's play *Orphée* (1925) and the film version he made in 1949. In Genet's 1961 play *Les Paravents* (The Screens) we also see the world of the dead, who are shown as detached from everything and laughing uncontrollably:

(From very far off, visible behind the screens, shadows arrive. Then the shadows pierce the paper and go through it: they are the soldiers, led by the general) [...]
THE GENERAL (laughing): Well, well! [...]
THE LIEUTENANT: And they make such a fuss about it! (He laughs complacently)[65]

Fellini and his co-writers made use of many models. Chief among them, clearly, was *The Divine Comedy*. Mastorna's journey, like that of Dante's hero, leads from Hell to Paradise. Everything starts off in a kind of hell ruled by chaos. The horror culminates with the scene where the dead die, falling asleep in the street. Then, after the nurse cries "Who can do something for Mastorna?", a sort of purification takes place, equivalent to Purgatory. The sequence of the cemetery and the passport photo already signal the start of a reparation process. Paradise will be reached once Mastorna is completely detached from the world. The air stewardess is the Beatrice figure, guiding the traveller ever upwards. However, even if the ultimate model is a mystical journey through different worlds, Fellini is realising the dream he cherished as an adolescent schoolboy: he depicts an anti-*Divine Comedy* where the next world is apparently as meaningless as this one.

The speech Mastorna makes on-stage at the awards ceremony recalls the message of Buzzati's story, *Il sacrilegio* [The Sacrilege]:

"I was deceived into believing in notions of judgement, reward and punishment, and I now realise that I've imposed on my life a completely imaginary direction which has prevented me from discovering its true meaning. What should I do? What can I do? Weep with disappointment, sorrow and bitterness? That wouldn't be enough, it would just mean I would disappear into the disgusting mire which is trying to stifle me."[66]

It is noteworthy, moreover, that the end of the screenplay also recalls Fredric Brown's story, *What mad universe*, the work Fellini had initially intended to film. Mastorna as prisoner of a crazy aeroplane, flown by the little Chinese girl while the actual pilot is asleep, resembles Brown's hero who is lost inside the imagination of an adolescent boy. Both these situations have the same meaning, namely that we find ourselves in a world completely devoid of sense.

The attraction of this project for a painter-filmmaker like Fellini is obvious: it was a case not of copying reality but of creating a new and completely different reality. The mixture of disparate settings, peculiar physical appearances, actors with ambiguous personalities – as well as tones moving between black, white and colour – were intended to create an entirely new visual effect.

And just as Dante evokes hell in order to settle scores with his living enemies, Fellini and his screenwriters use the realm of the dead to comment on the living. The gigantic fresco constitutes a cry of revolt against the religious view of the world which divides people into good and bad according to criteria which Fellini, Buzzati and Rondi reject. The whole screenplay is an initiatic path relating to life, not death. Its aim is to celebrate a human philosophy of complete indifference.

All the stages in Mastorna's journey are connected to detachment and indifference. He gradually renounces everything: possessions (his cello) but also his hope of meaning or reward (the awards ceremony). When he utters the words "It has nothing to do with me", proving his complete detachment, the jury is favourably impressed. Mastorna is allowed to proceed with his journey, leave Purgatory and make his way towards Paradise.

Finally with the revelation of the complete absurdity of the journey (the plane flown by the little girl while the old captain smiles in his sleep) Mastorna attains the highest state of indifference which Buzzati, more than Fellini perhaps, regards as the paradise of absolute wisdom.

> I'm tired, go wherever you like, I don't want to think any more.[67]

This makes the director's comment on Laurence Olivier's face, mentioned earlier, more comprehensible:

> By the end of the film, G. Mastorna could have Laurence Olivier's face, but not earlier.[68]

The film, written after the trauma caused Fellini by his therapist's death, may be seen as a sort of therapeutic process. Mastorna, and with him the public, learns to accept the notion of death.

Moreover the end of the film, Mastorna's return to life, is viewed by Ermanno Cavazzoni as a rebirth, or rather the soul's birth into a luminous and clear world:

> This is what eternity is. It reveals itself occasionally, without warning, when the mind is free and elevated, as if one were being born or reborn after a lengthy, painful, interminable sojourn in purgatory which is confusion, indecision as to which path to take, which identity to adopt. The destination is the birth into a luminous, clear world, the way the world looks on certain blissful days. Purgatory is beforehand, it's not an arrival point, but

a sojourn, preceding birth, amidst the chaos of possibilities, accompanied by all the lack of ease linked to indecision.

That is why I quoted Plato. It's as if Fellini had instinctively returned to the myth of Er (*The Republic X*): the soul which, before birth, dwells on the plains of Hades must with many risks and difficulties choose its identity; then it bathes in the river of Lethe where all this pain mingled with its memories of the underworld are washed away, whereupon the light and pure soul falls from the sky like a shooting star (it rises, according to the philosopher) and begins its life on this planet.[69]

It is death that gives life its meaning. Interestingly, we find here again images from the other two dream projects considered in this study. In *On répète Tête d'Or* the Last Post sounded during the aviator's funeral was intended to give the play its meaning. In *L'étrange mot d'...* (*The Strange Word of Urb ...*), Genet locates theatre in the middle of the cemetery and the cemetery in the middle of the city, just as he gives Death the central place in his great work.

In all three instances, Death is to be understood not as the end of life but as the sign of another world to which the heroes have privileged access. Simon Bar Yona, the Christ figure, holds the keys to this other world. For Genet too, the homosexual or the artist is the intermediary between the two worlds. And Fellini's *Mastorna* continues the theme of the artist as seer central to *Otto e mezzo* and his whole oeuvre.

In that film, his cinematographic "ars poetica", Fellini showed us why Maurice, the humble magician-entertainer, is preferable to Daumier, the illustrious philosopher. Maurice is not famous, just a music-hall magician who puts on shows in hotels with a partner, Maya, a mind reader. Yet he is the one who, at the end of the film, heralds or causes the rebirth of the director's inspiration, once the crisis is over. During this time the sinister intellectual, Daumier, pronounces a sterile speech on the virtues of silence. The artist-visionary allows the film to be shot, and is set against the hollow intellectual. *I Clowns* (*The Clowns*) (1970) ends with trumpet music summoning a clown to the realm of the dead. In *Prova d'Orchestra* (*Orchestra Rehearsal*) (1978) everybody admires the beautiful but very superficial pianist, while it is the fat harpist, the object of mockery, who mysteriously senses the approach of death. In *E la nave va* (*And the Ship Sails On*) (1983) the secret of the Maria Callas-like prima donna Edmea Tetoua's talent stems from a conception of the poet which is inspired by Jewish, Greek or Arabic tradition: a conduit for a voice from another realm. In Fellini's last film, *La Voce della Luna* (1990), all the heroes have visions or hear voices from the other world. This sheds further light on why the traveller in *Il viaggio di G. Mastorna* should be an artist: a cellist in 1966, a film director (Guido Zeta) in the revised screenplay and a clown in Milo Manara's graphic version. Like Orpheus, the artist-visionary is a bridge between the two worlds.

Apparitions of the phantom picture in the rest of Fellini's work

The first film to mention *Il viaggio di G. Mastorna* directly is, as has been mentioned, a short which Fellini made for American television in 1969, *Fellini: a director's notebook*. This autobiographical piece, accompanied by Fellini reading his text in English, opens with shots of the unused sets for *Il viaggio di G. Mastorna*, just as *Otto e mezzo* ends with the destruction of the huge unused set of the space station. Fellini shows us the aeroplane which was to land in the cathedral square in Cologne, the costumes and the wigs, lying unused in heaps in the workrooms. He remarks that his life seems to imitate his art, the fictional project dreamed of by the director in *Otto e mezzo*. Without dwelling on this subject, however, he moves on to the next film he is preparing to shoot, the *Fellini-Satyricon*. Still, he has made us aware that the artist is a seer, and a dreamed-of work can prefigure an unforeseen event in real life.

While *Mastorna* is only a fleeting presence in this film, its influence is far more clearly seen in *Toby Dammit* (1968), *Ginger and Fred* (1985) and *La Voce della Luna* (1990).

Toby Dammit

Toby Dammit (1968) is perhaps Fellini's finest film; it is certainly the least known. A French producer, Raymond Eger of Films Marceau had suggested that Fellini and two other directors make an 'omnibus' film based on three stories from Edgar Allan Poe's *Extraordinary Tales*. Initially the other directors were to be Ingmar Bergman and Akira Kurosawa, but in the end it was Roger Vadim and Louis Malle who had the dangerous privilege of sharing the billing with Fellini. And it really was dangerous because the two French directors' films – Vadim's *Metzengerstein* and Malle's *William Wilson* – served only as a foil for Fellini's genius.

Toby Dammit, conceived following Fellini's crisis, very clearly echoes *Il viaggio di G. Mastorna*. After lengthy deliberations Fellini and his new co-writer, Bernadino Zapponi, chose a short text from *Extraordinary Tales* called "Never bet the devil your head", to which the finished film shows only a distant resemblance. Toby Dammit keeps betting on his head with the devil, as a joke. One day the devil appears, disguised as an old man, at the entrance to a bridge barred by a turnstile. Toby bets the old man that he will be able to jump over the barrier. A steel bar cuts his head off, however. The mysterious old man carries off his trophy under his arm. The whole story is a kind of self-parody by Poe. At the end, for example, in order to recoup the costs of the funeral, the narrator has Toby Dammit exhumed and sells his flesh for dog meat.

Fellini made use of Poe's macabre and ironic pretext – and the means offered by Films Marceau – to relate the crisis he had just experienced, as well as to incorporate verbatim extracts from *Mastorna* in the magnificent screenplay.

In *Toby Dammit* a once-celebrated actor arrives in Rome to shoot a "metaphysical western". He is attacked by journalists before being welcomed by the film's ecclesiastical producers. These are no less worrying than the unfortunate leading man, who is exhausted and neurotic. While stuck in an enormous traffic jam, the symbol of a frenetic and paralysed society (a cinematic tour de force which Fellini would repeat in *Roma*) the artist has his palm read by a gipsy woman who foretells a sombre future.

During the award of a lifetime achievement prize he causes an uproar by denouncing the absurdity of this society based solely on external appearances. Fleeing the venue of the awards ceremony, he jumps into the new open-top Ferrari given him by the film's producers and begins a crazy, high-speed race through the streets of Rome and the surrounding area. There's a deafening noise of metal. Toby Dammit keeps driving but gradually comes to realise that he is dead. Perhaps this never-ending frenzied drive is his hell. The closing frames show the wire – reddened by his blood – which has decapitated him, and a little girl-devil playing ball with his head, a vision which has haunted him throughout the film.

Like *Il viaggio di G. Mastorna,* the film begins with a stranger arriving in a city and the two share the same ambiance, a world between life and death. Furthermore the artistic director was Pier Paolo Pizzi who had spent a long time working on *Mastorna* and thus simply carried on his research. The airport scenes with their mixture of different religions, as at the start of *Mastorna*, could have featured in the unrealised screenplay.

Terence Stamp, in the role of Toby Dammit, has an air of exhausted vampire about him, and all the other actors were chosen for their strange and unusual physical appearance. The ecclesiastics and the female journalist who questions the actor on television are reminiscent of characters from a horror film. With *Mastorna* Fellini aimed to create a 'metaphysical *James Bond*' and here the actor is in Rome to shoot a 'metaphysical western'. In particular it is the episode of the scandal at the awards ceremony which seems directly taken from *Mastorna*. In the screenplay the judging of the souls (rewards, punishments) is depicted as a huge television show, and a disappointed Mastorna protests against the absurd nature of this justice. Toby Dammit's outburst is directed not against the divine order but against a society based on spectacle. When invited on to the stage, like Mastorna, to receive his award from a beautiful presenter, the thoroughly inebriated Toby Dammit begins talking about his life:

> "It's not true. I'm not a great actor. No, it's not true, I assure you. I could have been one, I could. But I haven't worked in the last year. My director, my director complained because he said I was drunk. I don't know why I'm telling you this, or why they've brought me here (yelling). What do you want with me?
>
> And this woman (he laughs). She wanted to marry me. That's funny. Doesn't that make you laugh? I was sitting down, weeping. Yes, that happens to me often, especially when I've been drinking. I weep. Yes, I weep. It's the wine. It makes me sad. Too much light in here. But whisky whisky's something different, that's strange, yes, strange.
>
> A wonderful woman, she took hold of my hand, she stroked my hand. She said 'I'm here for you. The woman of your dreams, that's me'.
>
> I'm not waiting for you, though. I'm not waiting for anyone any more, do you get me?
>
> (To the public) I don't give a shit about you."

Then after causing a scandal he flees the venue, just like Mastorna.[70]

A further similarity between the two works lies in the fact that the beauty of the first sequences of *Mastorna*, like that of the closing sequences of *Toby Dammit,* depends entirely on ambiguity. From the start of the film, Mastorna is dead but is unaware of this. He gradually finds out he has woken up in a reality at once similar and deeply unfamiliar. This technique may owe something to the work Fellini did on Fredric Brown's story, *What mad universe,* whose hero little by little comes to understand that he finds himself not in reality but inside the consciousness of a teenage boy. At all events, it is the same effect used in *Toby Dammit.* The film begins with a voiceover describing Toby Dammit's arrival in Rome. His death, at the end of the film, comes as a surprise.[71]

After the frantic race through the streets of Rome and the car crash, Toby Dammit gets up. We, and he, believe he is still alive. Only thanks to various allusions – a brief glimpse of Cerberus (the dog which guards the gates of Hell in Greek mythology), strange echoes of voices – do the character, and the audience, gradually come to realise – as in *Mastorna* – that he has crossed over to the other side.

Furthermore, as in *Mastorna* it seems that nothing changes. The land in which Mastorna finds himself has railway stations, policemen and identity cards. In the realm of the dead Toby Dammit continues to drive his Ferrari like a maniac, just as he was doing a few minutes earlier when still alive. This time, however, the frantic, pointless race has become the symbol of his life, as it is of the life of every famous artist, perhaps, or even of every human being.

Ginger e Fred (1985)

In this film, made to measure for Giulietta Masina and Marcello Mastroianni, Fellini and his two co-writers, Tonino Guerra and Brunello Rondi, similarly reuse numerous elements from the screenplay for *Il viaggio di G. Mastorna*, notably the arrival in the enormous railway station and the television on the bus, its screen showing a marionette acting the *Divine Comedy*. Furthermore, the motel accommodating Amalia Bonetti and everyone taking part in the TV programme, the preparations for which are shown in the film, looks like the hotel where Mastorna sleeps in the realm of the dead: a building in the middle of nowhere. Similarly the whole sequence in which Amalia anxiously watches television in her hotel room is a parallel to that in which Mastorna nervously switches the television on in his hotel room while waiting for his departure. In particular, however, it is the scene in which Pipo wants to provoke a scandal during the television show that recalls the dream project. It is helpful at this point to give a brief outline of the plot. During the 1940s and 50s, Amalia and Pipo used to perform a tap-dancing routine copied from one by Ginger Rogers and Fred Astaire. They then split up but now, thirty years later, Italian television brings them together again for a major Christmas show devoted to impersonators. The only reason Amalia, now married and running a small factory, agrees to this is to see Pipo again after all these years of separation.

Pipo has lost his wits, however. During rehearsals for their dance routine he tells Amalia that he intends to cause national outrage on live television. He will stop dancing and speak out about his views on a society which turns him into a puppet.

A frantic team of make-up artists and dressers grab him, as in the case of Mastorna in the screenplay. On stage, an electricity failure – as in the hotel in *Mastorna* – interrupts the programme. Pipo's courage fails him and he does not voice his contempt to the whole world.

La Voce della Luna (The Voice of the Moon, 1990)

Fellini's last film, *La Voce della Luna*, perhaps comes closest to the dream project. Might this be why the director had so much difficulty in finishing it?

In October 1987, immediately after the triumphant success of *Intervista (Interview)*, which received a half-hour standing ovation at the Cannes Film Festival, Fellini embarked on a new project with Ermanno Cavazzoni, a novelist and professor at the University of Bologna. Cavazzoni's book, *Il poema dei lunatici (The Poem of the Lunatics)*[72] is the story of two visionary madmen, "lunatics" who are in contact with the next world. Savini and his paranoid friend "the prefect" believe they are being pursued by a group of old spies, drink "madmen's water" and speak to the moon. Fellini was attracted to this subject as it reminded him of the 'place between two worlds' of *Mastorna*.

Just as in the case of the dream project, Fellini had a village built, in the Dinocittà studios where the sets for *Mastorna* were also made. For the two leading roles, the "lunatics", he chose the very famous comic actors, Roberto Benigni and Paolo Villagio. He composed the screenplay with his old collaborator Tullio Pinelli but went on to improvise a lot during shooting. The film depicts the struggle experienced by several outcasts in contact with the other world who are crushed by the extreme cruelty of modern society. Ivo Salvini (not Savini as in Cavazzoni's book) has just been released from a psychiatric hospital. He hears voices. He is madly in love with Aldina, as blonde as the moon, who refuses to have anything to do with the semi-madman. The latter comes to gaze at her asleep in her room. She wakes and throws a shoe at him, which he then carries with him like a precious relic on his nocturnal wanderings. During the revolting Gnocchi festival, at which Aldina has been crowned Miss Wheat, he throws a plate of gnocchi at one of her admirers.

His friend, the prefect Gonnella, brilliantly played by Paolo Villagio, thinks a band of elderly men are spying on him. The two "lunatics" confront an apocalyptic, noisy and vulgar world which has no room for silence and poetry. Never was Fellini's criticism of the modern world so violent, so desperate. Advertising, television, domination by the purely material, mass-produced statues of the Virgin Mary, noise, sex, and the cruelty marking interpersonal relations make *La Voce della Luna* a very bitter film which is hard to watch. In its most poetic sequences, Gonnella, a latter-day Don Quixote, wants to wage war on the modern world. He goes into a large derelict building where young people are freaking out to disco music. He succeeds in stopping their trance-like state, and dances a waltz to the music of Strauss with his companion. But the wild music drowns everything out once more.

At the end of the film the men capture the Moon and shoot at her. This does not prevent the planet from appearing to Ivo Salvini a few minutes later to teach him a lesson about silence:

Se tutti facessimo un po' di silenzio, forse potremmo capire.[73]

As in *Il viaggio de G. Mastorna* the film's subject is what lies beyond the real. What Fellini tried to express in *Mastorna* by using the journey to the world of the dead he conveys in *La Voce della Luna* by means of liminal places affording access to the world beyond. The well links the two worlds. Celestial processions may be seen through the hole in the cemetery roof. What secrets may be discovered through the hole made in the road surface?

Just as the places are liminal, the characters encountered here exist at the edge of two worlds. Ivo Salvini, the prefect Gonnella, the instrumentalist, and the other 'lunatics' are bridges between these two worlds. They have visions and hear voices. In particular they hear the voice of the Moon. What does the planet represent in the film? The way in which the hysterical audience appeal to the captured moon comes through clearly in the televised 'supershow': "Take care of me! Help me!" The Moon is a metaphor for the Creator. Thus the gun shot aimed in its direction during the live television show given over to its capture appears to be the final avatar of the *Mastorna* awards ceremony. The protagonist there was expressing his disappointment at the traditional system of rewards and punishments. The episode recurred in *Toby Dammit* where Toby rebels in a smaller way against the showbiz society. In *Ginger e Fred* Pipo intends to interrupt the Christmas special to proclaim his disgust with society. Here in *La Voce della Luna* Fellini is repeating his metaphysical revolt against the Creator. A revolt which is, however, mocked and negated since the Moon reappears unharmed a few minutes later.

Other details also recall *Mastorna*. In that film the protagonist had two 'doubles': Armandino the naïve Neapolitan and De Cercis the atheist intellectual. At one point Fellini even thought of giving all three roles to the same actor. In *La Voce della Luna*, Ivo Salvini, Gonnella and the instrumentalist are the same visionary figure, divided into three.[74] In *Mastorna* the cemetery was depicted as full of life, where the dead, occupying their tombs, were visited by their families. The same notion recurs wholesale in *La Voce della Luna* where the instrumentalist's wife visits him in his tomb, bringing him his dinner. The closing words of the film return to the serene detachment propounded at the end of *Mastorna*. The Moon, back in place in the sky – thus negating the preceding episodes in which it was captured and killed – gives advice to the half-insane Salvini: one has to be indifferent to the world, move towards absolute indifference. "You have nothing to understand, you must only listen." This irony echoes *Mastorna* with its expression, in the closing part of the film, of indifference to both good and evil.

As in the case of *Il viaggio di G. Mastorna*, Fellini began having doubts about his work even before shooting began:

> In September 1988, the Maestro suddenly sank into emptiness once more. He admitted he no longer knew what he was trying to film. Nevertheless the building of a whole village was continuing at Dinocittà in the new Via Pontina studios named after their creator. To outwit his anxieties Federico made a show of monitoring progress, taking an interest in tiny details, the choice of a tie, a nail in the wall and so on. – It's as if I had to perfect something I couldn't see clearly, he said, turn an absence into something present. But I am wondering what that means. I can't even make a film about the director's crisis, because I've already done that.
>
> Notariani who was the overall organiser of the production tried everything to persuade him not to suspend the project; in particular he demonstrated how much had already been done. Federico's answer was that he was no longer able to direct his actors or visualise his characters. The situation was too much for Notariani and he fell ill, as did Cavazzoni. At a loss, the director went to his lawyer to put an end to the film with the least damage possible.[75]

This time, however, Fellini did complete the work and within a few months (March to May 1989). The result was a disappointment. This was to be his last film.

Aside from these four films directly inspired by *Mastorna*, there are sequences echoing passages of the unused screenplay scattered throughout Fellini's oeuvre. In *Roma* (1971) the women from a high class brothel descend in a lift; a VIP client whose identity is kept secret arrives; the other clients are immediately sent out. The sequence derives from *Mastorna* in which the kitchen of the dead Neapolitan La Cicciona turns out to be a brothel where the daughters of the mistress of the house arrive by lift. Then an important client appears and to preserve the anonymity of the newcomer, the other clients are dismissed.

The finale of *Prova d'orchestra* (1978) echoes that of *Il viaggio de G. Mastorna*. As the conductor brings down his baton the orchestra strikes up a swelling melody which ends the film on a peaceful note. In *Città' delle donne* (*City of Women*) (1980) an elderly servant woman puts the hero on her bicycle saddle, just as Iole, the old nanny, does in the

Mastorna screenplay. These analogies between individual details do nevertheless reveal that, consciously or not, in each new piece of work Fellini returns to his ideal screenplay. On a more general level, too, the themes of *Mastorna* provide the key to Fellini's overall oeuvre, in which the quest for the sacred has not been sufficiently recognized.

Fellini and the sacred

Spaghetti, women with enormous breasts, dreams: Fellini's stock in trade is all too well known. It reappears with every instance of his work and thereby ends up obscuring the true meaning of an oeuvre which is quasi-prophetic, a voice raging against the materialism of the modern world, an ongoing quest for the sacred.

It might initially seem surprising to speak of Fellini and the sacred. However the quest for the sacred is central to the director's output from *La Strada* (1954) to *Giulietta degli spiriti* (1965). Gelsomina in *La Strada* is a Christ figure, and Zampanò's cry of pain at the end of the film seems to signal that after her death Gelsomina has managed to disturb the thickness of this pure materiality.

Le Notti di Cabiria (1957) depicts the mystical search of the prostitute Cabiria who is moved by the purity and innocence of a child she sees taking part in a First Communion procession. One Sunday she goes to ask for a miracle but faith, like everything else, abandons her.

La Dolce Vita (1960) begins and ends with images of a Christianity which is dead and fossilized. The helicopter carries a heavy, blind Christ through the skies above Rome, a statue as rigid and lifeless as the huge dead fish which is caught at the end in front of the deeply despairing revellers. And Guido, like Cabiria or Marcello in *La Dolce Vita* is a man in search of meaning. His artistic crisis coincides with an existential one. Just as he wishes to find a meaning to his film he wishes to find a meaning to his life. In *Otto e mezzo*, as in *À la Recherche du temps perdu* which might have been one of the inspirations for the screenplay, several answers are entertained but rejected: sexual love (Carla), friendship (Giorgio), art. Guido gets very little from his meeting with the Cardinal. His memories of his religious education are very bitter ones. "There is nothing apart from the Church!" the Cardinal tells him. Christianity demands complete adherence and a total rejection of everything else. Priests believe sex comes from the devil. Fellini, however, sees sexuality, in the shape of the enormous Saraghina who lives on the shore, not as evil but as a facet of the infinite. Where Guido will find peace and fulfilment is in the gift of art and the acceptance of reality.

The following film, *Giulietta degli spiriti,* is yet another search for meaning but here the answers are much more clear cut. Its criticism of Christianity is more scathing, its attack on Giulietta's religious upbringing crueller. At the end of the film, Giulietta-Fellini will be strong enough to break with their religious past, free themselves from an oppressive morality and welcome "the voices of the earth". So what exactly are these supernatural forces which bring Giulietta so much joy at the end of her quest? Fellini's intention in *Mastorna* was to explore this answer in more depth, as for him every film was a search, an inner investigation, carried out through images.

Fellini is fighting on two fronts. On the one he is protesting against the whole of modern Western civilization, from a conviction that matter and reason are not everything. The very subject of *Il viaggio di G. Mastorna* is a rejoinder to those who hold that death is the end. On the other he completely rejects religion as practised in churches. Narrow-minded, tyrannical and ridiculous, priests – like atheist intellectuals – never come off well in his films.

Therefore, even if the discourse of revolt against Christian notions of reward and punishment is already present in Buzzati's story, Fellini was able to adopt it for himself and reject a religion whose morality is stifling.

Fellini, like Bergman incidentally, is in search of a middle way. The large number of books on spiritualism in his library show how interested the Maestro was in these subjects. *Mastorna* was intended as an investigation into what happens after death because Fellini was certain that something after death existed.

Mastorna may therefore be viewed as the ultimate stage in his search. In his subsequent work the sacred is less present. In the film he authored immediately after *Toby Dammit,* the *Fellini-Satyricon,* Fellini seems to have the same preoccupations. The film, shot immediately after Fellini's artistic crisis, similarly expresses a crisis. Encolpius is no longer able to have sexual intercourse. He believes that his impotence stems from the sacrilege he has committed in stealing a sacred child. He is cured by restoring contact with the earth (the enormous priestess with whom he has sex on the ground). It is impossible not to think of what Fellini was undergoing at this same time: was the crisis over *Mastorna* a result of 'sacrilege' (touching the taboo subject of the world of the dead)? There are some subjects (the world beyond) which must not be broached. And Fellini returned to the earth. His next films would evoke the sources of his inspiration (*I Clowns*) and the city (*Roma*) he loved above all. The sacred is still there but less and less prominently. If in his films the sea generally symbolises the infinite and the world beyond (the sea in *La Strada,* in *La Dolce Vita,* the shore next to which La Saraghina combs her hair) its waves are now present only in paper form (*Casanova*) or thanks to various artificial effects (*E la nave va*).

Two features of *Mastorna* run through Fellini's entire artistic output. Firstly, all Fellini's films aim to be summas, "large mirrors of the world". *Mastorna* may be seen as a "large mirror of the world and of all mirrors". In the land of the dead, all countries and all eras merge. Filming the land of the dead meant going even further than *Otto e mezzo* to film not only present reality but also all past realities. *Le Notti di Cabiria* is a repertory of all the means of seeking happiness: sexual love, fame, religion, magic, love. *Otto e mezzo* expresses the film director's childhood memories, his emotional life, and his struggles as a creative artist, and the end of the world and so on, and this is why the film within a film is so difficult to make. Casanova in *Fellini's Casanova* attempts to record *all* his sexual exploits. *Il viaggio di G. Mastorna* simply takes to an extreme that desire to create a 'totalising' artwork which is characteristic of Fellini's oeuvre.

These totalising works are also journeys and quests for meaning. This brings us to the second feature: the journey structure which gives its name to *Il viaggio di G. Mastorna* is actually found all over Fellini's work. While it is explicit in the titles of *Il viaggio di Anita* and *Il viaggio a Tulum* almost all of the other films are also journeys. The journey structure allows Fellini to emphasise the visual dimension of the film. The *Fellini-Satyricon* is a series of sequences which appear completely independent of one another and whose variety is justified by the three heroes' wanderings. *Fellini's Casanova* similarly depicts the central character's wanderings in Italy, France, England and Germany. The hero of *La Città delle donne* also travels, as do those of *E la nave va*, *Ginger e Fred* and *Intervista*. Even the films in which the characters do not really make a journey give the impression of a visit (*Roma*), an initiatic path. The journey formula which Fellini used in *Mastorna* lends itself particularly well to a totalising work of art. A hero travels from place to place, and these places are always magic because they are new.

※

At the end of *Giulietta degli spiriti* Fellini – in the figure of Giulietta – breaks free from Christianity and welcomes the voices of the earth. This marks a return, in a sense, to pagan roots. *Il viaggio di G. Mastorna* was the furthest Fellini ever went in denying the divine order. Because the outrageous cry of revolt in the awards ceremony is found in so many of his subsequent films it is tempting to suggest that Fellini was hoping for an answer. His whole artistic output appears to be a despairing question to the Creator, a plea for a meaning. A cry which is also one of alarm and horror addressed to his contemporaries.

Fellini or Jeremiah: in among the theatrical trappings, the frills or scornful cult of celebrities, almost all the films can be seen to predict a catastrophe looming for the Western world.

The dead fish and the sorrowful partygoers of the finale of *La Dolce Vita;* the global catastrophe in the film Guido is trying to make in *Otto e mezzo*; the hero's departure for Africa, as if fleeing a decaying world, in the *Fellini-Satyricon*; the amazing ballet of the barbarians on motorbikes arriving to invade and destroy Rome (Western civilization) in *Roma*. The enormous wrecking ball about to destroy the orchestra's rehearsal room – symbol of our own society – in *Prova d'orchestra*.

The sinking ship in *E la nave va* with its heaps of ridiculous singers belonging to a declining civilization, and the colossus with feet of clay evoked by Fred in *Ginger e Fred* (in which a simple power cut brings down the massive operation of the television studio) are the image of an exhausted and hollow world. *La Voce della Luna* similarly depicts a crazed society. Employing different metaphors each time Fellini goes on shouting in protest against a world which has lost its meaning. Thus *Mastorna*'s cry of horror is absolutely central to his work, a very secret work which has to be sought out beneath the fripperies of a sumptuous theatricality.

Conclusion

The central point of the work is the work as origin, the point which cannot be reached, yet the only one which is worth reaching.
  Maurice Blanchot, "The work and the errant word", in *The Space of Literature*, translated by Ann Smock (University of Nebraska Press, 1982, 50–55, p. 53)

The dialogue between Judaism and Christianity, which Claudel so often attempted to write, is central to his oeuvre. Genet's 'total' book, intended to found a new aesthetic and a new morality the principle of which was his difference, is the key to his theatre and his theoretical writings which aim to take alterity to its extreme. The film Fellini dreamed of making shows his faith in another world, an existence after death. At the same time the story violently contests the traditional notion of a heaven reserved for the just and a hell where sinners are punished. Fellini's unfilmed screenplay invites us – and for me this is a feature of every dream project – to reappraise a body of films to which an interrogation of the sacred is central, albeit systematically veiled. Claudel's project, Genet's 'total' book and Fellini's eschatological film, all three worked on for so long but finally left unfinished, as dream projects, 'impossible', have been used in this study as examples to demonstrate how far they constitute the taking to the limit of the remainder of the work. Are these three case studies sufficient to demonstrate the proposition with which this book opened? Are such struggles with cherished but ultimately unrealized works inevitable, obeying a sort of law of artistic creation? Is the phantom, impossible work always the centre of the whole oeuvre, the key to all the other works, which it nourishes? Does every creative artist have at the centre of his oeuvre such a dream project, an impossible work, never completed but revealing the deepest meaning of that artist's creative output?

Ideally it would be necessary to extend this preliminary research to include other artistic enterprises, broadening the scope to include not only literature but also music, painting, philosophy and science. There would have to be a way of identifying periods of sterility in creators' lives; these are inevitable but vary greatly in length, from five or six years for Genet, three for Fellini and almost twenty for Dreyer. Next is to examine personal diaries, letters, accounts of those close to the subject, to see whether the crisis is linked with a work which cannot be finished and which will be taken up again. After that would come finding outlines and versions of the continually restarted work among drafts, sometimes published but usually unpublished. Once the genesis and different stages of the work had been established, it would be time for the most difficult task, namely looking at the unrealizable work in relation to the remainder of the oeuvre in order to demonstrate that it takes this to the limit, and is its key. Before addressing the question of the mysterious phenomenon keeping the artist away from his essential creation, let us consider more briefly some other dream projects or 'impossible works', literary, musical, cinematographic, philosophical, pictorial, famous and less famous, a deeper analysis of which might help us understand a phenomenon which might well be inevitable to creation.

Alfred de Vigny's dream project: *La seconde consultation du Docteur Noir* (*The second consultation of Dr Noir*)

In the literary sphere, mention has already been made of Mallarmé's renowned *Livre*. A planned work by Alfred de Vigny, in which *Daphné* (1837) is only one stage, remaining unpublished in the writer's lifetime on his strict instructions, is equally significant. He may be said to have worked on the project his whole life. In 1816, at the age of 19, he wrote a tragedy about Julian the Apostate:

> I was a lieutenant of the royal guard, at the garrison in Versailles, in 1816, I think, when I wrote quite a bad tragedy about Julian the Apostate, which I burned recently.[1]

He continued to be obsessed by the character of Julian the Apostate:

> I can't get over the affinity I have always felt for Julian the Apostate. If metempsychosis exists, I have been that man.[2]

Julian the Apostate was to be the protagonist of *Daphné*: *La seconde consultation du Docteur Noir*. The penultimate entry in the *Journal*, in August or September 1863 – a matter of days before the poet's death on 17 September that year – is still concerned with the project:

> During a night of insomnia, Wednesday to Thursday 27 August: dream, plan and key idea for the *Seconde consultation* and for *Stello*. The aristocracy

of the Intelligence: this is and should be the only all-powerful one. On condition that we trust the sovereign Influence exercised for the (illegible) genius; brought down by the subterranean Intrigues of the horrendous miners which make their way by working like moles and sully instead of carrying and elevating the spirit of his people and his century. Develop the demonstration in three dramas which will be counterparts to those of *Stello*. Three mighty eagles and three moles. Invent three tales underpinned by the wide and deep historical tableau of an epoch, a country and a nature. For the first group, Turenne; look for the Mole and the Beaver.[3]

The work went through numerous metamorphoses between the first version, sketched by a very young man in 1816 and the project for the three dramas conceived by the dying poet almost fifty years later. *Daphné* (1837) was intended to follow on from *Stello: la première consultation du Docteur Noir* (*Stello: the first consultation of Doctor Noir*) (1832). The 'consultation' is a dialectical form, a dialogue between Vigny's heart (Stello, poetry which is superior to reality) and Docteur Noir (the reality of life).[4]

Vigny's aim in these two consultations was to provide an answer to two questions: should the poet have a political role? Should the poet have a religious role? The first of these is answered in *Stello*, while *La deuxième consultation*, which kept changing, was intended as an answer to the second. *Daphné* (1837) is both an anti-Christian novel and a plea for Christianity centring on the ambiguous character of Julian the Apostate. Vigny wrote six chapters, the fifth and longest of which is a series of letters sent by a Jew, Joseph Jechaïah, to his friend Benjamin Elul of Alexandria. The end of the text, where the two inseparable adversaries, Stello and Docteur Noir reappear, is astounding. It uses the historical event of the 1831 burning of the archbishop's palace in Paris to depict the triumph of materialism and the end of Western civilization.[5] Vigny did not publish it, however, and in 1842 he outlined a new version of the work, centring on a Jew who wishes to convert:

> The son of a rich Jewish banker wants to become a Christian because he is in love with a young Christian girl. He has three friends who wish to convert him to Catholicism but they almost cause him to die of sorrow as he can see, through their words, the hypocrisy of political mean whose only interest is power.[6]

As in the previous form of the text, the Jew – so often present in Vigny's work and in his *Journal* – is the symbol, as in the case of Claudel later, not of a religion but of the denial of all religion, the all-conquering

32. Photo of Alfred de Vigny (1797–1863), who was unable to bring his dream project, *Daphné*, on which he worked until his death, to its completion. (Photo: Félix Nadar).

33. Blue self-portrait by Arnold Schoenberg (1874–1951). Schoenberg worked on his opera *Moses und Aron* for decades but was unable to complete its final act. (Used by permission of Belmont Music Publishers, Los Angeles).

34. The Garabit viaduct, the area where *L'Enfer* of Henri-Georges Clouzot was shot and abandoned after the principal actor fled the production and the director suffered a heart-attack. (Photo: Graeme Churchard).

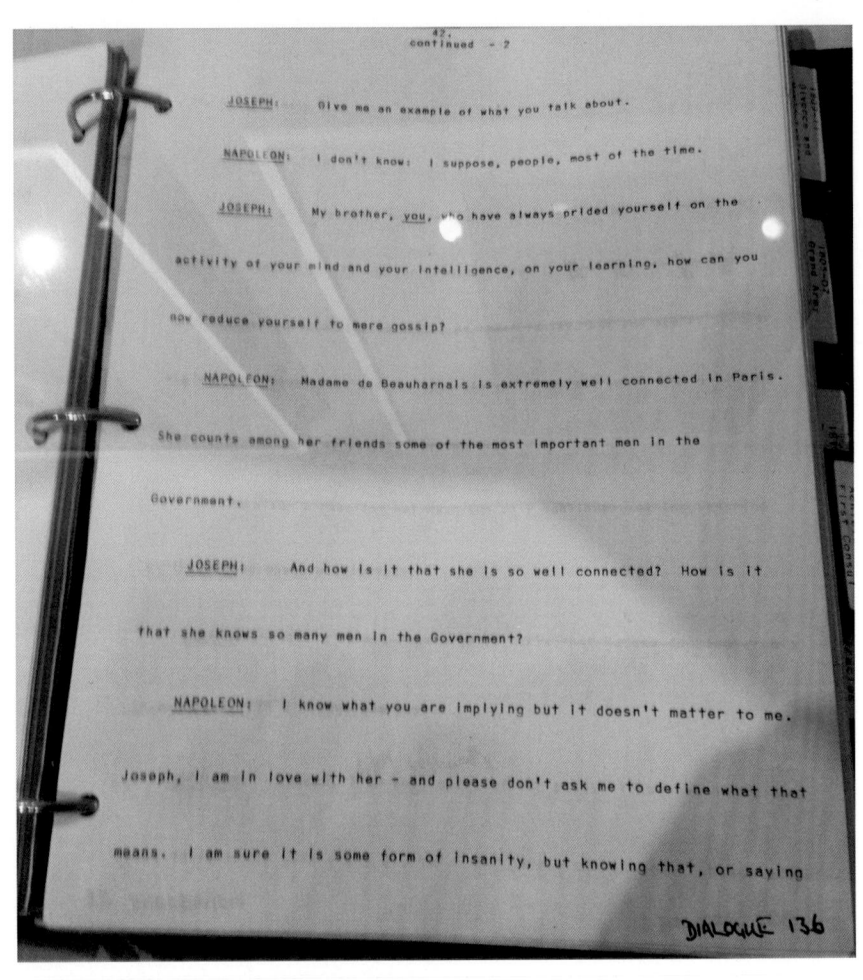

35. A page from the script of *Napoleon* – Stanley Kubrick's phantom picture. (Photo: William Beutler).

36. Bernard Dort (1929–1994), who sought to write an 'autotheatrography' (a biography of the spectator), is photographed by Antoine Vitez in his home.

37–38. *The Nymphéas* (*Waterlilies*) by Claude Monet (1840–1926). The painter never wanted to show the public his 'grandes décorations' project, and it was displayed only posthumously.

39. The dream project of Isaac Newton (1643–1727). In analysing the dimensions of the Tabernacle as set out in the biblical text, Newton sought to arrive at the secret of the entire Universe – a reality where physics and history merge. A page from Notes on the Jewish Temple (Courtesy of the National Library of Israel).

40. A page from a treatise on Solomon's Temple, *Prolegomena ad lexici prophetic partem secundam in quibus agitur De forma sanctuarii Judaici*. Newton believed that the architecture of Solomon's Temple held divine secrets that had long been lost. (The Grace K. Babson Collection of the Works of Sir Isaac Newton at The Huntington Library, Art Museum, and Botanical Gardens).

materialism dominating modern society. Furthermore, Vigny intended to finish with the presumably authentic story of a Miss Rothschild playing fast and loose with her father's dying wishes in order both to inherit and to marry the non-Jewish officer she loves. In 1844, Vigny returned to his 'second consultation': this time Julian the Apostate appears in the guise of a madman who believes himself to be Julian:

> Reflection and end of the 2nd consultation. [...]
> Docteur Noir reads Daphné's letters. The wretched man, terror stricken, goes mad and believes he is Julian redivivus [resurrected]. He thinks he has undergone metempsychosis and throws himself into the water in order to become the Emperor once more, in a reverse metamorphosis.[7]

Between 1849 and 1855 the spiritual direction of the *Seconde consultation* changed. In 1832, in *Stello*, Docteur Noir was fighting against 'those who create the fiction of the next world' and the Christian hope. In 1849 Vigny became aware of the social consequences which may be caused by the rejection of the spiritual world. He is fighting the 'senseless Positivists' in league with materialism and immediate gratification.[8]

> DAPHNÉ: Man has no time now for the wondrous in faith nor in poetry. Envy of everything is the predominant passion, which gives rise to the mania for equality. Faith in the supernatural order makes man and the globe greater.
> Libanius (a character in *Daphné*) thinks that the destruction of the supernatural order is the undoing of the nations; he tells Julian "The barbarians are healthier than we are, and of more use for the world's salvation".[9]

August of the same year saw Vigny thinking of one of the most surprising avatars of the work. His plan was to situate the material of the *Seconde consultation* not during the leadership of Julian the Apostate but in French Canada, also a victim of raging materialism wiping out any identity:

> DAPHNÉ: This is a populace of the prosperous Lower Empire. How it lives and dies: equality. Ruin, denial of castes first of all, then of inheritances, thirdly of birth right, fourthly of hereditary property, fifthly the destruction, confiscation and sharing out of property, even virgin, sixthly the envy and passion for equality. Names are replaced by numbers. The man becomes a monkey once more. The nation loses its way in the woods and snows.

Death of Monsieur de Montcalm and the English general. The same tomb. Equality after death.[10]

In 1853, while Vigny was correcting the proofs of the 10th edition of the *Première consultation* – and not allowing his editor Buloz to publish the text of the *Seconde consultation* written in 1837 – the *Journal* records a new form of the project, no longer taking place in the town of Daphné in Julian's time but "in the present day" in America.[11] In 1857 the project seemed to have been divided into two. On the one hand a modern novel about barbarianism ("it is stupidity which produces crimes and the majority of errors"[12]) and on the other a play, *Les Stoïciens* (*The Stoics*), where Saint Martin and Julian the Apostate are in dialogue:

> The drama is to be called *Les Stoïciens*. This work I have dreamed of for so many years has not yet attained its final form in my mind. It is drawing near. When my vision of it is sufficiently beautiful I will write it.[13]

Two years later Vigny was dazzled on discovering Buddhism, in Barthélemy Saint-Hilaire's *Le Bouddha et sa religion* (Buddha and his religion):

> Study of the *Bhagavala Pourana*. Admirable source of poetry and sentiment. An unexpected rapture seized me last night on reading, in the 36th chapter, the progress of the individual soul. The love of abstract contemplation has never been taken further than in this book.[14]

This had an immediate influence on the great work Vigny was planning:

> At Marcella, Julian will get to know an Indian sage who will explain the transmigration of souls to him and tell him that he has obtained from the Supreme Being the knowledge of his latest form.[15]

Even at the very end of his life, struck down by illness, Vigny was still dreaming of this work (Journal entries for 15 April 1863 and 19 May 1863) until, as has already been discussed, a new plan for the famed *deuxième consultation* came to him.

This consideration of the various stages of *La deuxième consultation du Docteur Noir* may provide us with the key to Vigny's innermost conflict and his ambivalent attitude towards Christianity. He rejects both official Catholicism and materialism. Strangely, just as he seemed able to envision the work clearly death prevented him from writing it:

La Deuxième consultation is the desire for a restoration of ancient morality and Roman strength, on the part of someone who did not dare, nor even always want, this. As if to prolong for eternity the doubt of this latter day Julian, death overtook him [Vigny] at the very moment he seemed to arrive at an honest decision and at clarity.[16]

Like Fellini in his hospital bed sketching Mastorna, or Pirandello dreaming about the scenery for *The Mountain Giants* in his final hours, the dying Vigny did not give up on the project which was a true obsession for him.

Arnold Schoenberg's 'impossible' opera

After showing him the first two acts of *Moses und Aron* (*Moses and Aaron*), Arnold Schoenberg confided in his friend the composer René Leibowitz his fears that this work, the most ambitious of all his compositions, might never be performed. Since that time, the work, which was never finished despite all Schoenberg's efforts, has become his best known composition, thanks to numerous stage productions (London 1965, Boston 1966, New York 1999, Stuttgart 2006, Vienna 2006), a film (Jean-Marie Straub and Danièle Huillet 1973) and a DVD documenting the magnificent 2006 staging by Reto Nickler at the Vienna Opera House.

The first draft of the opera is dated 1930 and the first two acts were completed in 1932. Act I begins with the episode of the burning bush where Moses receives the command to deliver the people of Israel. As in the biblical text, Moses states that he does not know how to speak – and the role is played not by a singer but by a speaker who says, not sings, the text. For Aaron (or Aron, in Schoenberg's spelling),[17] who will transmit Moses's statements, Schoenberg composed an extremely complicated part. "It is the most difficult role in the entire history of opera," according to Thomas Moser, who played Aaron in the 2006 production. The entire opera was to rest on the opposition between the spiritual conceptions of the two brothers. Moses is the thinker who is unable to put his ideas across. Aaron is the brilliant speaker who, in translating his brother's thoughts into words and images, betrays them.

Contrary to habit, Schoenberg had composed the text and score of the first two acts simultaneously, complete with full orchestration. After the episode of the Golden Calf, which is central to the opera and contains orgy scenes surprisingly bold for the 1930s, Schoenberg found himself unable to continue. In 1935, having fled Europe for the United States, he wrote the text of the third act but was not satisfied with it and did not compose the music. Aaron is arrested, accused of betraying Moses's ideas by images which were pleasing to the people but departed from the pure notion of a divinity to which images are alien. In Act 3 Moses asks the soldiers to release Aaron but the latter is then struck dead.

Even in the desert, far from the Promised Land (considered as an 'image'), the people can attain unity with the divinity. Schoenberg went on trying to complete the opera until his death but did not succeed. In fact Moses's spoken words in the second act make an admirable finale, the highpoint of the work, as Leibowitz writes:

> The fact that the work is unfinished does not appear to pose an obstacle or difficulty to understanding the opera. Indeed the end of the second act, where Moses tries in vain to find the words he lacks, is certainly one of the finest pages in the score as well as an entirely convincing and highly moving conclusion. After all is not Moses's despair also that of Schoenberg himself? And the speech which the protagonist lacks, is it not also that which the composer was unable to find to finish his work?[18]

More than *Pierrot lunaire* (1912) or *Die Jakobsleiter* (*Jacob's Ladder*) (1915–1926), the unfinished *Moses und Aron* is at the centre of Schoenberg's quest. The original solution which he adopted here, with the contrast between an actor (Moses) and a virtuoso singer (Aaron) takes what characterizes his lyric style to an extreme. In the same way as Wagner tried to resurrect on stage less the operatic recitative than the *paracatalogue* of Greek theatre, midway between speech and music, Schoenberg uses *Sprechgesang* in all his dramatic works. Following on from Wagner, in *Pierrot lunaire* in the gap between word and music he found a source of drama, which then becomes the theme itself of *Moses und Aron*. Aaron is a brilliant orator and this virtuosity is conveyed by the virtuosic nature of the score. Moses has no ability in speech, and so is unable to sing. His spoken words are in contrast to the musical flow of Aaron and the chorus. The last phrase of Moses's speech ("Wort! Das mir fehlt – Word – which I lack") closes that work and with it Schoenberg's whole oeuvre.

Moses und Aron is particularly illuminating where the composer's relationship to Judaism is concerned, something which is far more complicated than one might think. Schoenberg was born into a Jewish family but converted to Protestantism in 1898 when he was twenty-four years old. In the summer of 1921, however, while holidaying in Mattsee near Salzburg, he was driven out of the village by its inhabitants who did not want Jews there, even if they had become Protestants. This traumatic experience gave rise to a reflection which would bring him closer to Judaism again. First he wrote *Der Biblische Weg* (*The Biblical Way*) (1926) with its central character Max Aruns (Moses/Aaron) modelled on Theodor Herzl. Eventually in 1933 he reconverted to Judaism in Paris (Marc Chagall was his witness). This was Reform Judaism however. Right to the end his relation with observing Jewish laws remained ambiguous. The religion of **his** Moses is so pure as to defy any concrete form such as laws or the Promised Land. Having converted to Protestantism, Schoenberg returned to Judaism but rejected that faith as a collection of laws. What is Judaism as pure sentiment? Schoenberg was unable to finish his opera because he never really made a choice between Protestantism and Judaism. The opposition between the conceptions of the two brothers – Moses and pure religion as against Aaron and images and laws – corresponds to an internal conflict.

Luchino Visconti's dream project

In May 2013 Florence Colombani made a programme for France-Culture devoted to *Il viaggio di G. Mastorna*. This was the latest step in her research into 'impossible' films which had begun with her book on Visconti, *Proust–Visconti, histoire d'une affinité élective* (*Proust–Visconti, the story of an elective affinity*)[19] in which Colombani analyses how the project Visconti abandoned resonates throughout his creative output. From the opening words of her text, Florence Colombani places Visconti's dream project within a series of failed cinematographic projects which might well form the – hidden – centre of their creators' oeuvres:

> The history of the cinema is full of uncompleted projects, cancelled films and screenplays which remain mere words on the page. Greta Garbo tried to play *La Duchesse de Langeais* and Marilyn Monroe Grushenka from *The Brothers Karamazov*. Joseph L. Mankiewicz wished to turn Audrey Hepburn into a boy for *L'Aiglon* and Louis Malle to tell the story of Marlene Dietrich. Federico Fellini spent a lifetime contemplating *The Journey of Mastorna* in which Marcello Mastroianni would have played a dead man journeying through the afterlife. For years David Lynch has dreamed of adapting *The Metamorphosis*. The tale is often told of how Stanley Kubrick planned an amazing *Napoleon*, spending years gathering prodigious amounts of documentation with legendary exactitude, creating models of the great imperial battles, debating his choice of actor – Al Pacino or Jack Nicholson? Kubrick never shot the film but went on carrying it within him

to the extent that its traces can be seen even in the battles of *Barry Lyndon* (1975) and the sexual anxiety of the hero in *Eyes wide shut* (1999). It is characteristic of the phantom film that it draws attention to "that which, because it was not expressed there, was reinvested somewhere else".[20]

At the end of the 1960s Nicole Stéphane, having obtained the adaptation rights to Proust's novel, contacted Luchino Visconti. The screenplay was written. The prestigious casting was in place: Marlon Brando was to play the Baron de Charlus and Greta Garbo the Duchesse de Guermantes; Albertine would be brought to life by either Catherine Deneuve or Charlotte Rampling. Visconti was looking for locations. However, perhaps fearing this would be his last film, his final work, Visconti abandoned the idea of directing it, to the producers' despair. Florence Colombani demonstrates the underlying presence of this phantom film in Visconti's subsequent films: *Death in Venice* (1971), *Ludwig* (1973), *Conversation Piece* (1974).

Baron de Charlus may be seen in *Ludwig*, in *Death in Venice* (Gustav von Aschenbach) and in *Conversation Piece* (the professor). The figure of Sandra, in that same film, recalls Proust's Gilberte, known to Visconti since his adolescence, in her denial of her Jewish origins and ambiguous relationship with her father. Madame Swann and her flowers reappear in *The Leopard* (1963), *Death in Venice*, *Ludwig* and *Conversation Piece*. Sophie Von Essenbeck in *The Damned* (1969) seems to be modelled on Oriane de Guermantes, and the hotel manager in *Death in Venice* a deliberate calque on the manager of the Grand Hotel in Balbec. In Proust as in Visconti "the body is an object of pleasure and desire at the very moment it is destroyed".[21] Proust's influence is evident up to Visconti's last film. Pierre Tosi, the costume and set designer– who worked with Fellini on *Mastorna* – is of the view that *The Innocent*, an adaptation of a novel by Gabriele d'Annunzio, is also an echo of *À la recherche*:

> Without daring to say it, Luchino wanted *The Innocent* to be Proustian [...]. In the salons of *The Innocent*, a longing for Proust may be felt: they are not of d'Annunzio, they don't belong to the Rome of the 'little duke', they are the musical salons of the Guermantes and the Verdurins.[22]

Florence Colombani is delighted that Visconti refused to make his grand project, the film adaptation of *À la recherche*:

After all, by tearing himself away from the wearisome banality of literal adaptation, Visconti allowed Proust to seep into the entirety of his work, an incalculably more exciting exercise.[23]

Visconti's film *À la recherche du temps perdu* does not exist, but its ghost runs through his masterpieces which remain steadfastly faithful to that famed and magnificent 'Proustian sentiment'. Is it not the case that what Visconti gives us – a rereading, a reinvention of Proust – is infinitely more precious than a literal adaptation?[24]

The list of phantom films obsessing their creators could go on and on. In 2009 Alison Castle published a huge tome, *Stanley Kubrick's Napoleon: The greatest movie never made*.[25]

Kubrick employed an army of researchers supplying him with photos, copies of uniforms and meticulous historical details. The cost of the project together with the failure of another film about Napoleon, Sergei Bondarchuk's 1970 *Waterloo*, led an alarmed MGM to cancel the project. As noted by Michel Ciment, however, the research undertaken for *Napoleon* enriched the rest of Kubrick's works. In particular Kubrick's desire to shoot the film in natural light, which led his production director Jan Harlan[26] to search the world for film sufficiently sensitive to shoot even dimly lit interior scenes, would later benefit *Barry Lyndon*.

Was *Napoleon* really an impossible work, however? It seems likely that with the necessary budget at his disposal Kubrick would have made the film. Henri-Georges Clouzot's 1964 film, *L'Enfer (Inferno)*, on the other hand, remained unfinished, officially for technical reasons but it appears that the ambitious nature of the project itself posed obstacles to its realization.

After the shock provoked by Fellini's *Otto e mezzo*, Clouzot decided to break with classic formalism. He had a limitless budget from Columbia, his American production company. Clouzot accumulated hundreds of hours of trial film, in black and white and in colour. He wanted to make a film imbued with contemporary art. Shooting was a disaster. The leading actor, Serge Reggiani, fell ill and the shoot was broken off when the director suffered a heart attack. In 1994 Claude Chabrol used the film's screenplay for a remake, which was, however, minus its essential feature, the effects wanted by Clouzot. Serge Bromberg and Ruxandra Medrea found dozens of cans containing Clouzot's test reels and in 2009 made a documentary tracing the complicated history of the unfinished – or perhaps unfinishable? – film, *L'Enfer d'Henri-Georges Clouzot*.

There is, too, the documentary film *Lost in La Mancha* by Keith Fulton and Luis Pepe which traces Terry Gilliam's unsuccessful attempts to film Cervantes' *Don Quixote*.[27] To this already considerable list might be added *Megapolis*, on which Coppola worked for so long, or Dreyer's *Jesus*, his final project which he was unable to complete.

Louis Malle's film, *My dinner with André* (1981), based on the play by André Gregory and Wallace Shawn, depicts a particularly fierce struggle with a work which the director, André Gregory, speaking in his own name in the film, cannot manage to create. After an especially brilliant period, the theatre director, a friend of the famous Polish director Grotowski, finds himself unable to keep on directing in the traditional setting. He goes off to the Sahara with a Tibetan monk, in the aim of creating a dramatic adaptation of *Le Petit Prince* (*The Little Prince*). There he devotes himself to all sorts of experiments on the borderline between theatre and ritual. The last of these, being buried alive, is so traumatic for him that he comes out of it changed and healed, returning to the theatre.

This phenomenon has already been observed in the cases of Genet and Fellini. The struggle with the impossible creative work gives rise to a period of distress followed by a kind of rebirth: a pattern which it is tempting to apply to any artistic career. An initial, extremely fertile period is followed by a crisis linked to a struggle with a work which is particularly difficult to express. If the creative artist comes through this crisis, he emerges changed. His manner is no longer the same.[28]

The dream project of Bernard Dort

The stock image of Bernard Dort (1929–1994) is all too well known. It has even gone down in history in *L'Impromptu d'Alma* (1956), Ionesco's play in which Dort appears as Bartholoméus II, alongside Roland Barthes, Bartholoméus I. Barthes and Dort are two pedants who, Brecht book in hand, come to stifle Ionesco's inspiration along with that of all other theatrical artists. It is true that Dort made Bertolt Brecht known in France and fought to impose his system. This cliché, however, hides a much more complex and interesting reality. Dort was a teacher worshipped by his students at the Sorbonne, in Louvain, in Strasburg and at the Conservatoire, as well as a very diligent and influential theatre critic, a 'universal witness' who every evening, for as long as he was able, attended and reported on European theatre and also a philosopher of the dramatic. The articles he selected for his collections (*Lecture de Brecht, Théâtre public, Théâtre réel, Théâtre en jeu, La représentation émancipée, Le spectateur en dialogue*) are the tip of a much bigger iceberg comprising literary film analysis, translations and novels. He was unhappy about how scattered his writing was and wanted to produce a bigger work, a biography of the spectator, described in Chantal Meyer-Plantureux's notable study of Dort,[29] in the following terms:

> He dreamed of writing the biography of the spectator he had been for twenty-five years. The tone is set by the very first sentence: "paradoxically it was radio which gave me one of my first and most vivid theatrical pleasures. I was a schoolboy".[30]

He wrote almost two hundred pages but had difficulty in going on, as his *Journal* attests:

> I am feeling my way forward. More impossible than ever to map out, make plans for each chapter or such and such a development... [...]. Of course ... the pleasure of the theatre ... But Barthes's "pleasure of the text" made a detour by way of theory – by what might be called "theory-fiction". I refuse more or less subconsciously (also I'm not capable of it) to do likewise.[31]

Several years later he would return to this project with his chronicles for *Le Monde*, speaking subjectively once more, a spectator attempting to define the pleasure of the theatre.

When the finest of these chronicles were collected as *La représentation emancipée* Dort composed an 'impossible' preface, which was also connected with the planned biography of the spectator:

> I wanted to write a preface for *La représentation emancipée*. I could not. Not that I didn't conceive and draft many possible prefaces. One began thus: "My liking for the theatre has always been split between two sentiments: the desire for communion and the delight in difference" [...] In short, I would have had to write my biography of the spectator: that was too much for a preface.[32]

And after considering several ways of writing the preface, he ends with a clever trick:

> ... Here I am on the verge of being caught at my own game: this impossible preface is threatening to turn into a statement of intentions. Let's leave it there and say it's just a foreword.[33]

Shortly before his death which he knew to be approaching he made plans for a trilogy, even signing a contract with a publisher. The first volume was to be called *Le spectateur* (*The spectator*),[34] the second *Le Théâtre impossible* (about the utopia of the theatre) and the third *L'acteur* (*The Actor*).

A consideration of Dort's dream project, this never completed 'autothéâtrography'[35] allows a better understanding of his oeuvre and its contribution. Bernard Dort was not simply a theatre critic, nor was he only an expert in theatre studies. This difference may perhaps explain the awkwardness he felt with his former students, some of whom had become the theatre studies specialists of their generation, next to whom he felt out of place. The work he was unable to realize, using theatre to interrogate himself and, by extension, the mechanisms of artistic creation, reveals another Bernard Dort, the man behind the unpublished *Journal* and the unfinished novels: a writer. He used the rather old-fashioned term 'essayist', but that was probably to make fun of himself, as usual. Dort's discovery of Brecht, with whom he is always associated really masks his true image. The dream project reveals that he is a writer, who uses theatre to create texts which are often intensely poetic. This friend – and doubtless rival – of Roland Barthes, in the shadow of Maurice Blanchot, this brilliant spectator wanted by way of his own impressions to define a theory of artistic creation. He had the very painful feeling of having failed. A quarter century after his death, however, on reading his works it is possible to see that these text-poems, which should be published together, from *Le théâtre public* to *Le spectateur en dialogue,* constitute just such a work as he dreamed of, being both the theatrical novel of the twentieth century and an attempt to define the act of theatre. Bernard Dort or, secretly, a poet of refined grace.

Monet's grand waterlilies project

One might argue that had Dort lived longer he would have finished his major project. It seems more likely to me that the reverse is true: it was the very nearness of death that caused him to undertake, against his habit and will, a project he felt was essential. That said, it is important to distinguish between a work which is unfinished because of factors external to the artist's will and dream projects which are begun again, reworked and left unfinished endlessly, such as Mallarmé's *Livre* and Claude Monet's *Nymphéas* [*Waterlilies*].

This latter project appears to me to be the most significant project of all and thus its characteristics and various stages will be briefly recalled here. The great artistic enterprise of Monet's 'waterscapes' began in 1893. The artist had a "water garden" made. This was a small pool with waterlilies on it, surrounded by weeping willows and poplars. Its most prominent feature was a little green-painted bridge. Two years later in 1895 this water garden began to appear in Monet's work. In 1897 he formed the plan of a cycle of paintings on the subject of the Nympheas. The artist showed his initial studies to journalist Maurice Guillemot, who describes them thus:

> Imagine a circular room whose walls beneath the dado rail would be entirely filled by a horizon of water spotted with these plants, walls of a transparency, now green, now mauve, where the tranquillity and silence of the still water reflect spreading blooms; the shades are imprecise, deliciously nuanced, as delicate as a dream.[36]

In 1900, twelve *Bassins aux Nymphéas* (*Pools with waterlilies*) were shown at the Durand-Ruel gallery in an exhibition called 'Some recent works by Claude Monet'. In 1901 Monet bought a new piece of land to extend the 'water garden' he used as a model. In 1903 new variations did away with the bank and bridge leaving only the surface of the water and the flowers visible. Six years later Monet was still exploring this formula in echoes of the 1897 project. The framing cuts out the edges of the water garden. The surface is vertical. Variety comes from the lighting and the interplay of colours. In 1907 he was preparing for a new exhibition restricted to the *Nymphéas* "the whole effect of which depends on their being shown as a group".[37] However he postponed the exhibition to the following year and destroyed the paintings with which he was not satisfied.

> I have five or six possible canvases at the most, and have just destroyed thirty, to my great satisfaction.[38]

At this point he composed several canvases, declaring himself more or less happy with them. However this happy period was followed by one of crisis. He destroyed new paintings. Then in despair he told the gallery owner, Durand-Ruel, that he was definitively giving up the idea of the exhibition. During the summer he began painting again and wrote to his friend, the art critic Gustave Geffroy:

> These landscapes of water and reflections have become an obsession. They are beyond my strength in my old age, and yet I still wish to succeed in conveying what I feel. I've destroyed some . . . I start on more . . . and I hope that something will come out of all these attempts.[39]

New bouts of despair followed, and a new period of destruction. However in 1909 the exhibition did actually take place, with the title "Les Nymphéas, séries de paysages d'eau" ("Waterlilies, a series of waterscapes"). The canvases, completely taken up by water, marked a revolution in the concept of an exhibition. They represented variations on a theme, and the individual paintings had no names. Paradoxically the death of Monet's wife in 1911 and of his son in 1914, his fear of losing the sight in his right eye and the outbreak of war sent him into a renewed passion for work which even the German invasion could not halt. Refusing to leave Giverny he threw himself into the 'grandes decorations' project, developing that which he conceived in 1897:

> It is the same project as I had thought of long ago: water, lilies, plants, but on a very large surface.[40]

He had a studio constructed especially so that he could paint the series of very tall canvases arranged in an oval:

> I am obsessed by what I have undertaken to do here.[41]

He was occupied with this project until his death in 1926, experiencing periods of exaltation alternating with others of deep discouragement. In 1918, through the offices of his friend and neighbour Georges Clemenceau, he offered the huge art work to the French state which would in return oversee the building of a suitable home for it.

Fourteen oval pictures were ready by this point, but Monet constantly changed his mind about the manner in which they should be displayed. By 1924 the Orangerie galleries were ready to receive the large scale work but Monet refused to hand it over as he felt it was not yet finished. He went on working at it intensively, destroying many paintings in the process. In 1925 he decided to put a definitive end to the plan. Finally he agreed to deliver his art work as it was, "in spite of the very incomplete nature of his work". He died in 1926 without ever having shown the public the results of this immense project he still considered unfinished and which was not displayed until 1927, a year after his death.[42]

With his *Nymphéas* project, Monet takes his creative work as far as it can go. In it we see an artist revolutionising painting: those huge oval canvases in which the public immerses itself are completely different from painting as it is still practised today. Moreover this profoundly innovative aspect, revealed by an analysis of the project, leads us to view the rest of Monet's work with a different eye.

The same may be said of other instances of dream projects. Analysis often allows an unexpected aspect of the creative artist to be discovered, an aspect which in turn sheds completely new light on the rest of their oeuvre. The stock image of an artist often prevents us from really reading their work. *Mastorna* thus makes it possible to look beyond buttocks and spaghetti to discern in Fellini an auteur on a quest for a new form of the sacred. Genet's *La Mort* illuminates his theatre and his theoretical and political writings: an attempt to forge a new morality and a new aesthetic founded on difference. The fourth part of Claudel's *Coûfontaine* trilogy shows us the writer listening to the Other, searching for a position beyond the opposites. It throws light on the positive role given to Evil in his works. The project *La seconde consultation du Docteur Noir* invites us to read Vigny in a different way, just as Dort's *Autothéâtrographie* helps reveal another Dort, far removed from Brecht and his system.

Sir Isaac Newton's dream project

The father of modern science, Sir Isaac Newton (1642–1727), also had a dream project. In addition to his works on optics and physics, where he launched the revolutions which founded modern science (e.g., refraction of light, gravitation, calculation of the infinitesimal), Newton wrote a great deal, almost covertly, without publishing his research, on the Temple of Solomon and the dimensions of the Tabernacle. In analysing the dimensions of the Tabernacle as set out in the biblical text, he sought to arrive at the secret of the entire Universe – a reality where physics and history merge.

In several libraries around the world, and in particular in the National Library of Jerusalem, there exist thousands of pages – now available online – of unpublished texts, where Newton tries to probe the secrets of the Tabernacle, of the Temple of Solomon and the Third Temple, as described in the prophecies of Ezekiel (chapters 40–45).

During Newton's lifetime, he did not publish any of these manuscripts, as they seem to expose theological opinions which might have cost him dearly. He seems not to believe in the Holy Trinity and also to believe that the Jewish people still play a central role in the manifestation of the divine plan. One year after his death (1728), *The Chronology of Ancient Kingdoms Amended* was published,[43] a work in which Chapter V speaks of the Temple and its dimensions. Five years later (1733), another volume where Newton made apocalyptic calculations, *Observations upon the Prophecies of Daniel and The Apocalypse of St John,* was published.[44] In 1737, another work appeared, in which

Newton compared the cubit, the measure of biblical dimension (used for the construction of the Tabernacle and the Temple) to the different measures used by the peoples of Antiquity: *A dissertation upon the Sacred Cubit of the Jews and the Cubits of the Several Nations*,[45] a subject of considerable importance for the dimensions of the Tabernacle, in which he sees the ultimate secrets of the cosmos.

Hundreds of manuscripts remained unpublished among the papers he left after his death. In 1872, these manuscripts were donated by Newton's family to the University of Cambridge. The University accepted the scientific papers but refused the very numerous manuscripts that dealt with Prophecy and the Temple. The University of Oxford was asked if it was interested in the manuscripts, but it refused them as well. In 1936, this significant body of material (339 manuscripts) was put up for public sale at Sotheby's by the Duke of Portsmouth who had inherited it from Newton's great-niece. It was acquired by thirty-three different buyers. One of them, Abraham Shalom Yahuda, who was an acquaintance of Albert Einstein, sought, with the support of his eminent friend, to resell them to different American universities, such as Yale and Harvard, but, once again, no University was interested in these theological writings.

The explanation for this refusal by the universities and the academic world of the time seems to be based on the notion that the brand image of the father of modern science must not be damaged by strange, mystical writings that some say were written after the nervous breakdown of 1693, by an aging and sick Newton. And Abraham Shalom Yahuda, who did not find a buyer, would eventually, on his deathbed, bequeath the manuscripts to the National Library of Israel in Jerusalem which has made them available online.[46] They can also be accessed at the Newton Project website.[47]

Since the 1960s, when these manuscripts became accessible, several researchers have analysed Newton's theological writings, which seem to bear witness to a great project, one that possesses the characteristics of the dream projects we have described in this work: he worked on it throughout his life but never completed it such that he could arrive at publication. This massive project sought to encompass the scientific, historical and esoteric into a single system.

The first researchers to have studied Newton's unpublished manuscripts are: Frank E. Manuel,[48] B.J.T. Dobbs,[49] Richard Westfall[50] and David Castillejo.[51] Matt Goldish, in his doctorate published under the title: *Judaism in the Theology of Sir Isaac Newton*,[52] emphasises the interest that Newton took in the symbolic meaning of the measures of the Tabernacle and the Temple. Newton imagines the Temple as a perfectly symmetrical structure around a central fire, symbol of the sun around which the stars move (MS Yahuda, 41, p.62). In another manuscript (MS Yahuda, 9.2), Newton reads the Temple ceremonies as "the shadows of events to come".

An Israeli researcher, Ayval Leshem Ramati, compares Newton's research to that of Lurianic Kabbalah:

> The central altar representing the place of the sun in the solar system and God's spiritual governance over matter is related to the intricate relationship between gravity and inertia. Here once again, the Hebrew words relating to inertia and heaviness versus gravity and attraction are revealing. Heaviness in Hebrew is כובד (koved) whilst "honor" is כבוד (kavod). According to the writings of the Lurianic Kabbalah, the central altar in the Temple was the place where the Priests burned the heaviness (koved) of materiality of the people of Israel transforming it into spiritual honor (kavod) that returns to God. Indeed the numerology of the words כובד and כבוד is 32 which is also the numerology of heart (לב). The central altar was placed at the heart of the Temple to represent and remind the people of Israel that God's heart, namely God's love governs the world. Love is the gravitational attraction between bodies and souls towards unity, and in order that this divine love will sustain Creation at its best, people must honor (kavod) and respect God alone and love their neighbor.[53]

Tessa Morrison has also studied Newton's interest in the Temple.[54] Her research is mainly based on a manuscript by Newton at Babson College, Massachusetts, *Prolegomena ad Lexici Prophetici partem secundum in quibis agitur De forma Sanctuarii Judeici*. In this manuscript, Newton compares the mathematical relationships that pertain between the three structures of the Tabernacle, the Temple of Solomon, and the Temple of Ezekiel, seeing a triple analogy between these three. For him, the Temple is a living structure which evolves according to the degree of purity of the community.[55]

Over the course of the last fifty years, researchers who have studied Newton's dream project relating to the Temple have seen it as the key to understanding his scientific work. To appreciate Newton's work, one needs to recognise the principles which he believed govern the material world, the spiritual world and history. Abandoning a purely materialistic science, we turn toward a new approach to science, one which would not deny the spiritual but would seek to understand it, arriving at a position where physical laws (such as gravitation) are only the material manifestation of more general laws.

In Balzac's *Le chef d'oeuvre inconnu*, Maître Frenhofer burns his painting without ever agreeing to show it publicly. In Louis Malle's film *My dinner with André*, André Gregory does not complete the production of *Le Petit Prince* which has taken him to the Sahara. If he had not died, Monet might have destroyed his series of *Nymphéas* paintings, in the same way as Genet tore up the drafts for *La Mort* – and as he might have destroyed the proofs of *Le Captif amoureux* had he lived long enough. In his Will, Bernard Dort requested that all his unpublished works should remain unpublished. How might the mysterious phenomenon which keeps a creative artist from his essential work be explained? "It will be your last work," Fellini was told by the clairvoyant Rol during anguished preparations for *Mastorna*. And Visconti experienced similar feelings with respect to his *À la recherche* adaptation:

> A superstition, a fear of the final work can be sensed. As if, having adapted Proust, Visconti would risk finding out that his artistic trajectory was at an end, that he could create nothing new. Suso Cecchi d'Amico hints as much in the preface to the screenplay for *À la recherche*: the project fascinated and at the same time frightened Visconti who, having studied and admired Proust since his youth, veritably idolised him.
>
> "This will be my final film," he always said at the end of each of our conversations.[56]

The fear of the definitive work, which might put an end to an artistic career because there would be nothing which could be added to it, might provide an explanation on a psychological level for the paradoxical behaviour of the artist where his essential work is concerned.

The (over)ambitious nature of the projects might also be a possible explanation of the phenomenon. All the projects considered in this study are grandiose. Mallarmé envisaged his *Livre* as having five volumes, like the five parts of the Bible, intending it to be read as a secular Mass. Genet's book was to be a new Bible, founding a new aesthetic and a new morality. Fellini's film would put forward a new vision of life after death. It, like the works of Genet, Claudel or Visconti, is a "great mirror of the world and all its mirrors", encompassing all facets of reality. The final avatar of Bernard Dort's work (the trilogy of the spectator, of the impossible theatre, and of the actor) would account for the entire phenomenon of theatre.

More profoundly, the works are attempts to attain a point situated beyond the dualities of usual logic. In the stunning vision experienced by Claudel during the stormy night in Guadeloupe the author was striving to express a state where Good and Evil would be equivalents. The positive role of Evil is a theme which subtends the various avatars of his dream project. The world appears to be bad and meaningless but the poet whose role it is to explain wishes to teach us that Evil is only a stage on the way to Good, that it is useful and creates connections. In his grand project *La Mort* Genet also dreams of a work in which opposites would be identical. Besides, his entire oeuvre is like a fan in its structure: opened out, it is everything, and nothing when folded again. The answer proposed by Buzzati and Fellini at the end of *Mastorna* is an absolute indifference to the world, which also reaches a point beyond human reason. I can be happy only if everything is alike to me, if I can no longer feel the difference between what seems good and what seems bad. However, art is not philosophy; it cannot adequately express such complex thought without becoming tedious.

Another feature common to the three works considered in this book is that they are all concerned with death. The characters in *On répète Tête d'or* rehearse the play during the funeral of the English airman. The Last Post sounded by the British army "is going to explain everything". *La Mort* is the title of Genet's dream project, dedicated in its entirety to interrogating le Néant. And the world after death is the actual subject of Fellini's project. In all three artistic enterprises, these three artists, among the greatest of the twentieth century, fail in their attempt to realize the Other world. Is this to be seen as a failure of Western art to apprehend transcendence, or as overweening ambition on the part of an artist who, believing he is a superman, a prophet, a visionary, dares to conceptualize something which lies beyond the dualities and is reserved for the divinity alone? As in the story of the Tower of Babel where the overambitious architects whose construction aimed to reach up to the Heavens are scattered, Mallarmé did not accomplish his new Mass, Genet did not seal his new Bible and Fellini did not show us his new world beyond, neither Hell nor Paradise.

The presence of Midnight

In his *Cahiers (Notebooks)*[57] Valéry senses that the work he has not made is ultimately more significant than that which he has created:

Station on the terrace –
I went up on to the terrace, to the highest point of the place where my mind dwells – the place to which age, reflections and expectations have led – those borne out by events, those that have come to nought, the brilliant moves, the failures, – the people, the names, the critical reviews and so forth long forgotten.
And in the night sky of poetry, subject only to the laws of the Universe of language, there gleam the constellations that rise, and set, and will reappear . . .
There I can see *Hérodiade*, there *L'Après-midi*, the *Tombeau de Gautier* and so on, but they no longer bear the authors' names. The individuals *no longer matter*.
And while I was contemplating these 'signs', the question outlined above *came upon me* –
It came upon me like a moment of stillness and silent potency, like a great bird suddenly alighting on my shoulders, abruptly transformed into a dead weight. But I felt this great bird's weight to have the strength to carry me off. And this it did, lifting away me and my 70 years, me and my memories, my observations, my preferences and my fundamental injustice.
And above all else I saw the full value and the beauty, the accomplished excellence of *everything I have not done*.
There is your work – a voice said to me.
And I saw all I had not done.
And I knew ever more clearly that I was not he who had done what I have done – rather, I was he who had not done what I had not done – . In this way, what I had not done was perfectly beautiful, perfectly consonant with the impossibility of doing it,
and this (unbeknown to others) – I could see, I could conceive, and even (I might say) could hold and touch with extraordinary and extreme Precision. [...]
Such was my work.
Toil, suffering, events, the sweet moments or bitter blows of life, the hopes most of all, but also the times of despair, the nights without respite of sleep, charming friends, women wonderfully present, the passing hours, days – sudden centuries, foolish mistakes, difficult times – this – all this, for so many years – was necessary; it took all this, and the disgust or the disdain, the regret or the remorse, and the blending and the rejection of all this, for there to emerge, hollowed out from the mass of existence, from the welter of experiences merged and welded together – *this* wondrous core, this final – intolerable – masterpiece hewn from *negations* – and the triumph of impossible purity![58]

Conclusion 125

Might Art itself always ultimately be an impossible oeuvre? This is a theme central throughout the work of Maurice Blanchot, leading on from Mallarmé and Valéry:

> Such is the central point. Mallarmé always comes back to it as though he were returning to the intimacy of the risk to which the literary experience exposes us. This point is the one at which complete realization of language coincides with its disappearance. Everything is pronounced ("Nothing", as Mallarmé says, "will remain unproferred"); everything is word, yet the word is itself no longer anything but the appearance of what has disappeared – the imaginary, the incessant, and the interminable. This point is ambiguity itself.
>
> On the one hand, in the work, it is what the work realizes, how it affirms itself, the place where the work must "allow no luminous evidence except of existing." In this sense, the central point is the presence of the work, and the work alone makes it present. But at the same time, this point is "the presence of Midnight," the point anterior to all starting points, from which nothing ever begins, the empty profundity of being's inertia, that region without issue and without reserve, in which the work, through the artist, becomes the concern, the endless search for its origin.[59]
>
> The writer never knows whether the work is done. What he has finished in one book, he starts over or destroys in another. Valéry, celebrating this infinite quality which the work enjoys, still sees only its least problematic aspect. That the work is infinite means, for him, that the artist, though unable to finish it, can nevertheless make it the delimited site of an endless task whose incompleteness develops the mastery of the mind, expresses this mastery, expresses it by developing it in the form of power. At a certain moment, circumstances – that is, history, in the person of a publisher or in the guise of financial exigencies, social duties – pronounce the missing end, and the artist, freed by a dénouement of pure constraint, pursues the unfinished matter elsewhere.[60]

Two legends, one Greek and the other Chinese, seem to illustrate the failure inherent in artistic creation. The first is the celebrated myth of Orpheus. Eurydice, Orpheus's wife, is the inspiration for the poet's songs. Suddenly he loses her to death. How can he continue singing without Eurydice? He finds her and persuades the rulers of hell to let him take her back to the land of the living. There is one condition, however, laid down by Pluto: if Orpheus looks Eurydice in the face – if he understands what makes him sing, understands the nature of his inspiration – he will lose her. As years and works come and go, the artist eventually succeeds in expressing the essential, in contemplating Eurydice. However

– and this, for me, is the meaning of the myth – the poet cannot look at what makes him sing without risking being compelled to fall silent. The ultimate work of art is thus impossible.

The Chinese legend is different but comes to the same conclusion. An emperor commissions a painting of a dragon, and the artist sets to work. After some years the emperor is astonished to have heard nothing of the project and so sends the artist a messenger. The artist shows him several sketches in which the dragon is depicted in increasing detail, eventually appearing to leap off the page. Gradually, though, the picture becomes more abstract; details disappear, until finally there is only one line on the blank page. This is the essence of a dragon. Usually the story ends with this single line on the page. What is forgotten, however, is that the painter still has not sent this one line to the emperor; he feels deep down that even this one line is too much. The only true picture of the dragon is the blank page; the finest of symphonies is silence; the finest drama is chaos. In its most perfect form, art returns to nothingness. Might every true work of art be impossible?

Notes

Introduction
1 Honoré de Balzac, *The Unknown Masterpiece* in Honoré de Balzac, *The Girl with the Golden Eyes and Other Stories*. A new translation by Peter Collier, Oxford University Press, Oxford, 2012, pp. 49–50.
2 *Ibid.*, p. 57.
3 *Ibid.*, p. 62.
4 Letter from Mallarmé to Théodore Aubanel on 26 July 1866, in Stéphane Mallarmé, *Correspondance* (1862–1871), Gallimard, Paris, 1959, p. 222. The translation of this quotation, like all others not otherwise attributed, is by Melanie Florence.
5 Letter from Mallarmé to Henri Cazalis on 14 May 1967, *ibid.*, p. 242.
6 Letter from Mallarmé to Eugène Lefébure on 17 May 1867, *ibid.*, pp. 245–247. Mallarmé occasionally speaks of the *oeuvre*, which, in French, is a feminine noun, in the masculine, as in "le grand Oeuvre" of the alchemists.
7 Letter from Mallarmé to Verlaine on 16 November 1885, in Stéphane Mallarmé, *Correspondance* (1871–1885), Gallimard, Paris, 1965, pp. 301–302.
8 Letter from Mallarmé to Émile Verhaeren on 15 January 1888, *ibid.*, p. 24.
9 Paul Valéry, *Oeuvres* I, *Pléiade*, Gallimard, Paris 1975, p. 623.
10 Letter from Mallarmé to Henri de Régnier, spring 1898, cited by Eric Benoit, *Mallarmé et le Mystère du "Livre"*, Champion, Paris, 1998, p. 12.
11 Letter from Pirandello to Marta Abba, in *Théatre III*, Gallimard, Paris, 1985, p. 1568.
12 Stefano Pirandello, *ibid.*, p. 1545.
13 Jean-Paul Sartre, *Saint Genet, actor and martyr*, translated from the French by Bernard Frechtman, Heinemann, London, 1988, p. 576.
14 Jean Genet, *Fragments*, in Jean Genet, *The Criminal Child: Selected Essays*, Translated by Charlotte Mandell and Jeffrey Zuckerman, NYRB, New York, 2020, pp. 38–58.

CHAPTER ONE
A Dialogue Long Dreamt Of
1 First published in English translations by John Heard in the American journal *Poet Lore*, Summer 1944, v. 50 (2) pp. 100ff., Fall 1944, v. 50 (3)

pp. 195ff., Winter 1944, v. 50 (4) pp. 291ff.. Subsequently published as Paul Claudel, *Three Plays*, tr. by John Heard. John Luce, Boston, 1945.
2. Paul Claudel, *Journal*, tome 1, Gallimard, Paris, 1969, pp. 832–833.
3. Paul Claudel, *Crusts*, tr. John Heard, in *Poet Lore*, Fall 1944, v. 50 (3), p. 251.
4. The three existing plays depict what so many other works of the time show: the decline of the old nobility. *A la recherche du temps perdu* (*In Search of Lost Time*) ends with the party given by Gilberte de Saint-Loup, an elegant aristocrat connected to the Guermantes family, who is none other than the daughter of a Jew, Swann, and a high-class prostitute, Odette. Already in the middle of the nineteenth century Wagner's Ring cycle shows an aristocratic family, the Gibichungen, one of whose members, the traitor Gunther, has 'nibelungen' roots; in Wagner this word may well be a way of referring to the Jews. In Jean Renoir's film *La Règle du jeu* (*The Rules of the Game*) (1939) – a 'masterpiece of political ambiguity' as Lucien Rebatet calls it – the Comte de la Chesnaye is a scion of the Rosenthal banking family. In the Coûfontaine trilogy, the 'noble' Pensée is only the granddaughter of the peasant Turelure and Habenichts, the Jewish businessman. "The name hides everything," writes Claudel, who also demonstrates how the French aristocracy (the best thing in the world) is invaded by the Jews (the worst thing in the world). However already with the character of Pensée we see a change of direction in Claudel's imagination. Pensée the pathetic blind woman is no longer the monstrous Sichel.
5. Paul Claudel, "Préface à la representation du cycle dramatique des Coûfontaine," 1920, *Théâtre II, op. cit.*, p. 1419.
6. Paul Claudel, "Comment j'ai écrit *Le Père Humilié*", 1946, *Ibid.*, p. 1455.
7. *Ibid.*, p. 1452.
8. *Journal*, tome 1, Gallimard, Paris, 1968, pp. 832–833.
9. Paul Claudel, *La Parabole du Festin, Théâtre II, op. cit.*, pp. 1192–1193.
10. *Proverbs*, chapter 9, 1–6, Holy Bible, New Revised Standard Version, Oxford, 1995.
11. Paul Claudel, *La Sagesse ou la Parabole du Festin, Théâtre II, op. cit.*, p. 1210.
12. The letters to Darius Milhaud, the musician, and Audrey Parr, the set designer for the project, reveal how ambitious the great stage production was intended to be. Those letters written to Ida Rubinstein went missing when the artist's private residence in Place des États Unis was sacked in 1940. The letters have been discovered recently by Pascal Lécroart and have been published in the *Bulletin de la Société Paul Claudel*, 2019–20, no. 228, pp. 9–54.
13. Letter from Claudel to Audrey Parr in August 1935, *Cahiers Paul Claudel XIII*, Gallimard, Paris, 1990, p. 332.
14. In a weekly read by the young Claudel, Michel Lioure has found an engraving featuring a plumed diadem which might have inspired the young

man (see *Tête d' Or de Paul Claudel*, Annales littéraires de l'Université de Besançon, 1984, p. 64).
15 See my analysis in *Claudel metteur en scène*, Presses Universitaires de Besançon, Besançon, 1998, pp. 293–314.
16 *Samuel* I, chapter 31, 5.
17 Paul Claudel, *Oeuvres en Prose (Prose Works)* Gallimard, Paris, 1965, p. 540.
18 Paul Claudel, *Théâtre II*, op. cit., p. 257.
19 *Ibid.*, p. 1250.
20 Paul Claudel, *On répète Tête d'Or*, in Michel Lioure, *Tête d'Or de Paul Claudel*, Annales littéraires de l'Université de Besançon, Besançon, 1984, p. 291.
21 *Tête-d'Or. A Play in Three Acts by Paul Claudel*. Translated from the French by John Strong Newberry, Yale University Press, New Haven, 1919.
22 Michel Lioure, op. cit., pp. 73–81.
23 Similarly, in *Le livre de Christophe Colomb* (*The Book of Christopher Columbus*) the explorer's desire to discover new places corresponds to a call from the beyond.
24 Paul Claudel, preface to the 1950 edition of *Tête d'Or*, *Théâtre I*, op. cit., p. 1250.
25 Henri Serouya, *La Kabbale*, Grasset, Paris, 1947.
26 Paul Claudel, *Journal, tome II*, Gallimard, Paris, 1969, pp. 707–708.
27 Paul Claudel, *L'Évangile d'Isaïe*, Gallimard, Paris, 1951, p. 324, cited by Pierre Brunel, "*Tête d'Or 1949*", in *Revue des Lettres modernes*, 1965, nos. 114–116, p. 49. The image of the melded bodies evokes the ovens of the crematoria – and the centrality of Death in the prison camp in the 1949 version of *Tête d'Or* also evokes the concentration camps. Moreover when Claudel describes his new project to Honegger, he speaks of "concentration camp" rather than "prison camp."
28 Letter of 2 September 1950 from Claudel to Barrault, *Cahiers Paul Claudel X*, Gallimard, Paris, 1974, p. 217.
29 Here is the text of the *Paris Match* article: "A French prisoner of war tells me how human community had been revealed to him while he was captive. "Overnight we had been stripped of all our goods, all our advantages, everything enjoyable about our past lives. We no longer had anything. But out of all the wretchedness sprang up an admirable burst of fellow feeling. When a man was ill, the others did his work. When someone received a parcel he shared it at once. It was an intoxicating new initiation but a very healthy one. We had a sense of human community. [...]
"A German ex-prisoner of war described his experiences in near-identical words: 'In human terms, we are all alike. We may have different attitudes. We all belong to the same humanity. We concluded that we all had to work together. We must extend a hand to each other.'" (Paul Claudel, *Journal*, tome II, Gallimard, Paris, 1969, pp. 747–748.)
30 Paul Claudel, *On répète Tête d'Or*, op. cit., p. 294.

31 Letter of 2 September 1950 from Claudel to Barrault, *op. cit.*, p. 217.
32 *On répète Tête d'Or*, *op. cit.*, p. 292
33 *Ibid.*, p. 296.
34 *Ibid.*, p. 288.
35 Paul Claudel, *Mémoires improvisés*, Gallimard, Paris, 1954, p. 51.
36 Paul Claudel, *Tête d'Or (first version)*, *Théâtre I*, *op. cit.*, p. 65.
37 Arthur Honegger, "Ma Collaboration avec Paul Claudel", *N.R.F.*, September 1955, p. 559.
38 Paul Claudel, *On répète Tête d'Or*, *op. cit.*, p. 295.
39 *Idem*.
40 *Ibid.*, pp. 296–297.
41 *Ibid.*, pp. 297–298.
42 Jules Renard, *Journal*, Gallimard, Paris, 1935, p. 386. Regarding the phrase "houses" that appears above: this is based on the fact that the French phrase (used by Claudel's questioner), "mais la tolérance," plays on (i.e., is linguistically similar to) the expression "maisons de tolérance" which is the French for brothel. As such, when Claudel responded, "there are houses for that," he was making a play on words, dismissively implying that there are "houses of ill repute" for tolerance.
43 Letter of Claudel to Péguy of 10 August 1910, cited in Henri de Lubac and Jean Bastaire, *Claudel et Péguy*, Aubier, Paris, 1974, pp. 131–133.
44 Paul Claudel, *Au milieu des vitraux de l'Apocalypse*, in *Le Poète et la Bible*, v. 1, Gallimard, Paris, 1998, p. 150. Note that Claudel is inverting Isaiah's curse in the first citation (from chapter 49, 26), as Isaiah issued this curse to "your oppressors," whereas Claudel wishes it upon "you." The second citation is from Ezekiel (chapter 28, 18), from a prophecy directed against another nation (Tyre), inverting this upon Israel, as well.
45 Letter from Claudel to the 1936 World Jewish Congress, in *La Figure d'Israël*, *Cahiers Paul Claudel VII*, Gallimard, Paris, 1968, p. 323.
46 In his *Journal d'Occupation* (*Occupation Diary*) Cocteau, for example, only rarely mentions the persecutions of the Jews. Colette, his neighbour, was however married to a Jew who wore the yellow star (but not visibly enough, according to the poet). She told him about the suicide of the Jewish wife of a playwright, Léopold Marchand, who chose death rather than hamper her husband's career. Cocteau bears witness but does not sympathise.
47 Claudel, *L'Évangile d'Isaïe*, *op. cit.*, p. 316.
48 *Ibid.*, p. 347.
49 Paul Claudel, "Entretiens avec André Chouraqui", *Cahiers Paul Claudel VII*, Gallimard, Paris, 1968, p. 175.
50 Paul Claudel, *The Tidings brought to Mary: A mystery*. Translated from the French by Louise Morgan Sill, Yale University Press, New Haven, 1916.
51 Paul Claudel, *The Satin Slipper, or The Worst is not the surest*. Translated by John O'Connor, Sheed & Ward, London, 1931, p. 305.
52 Paul Claudel, *L'ours et la lune*, *Théâtre II*, *op. cit.*, p. 632.
53 Paul Claudel, *On répète Tête d'Or*, *op. cit.*, p. 289.

54 Paul de Saint Victor, *Les Deux Masques*, Calmann-Lévy, Paris, 1880, vols. 1–3.
55 *Ibid.*, v. 1, p. 540.
56 Paul Claudel, prologue to *Protée*, from 2 February 1955, *Théâtre II, op. cit.*, p. 1432. This prologue was written for the occasion of the premiere of *Protée* at the Comédie de Paris, on 25 February 1955, two days after the poet's death.
57 *Tête d'Or* first version, *op. cit.*, p. 31.

CHAPTER TWO
A Triply Murderous Work

1 *Le Condamné à mort (The Man Sentenced to Death)* 1942; *Chants secrets (Secret Songs)* 1945; *La Galère (The Galley)* 1947; *Poèmes*, 1948.
2 *Notre-Dame-des-Fleurs (Our Lady of the Flowers)* 1943; *Miracle de la Rose (Miracle of the Rose)* 1946 ; *Pompes funèbres (Funeral Rites)*, 1947; *Querelle de Brest (Querelle of Brest)*, 1947; *Journal du Voleur*, 1948.
3 *Les Bonnes (The Maids)*, 1947; *Haute surveillance (Deathwatch)* 1949.
4 Jean Genet, 'Interview with Madeleine Gobeil', in *The Declared Enemy: Texts and Interviews*, edited by Albert Dichy. Translated by Jeff Fort, Stanford, Stanford University Press, 2004, 2–17, p. 12.
5 Jean Cocteau, *Le Passé défini*, Gallimard, Paris, 1983, p. 318.
6 Jean-Paul Sartre, *Saint Genet, actor & martyr*, translated from the French by Bernard Frechtman, Heinemann, London, 1988, pp. 576–578. *Un coup de dés jamais n'abolira le hasard (A Throw of the Dice will Never Abolish Chance)* is what remains of Mallarmé's dream project, first printed in 1914. *The Seven Pillars of Wisdom* is a book by Lawrence of Arabia, published in 1926. *Eupalinos ou l'Architecte (Eupalinos or the Architect*, published in 1921) is a text by Paul Valéry on the process of creation.
7 See the fine study by Myriam Bendhif-Syllas, *Genet-Proust: Chemins croisés*, L'Harmattan, Paris, 2010.
8 Edmund White, *Genet: A Biography*, Chatto & Windus, London, 1993, p. 428.
9 Letter from Genet to Sartre in around 1952, *ibid.*, p. 384. The phrase translated as "without end" is "sans fin" in the original French, which is a word play which means to hint at sexuality without purpose, i.e., that does not produce offspring.
10 Jean Genet, *Fragments*, in *The Criminal Child and other essays*. Translated by Charlotte Mandell and Jeffrey Zuckerman, NYRB, New York, 2020, p. 38.
11 In 1936, when Genet was living in Brno, Czechoslovakia (now Czech Republic), he gave French lessons to this young Jewish woman, with whom he went on to correspond from May-November 1937, when he returned to France. The letters to Ann Bloch were discovered and published in 1987 by Friedrich Fleming under the title *Chère Madame*. These letters destroy the

myth of the unlettered artist discovering his artistic vocation while imprisoned in 1942. By writing these letters, Genet, back in 1937, proves his tremendous knowledge of French literary culture.
12 *Ibid.*, p. 50.
13 *Ibid.*, p. 43.
14 *Ibid.*, p. 51.
15 *Paris Presse*, 30 December 1952.
16 *Fragments, op. cit.*, p.44.
17 *Ibid.*, p. 45.
18 *Ibid.*, p. 39.
19 *Ibid.*, p.58.
20 *Ibid.*, p. 38.
21 *Ibid.*, p. 118..
22 *Ibid.*, p. 38.
23 *Ibid.*, p. 77.
24 *Idem.*
25 *Ibid.*, p. 92.
26 Letter from Jean Genet to Jean Cocteau around 1954, in *Cocteau, Le Passé défini*, v. III, Paris, Gallimard, 1989, pp. 247–248.
27 Jean Genet, 1956 interview with Robert Poulet, published in *Aveux spontanés*, Plon, Paris, 1963, p. 109.
28 Carole Weisweiller, *Cocteau: les années Francine* (1950–1963), Éditions du Seuil, Paris, 2003, p. 120.
29 Jean Genet, words reported by Jean Cau in *L'Express* magazine, 5 November, 1959, p. 37.
30 Programme for the Schlosspark Theater, May 1961, quoted by Richard Coe in "Jean Genet: a checklist of his works in French, English and German", *Australian Journal of French Studies*, vol. VI, 1969, p. 125.
31 Letter addressed by Jean Genet to Bernard Frechtman in October 1959, in *Théâtre complet, op. cit.*, p. 927. Rosica is Rosica Colin, the representative of Genet's rights in Germany, and Mayer, Andreas Mayer, Genet's German editor.
32 Letter from Mallarmé to Vittorio Pia, on 27 November 1886, in Eric Benoit, *op. cit.*, p. 18.
33 Jean Genet, "Interview with Antoine Bourseiller", in *The Declared Enemy*, *op. cit.*, 186–193, p. 189. In Bourseiller's working notes during preparation for the interview, Genet noted: 'Two days ago I told you God had no place in my life. The truth may perhaps be different: if I don't believe in God, I still behave all the time as if I am activated by Him and as if He has His eyes on me day and night." ("Entretien avec Antoine Bourseiller" in *L'Ennemi déclaré*, Gallimard, Paris 1991, p. 399).
34 Jean Genet, *Prisoner of Love*. With an introduction by Ahdaf Soueif. Translated from the French by Barbara Bray, NYRB, New York, 2003.
35 Jean Genet, *La Sentence*, Gallimard, Paris, 2010, p. 10.
36 *Ibidem*, p. 30.

37 *Ibidem*, p. 26.
38 *Ibidem*, p. 38.
39 "Put all the images in language in a place of safety and make use of them for they are in the desert, and it's in the desert we must go and look for them" p. vii (manuscript note at the top of the final proofs of *Le Captif amoureux*). This text written by Genet himself shows he planned to rewrite *Le Captif amoureux* which was published after his death.
40 Jean Genet, *Prisoner of Love*, op. cit., p. 132.
41 *Ibidem*, p. 184.
42 Jean Genet, *The Balcony*, translated by Barbara Wright and Terry Hands, Faber & Faber, London, 1991, p. 117.
43 Jean Genet, *Fragments*, op. cit., p. 92.
44 Jean Genet, *The Balcony*, op. cit., p. 127.
45 Jean Genet, *Fragments*, op. cit., p. 79.
46 For a more extensive treatment of these topics, see my *Le Maître fou: Genet théoricien du théâtre*, Nizet, Saint Genouph, 2009.
47 Jean-Paul Sartre, *Saint Genet: actor and martyr*, op. cit., p. 576.
48 Jean Genet, *Funeral Rites*. Translated by Bernard Frechtman, Faber, London pp. 127–128.
49 Jean Genet, *Querelle of Brest*, Grove Press, NY, 1974.
50 Jean Genet, "What remained of a Rembrandt ... " in *Reflections on the theatre and other writings*, translated by Richard Seaver, Faber & Faber, London, 1972, pp. 77–91, p. 80.
51 Jean Genet, *The Screens*, translated by Bernard Frechtman, Faber, London, 1963, pp. 133–134.
52 Letter from Jean Genet to Bernard Frechtman on 21 November 1957, in *Théâtre complet*, Gallimard, Paris, 2002, p. 913.
53 Jean Genet, 'Interview with Antoine Bourseiller' in *The Declared Enemy*, op. cit., p. 187.
54 Jean Genet, "The Brothers Karamazov" in *The Declared Enemy*, op. cit., p. 184f.

CHAPTER THREE

A Metaphysical 'James Bond Film'

1 Liliana Betti, *Fellini*, Little Brown and Co, Boston, 1979.
2 Tullio Kezich, *Fellini*, Caminia, Milan, 1987, pp. 357–376.
3 I am grateful to Umberto Rondi, Brunello Rondi's son, for providing me with access to this work.
4 Genet's letters to his agent, Bernard Frechtman, lift the lid on the financial side of his artistic creation, an essential aspect which is generally kept hidden in a still-Christian civilization which regards money as dirty. In the selection of letters between Genet and Frechtman published by the Pléiade, Genet's very detailed financial accounts are omitted and only notes on literature are highlighted.

5 Federico Fellini, *Il viaggio di G. Mastorna*. A cura di Ermanno Cavazzoni, Bompiani, Milan, 1995; Federico Fellini, Dino Buzzati et Brunello Rondi, *Le Voyage de G.Mastorna* traduit de l'italien par Françoise Pieri avec la collaboration de Michèle Berni Canini, Éditions Sonatine, Paris, 2013. *The journey of G. Mastorna: the film Fellini didn't make*, Federico Fellini; with the collaboration of Dino Buzzati, Brunello Rondi and Bernardino Zapponi; translated and with a commentary by Marcus Perryman, Berghahn Books, New York, Oxford 2013.
6 Bernardino Zapponi and Tonino Guerra also touched up the screenplay, much later on when Fellini had bought back the rights and was once more thinking of making the film. Their names are not mentioned in the present edition, however.
7 Federico Fellini, *The Book of Dreams*, edited by Tullio Kezich and Vittorio Boarini ; with a contribution from Vincenzo Mollica. Rizzoli, New York, c. 2008 p. 534.
8 Aldo Tassone, "*La vie . . . est aussi la mort*, le chef-d'oeuvre inachevé de Fellini", in *Le voyage de G. Mastorna*, Éditions Sonatine, Paris, 2013, p. 18.
9 *Ibidem*.
10 Ermanno Cavazzoni, "Les Purgatoires du XXe siècle" in *Le Voyage de G. Mastorna, op. cit.*, p. 192.
11 *Ibidem*, p. 204.
12 Jean-Paul Manganaro, *Fellini romance*, POL, Paris, 2009.
13 He was to play an important role in this story because as a doctor he was the one to diagnose the illness which paralysed the director and ended the project for good.
14 Tullio Pinelli, who had collaborated with Fellini on screenplays for other directors, had been his co-writer since his first film, *Luci del varietà* (Variety Lights). Ennio Flaiano came on board only with *La Strada*.
15 His output includes sixty screenplays including ten for Fellini, several novels: *Tempo di uccidere* (A Time to Kill) (1947), *Una e una notte* (One and one night) (1959), *Un marziano a Roma* (A Martian in Rome) (1971), several theatrical works and some essays. He worked on the adaptation of *À la recherche du temps perdu* (*In search of lost time*) which no doubt had considerable influence on *Otto e mezzo* which displays all the elements of Proust's work.
16 The role of Fellini's co-screenwriters is often underplayed in studies of his creative process. After abandoning Ennio Flaiano and Tullio Pinelli, Fellini never really succeeded in getting on with Dino Buzzati. His career really only took off again when he began collaborating with Bernardino Zapponi on the screenplays of *Toby Dammit* and *Satyricon*.
17 Dario Zanelli, *L'inferno immaginario di Federico Fellini, op. cit.*, pp. 69–70. A passage like this proves that these conversations, probably recorded without Fellini's knowledge, were not intended for publication. This is why Zanelli's slim book is so valuable.

18. Fellini, reported in Charlotte Chandler, *I, Fellini*, Bloomsbury, London, 1995, p. 163.
19. Fellini always presented his links with Ernst Bernhard as purely those of friendship. However bills found among the psychologist's papers are evidence of a treatment process interrupted by the therapist's sudden death. It was in the aftermath of Bernhard's death that Fellini began working on the screenplay.
20. Note however that the story's central element, the hero's gradual realisation of a completely unforeseeable reality which is the fruit of a teenager's imagination, constitutes the best part of the screenplay for *Mastorna*, the hero's progressive discovery that he is in the land of the dead. Furthermore, the climax of the screenplay – Mastorna in the aeroplane flown by the little Chinese girl – connects in its symbolism to Brown's text, a man lost inside the absurd imagination of a child.
21. Account of Brunello Rondi, in *L'inferno immaginario, op. cit.*, p. 63.
22. Letter from Fellini to Dino De Laurentiis, in *Le Voyage de G. Mastorna*, *op. cit.*, p. 167.
23. *Ibid.*, p. 67.
24. Dario Zanelli, *op. cit.*, p. 68. It is noteworthy that neither Rondi nor Fellini mentions Buzzatti's short story, *Il sacrilegio,* which was, however, the film's starting point.
25. *Ibid.*, pp. 73–74.
26. Almeria, whom Buzzati had married in 1964, sees writing the film as responsible for the illness he contracted almost immediately and from which he would die in 1972. She was often asked for the screen rights for theatre but steadfastly refused to grant them until 2019, when the film was converted into a play by Comédie-Française under the direction of Marie Rémond.
27. This is the subject of the short film made by the director, *Fellini: A director's note-book.*
28. Liliana Betti, *Fellini, op. cit.*, pp. 124–125.
29. *Ibid.*, p. 125.
30. Dario Zanelli, *op. cit.*, p. 71.
31. After Fellini's death an open letter from Rol to Giulietta Masina appeared in the Italian press in which the former claimed he had never advised Fellini not to make the film, merely to change its title. And indeed this is what Fellini did when he published the screenplay as a graphic novel. The title became *Viaggio di G. Mastorna ditto Fernet* (The Journey of G. Mastorna, known as Fernet). The addition of "ditto Fernet" was to follow the spiritual master's advice: the slightly altered title was supposed to make the work escape its destiny. Fernet was the name of a famous French clown.
32. Liliana Betti, *op. cit.*, pp. 129–130.
33. Dario Zanelli, *op. cit.*, pp. 77–78.
34. Giorgio De Michele was Fellini's lawyer.
35. Liliana Betti, *Fellini, op. cit.*, p. 122.
36. *Ibid.*, p. 124.

37 Liliana Betti, *op. cit.*, p. 126.
38 *Idem.*
39 Jean Genet, *The Tightrope Walker, op. cit.*, p. 116.
40 Liliana Betti, *op. cit.*, p. 129.
41 It should be noted that the clairvoyant Rol had asked Fellini to alter the work's title.
42 Maite Carpio's fine film ends with this mysterious outline drawn in the margin of a text.
43 Fellini, in a letter to Dino De Laurentiis, in *Le Voyage de Mastorna, op. cit.*, p. 167.
44 The French translation was published in 1996 by Éditions Casterman. The English version was published in the volume *Manara Library volume 3: Trip to Tulum and Other Stories*, Dark Horse, NY, 2018.
45 Fellini, *Le Voyage de G. Mastorna, op.cit.*, p. 187.
46 The passengers' questions and remarks have been scored out in the typescript, along with several announcements by the stewardess about a departure scheduled for the next day.
47 In the screenplay revised with Bernadino Zapponi and later with Tonino Guerra and published in 1995 by Kezich, this is the most reworked scene. Instead of a birth, Mastorna witnesses a domestic scene. One of the actors, playing the role of a woman, addresses him directly. It becomes evident that the scene is one from his past. In Germany he broke up the marriage of one of his admirers. In Milo Manara's graphic version Fellini reverts to the much more meaningful first version, featuring the birth, with which the theatricality of the realm of the dead culminates, just as the theatricality of the land of the living culminates in death.
48 The screenplay contains a very detailed description of the programmes, but this has been crossed out. In the graphic version, the TV announces the air disaster but Mastorna does not understand it. This is the point at which the first instalment ends, and was not continued.
49 Fellini, first letter-treatment, in *Le Voyage de G. Mastorna, op. cit.*, p. 162.
50 In the typescript from 1966 the scene takes place in a car but Fellini changed this to a bus in a handwritten note. And the letter sent to Dino De Laurentiis does indeed describe a journey in a half-empty bus, lit from the inside with a strange light.
51 Each version gives a different number of decks: the screenplay says 'four', the letter-synopsis 'five' and 'eight' is the number cited by Liliana Betti, going by the log book Fellini kept for *Mastorna*. It was the accidental collapse of this stupendous piece of the set (a multi-decker carriage) which caused the director's own collapse, as he was floored by so many unforeseeable accidents.
52 Fellini, F.; Buzzati, D. and Rondi, Brunello, *The Journey of G. Mastorna, The Film Fellini didn't make*, Berghahn, New York-Oxford, 2013, pp. 45–46.
53 Possibly a homage to Dino De Laurentiis, himself a Neopolitan.

54 *Ibidem*, p. 60.
55 *Ibidem*, p. 62.
56 Fellini, F., second letter-treatment in Dario Zanelli, *op. cit.*, p. 40.
57 Fellini, Buzzati, Rondi, *Fellini. Mastorna, op. cit.*, pp. 80–81.
58 *Ibidem*, p. 87.
59 Fellini wanted the famous clown Toto for this role.
60 Fellini, letter-treatment, Dario Zanelli, *op. cit.*, pp. 45–46.
61 Fellini, Buzzati, Rondi, *Fellini Mastorna op. cit.*, p. 116.
62 Fellini, letter-treatment, Dario Zanelli, *op. cit.*, pp. 49–50.
63 Fellini, first letter-treatment, in *Le Voyage de G. Mastorna, op. cit.*, p. 186.
64 Fellini, F., Buzzati, D and Rondi, B., in *Fellini Mastorna, op. cit.*, p. 135.
65 Jean Genet, *The Screens*, trans. by Bernard Frechtman, Grove Press, NY, 1962, pp. 158–159.
66 Fellini, F., Buzzati, D., and Rondi, B., *Fellini Mastorna, op. cit.*, p. 97.
67 *Ibidem*, p. 128.
68 Liliana Betti, *op. cit.*, p. 125.
69 Ermanno Cavazzoni, "Les purgatoires du XXème siècle" in *Le Voyage de G. Mastorna*, p. 206. In Genet's *J'étais et je n'étais pas* we also find the idea that the soul is infinite **before** it becomes incarnate in a body..
70 It may be supposed that this wish to disrupt the order of an awards ceremony also has a root in Fellini's own life. In the preceding years, from 1954 to 1964, *La Strada, La Dolce Vita* and *Otto e mezzo* had received dozens of international prizes. Each time, Fellini had to travel in order to receive them, and to listen to and give speeches. These occasions must have been a sore trial to someone who was only at ease in his work.
71 Billy Wilder, much admired by Fellini, used the same effect in *Sunset Boulevard* (1949) where the narrator is a ghost: the hero, who is recounting his death to the viewers, will be killed at the end of the film.
72 Translated into English as *The Voice of the Moon* translated by Ed Emery, Serpent's Tail, London, 1990.
73 If we were all silent for a while, we might be able to understand something.
74 As early as *Otto e mezzo* Maurice the artist-visionary and Daumier the intellectual are two antagonistic facets of the same Guido.
75 Bertrand Levergeois, *Fellini, La Dolce Vita du Maestro*, éditions de l'Arsenal, Paris, 1994, pp. 280–281.

Conclusion

1 Alfred de Vigny, *Le journal d'un poète*, entry for 5 November 1832, in *Oeuvres complètes*, tome II, Gallimard, Paris, 1960, p. 970.
2 *Ibid.*, entry for 8 May 1837, p. 988.
3 *Ibid.*, August or September 1867, p. 1392.
4 My account of the stages the project went through is based on Georges Bonnefoy's remarkable thesis, *La pensée religieuse et morale d'Alfred de Vigny*, Hachette, Paris, 1944.

5 Alfred de Vigny, *Daphné*, *Oeuvres complètes*, tome II, *op. cit.*, p. 856.
6 Georges Bonnefoy, *La pensée religieuse et morale d'Alfred de Vigny*, Hachette, Paris, 1944, p. 197.
7 *Ibid.*, p. 1225.
8 *Ibid.*, p. 1280.
9 Vigny, *Le Journal d'un poète*, entry for 21 August 1851, *op. cit.*, p. 1286.
10 *Ibid.*, entry for March 1853, p. 1306. Monsieur de Montcalm was a French general.
11 *Ibid.*, entry for March 1853, p. 1306.
12 *Ibid.*, January 1857, p. 1358.
13 *Ibid.*, entry for 5 February 1857, p. 1323.
14 *Ibid.*, entry for 24 February 1859, p. 1348.
15 *Ibid.*, entry for 5 October 1859, p. 1348.
16 Georges Bonnefoy, *La pensée religieuse et morale d'Alfred de Vigny*, *op. cit.*, p. 396.
17 Schoenberg modified the spelling of the name Aaron, so that the work's title should have twelve letters, not thirteen, a number to which he had a pathological aversion.
18 René Leibowitz, *Schoenberg*, "Solfèges", Seuil, Paris, 1969, p. 126.
19 Florence Colombani, *Proust-Visconti, histoire d'une affinité élective*, Philippe Rey, Paris, 2006.
20 *Ibid.*, pp. 9–10. The quotation is from Michel Ciment's book on Kubrick, Calmann-Lévy, Paris, 1999.
21 Florence Colombani, *op. cit.*, p. 96.
22 Caterina d'Amico de Cawalho et Guido Vergani, *Piero Tosi, costume e scenografie*, Leonardo Arte, Venise, 1977, p. 169, cited by Colombani, *op. cit.*, p. 107.
23 Florence Colombani, *op. cit.*, p. 19.
24 *Ibid.*, back cover.
25 Alison Castle, *Stanley Kubrick's Napoleon: the greatest movie never made*, Taschen, Cologne, 2009.
26 Jan Harlan was Kubrick's brother-in-law and also the nephew of Veit Harlan, director of *Jud Süss* (1940) and *Kolberg* (1945), the monumental war film depicting the German people's resistance to Napoleon's army. Kubrick, an American Jew, was thus giving a rejoinder to the great Nazi director's supreme effort.
27 After nearly thirty years and numerous attempts, Gilliam finally produced the film in 2018 as *The Man who killed Don Quixote*.
28 Even if the artist has changed to another style or medium following his crisis, the researcher can still look for links between the two creative periods, before and after the crisis, and demonstrate the ways in which they are both different and connected: the link between Genet's novels and his plays, which are separated by the crisis of the early 1950s; that between Fellini's films pre- and after *Mastorna*; the links between Racine's secular dramas and his sacred ones, written after he had given up the theatre for a lengthy period.

29 Chantal Meyer-Plantureux, *Bernard Dort, un intellectuel singulier*, Seuil, Paris, 2000.
30 *Ibid.*, p. 197.
31 Bernard Dort, *Journal*, entry for 25 February 1977, cited by Chantal Meyer-Plantureux, *idem*.
32 Bernard Dort, *La représentation emancipée*, Actes Sud, Arles, 1988, p. 11.
33 *Ibid.*, p. 18.
34 Published posthumously as *Le spectateur en dialogue*, POL, Paris, 1996.
35 The 'autothéâtrographie' is his spectator's autobiography.
36 Maurice Guillemot, *Revue illustrée*, 15 March 1898, cited in the catalogue for the exhibition *Le Cycle des Nymphéas*, Réunion des Musées nationaux, Paris, 1999, p. 30.
37 *Ibid.*, p. 35.
38 *Idem*.
39 *Ibid.*, p. 36.
40 *Ibid.*, p. 43.
41 *Ibid.*, p. 44.
42 A comparison could be drawn to Kafka, whose three novels, *The Trial*, *America* and *The Castle* were left unfinished, and were published by Max Brod only after the author's death.
43 Republished in London, *Histories and Mysteries of Man*, 1988.
44 Republished in Lewiston, E. Mellen Press, 1999. Several movies have been made based on the predictions made in this book, such as *Secret Life of Isaac Newton*: https://www.youtube.com/watch?v=s2YZN2L700Q.
45 A translation from the original Latin is available online at The Newton Project:
http://www.newtonproject.ox.ac.uk/view/texts/normalized/THEM00276.
46 https://web.nli.org.il/sites/NLI/Hebrew/collections/Humanities/newton/Pages/list.aspx
47 http://www.newtonproject.ox.ac.uk/texts/newtons-works/religious
48 Frank E. Manuel, *Isaac Newton, Historian*, Cambridge, 1963.
49 B.J.T. Dobbs, *The Foundation of Newton's Alchemy*, Cambridge, 1975.
50 Richard Westfall, *Never at Rest: A Biography of Isaac Newton*, Cambridge, 1980.
51 David Castillejo, *The Expanding Force in Newton's Cosmos as Shown in his Unpublished Papers*, Madrid, 1981.
52 Kleuwer Academic Publishers, 1998.
53 Ayval Leshem Ramati, "Newton and the Kabbalah: on the secrets of the Creation hidden in the Temple", *Parcours Judaïques* 10, Paris, 2006, p. 123.
54 Tessa Morrison, *Isaac Newton's Temple of Solomon and His Reconstruction of Sacred Architecture*, Birkhaüser, Basel, 2011.
55 According to Jewish tradition, the Cherubim, when Israel acts according to the will of the Creator, turn to each other and kiss. Otherwise, they turn away from each other. The degree of purity of the people has an action on the form of the Temple.

56 Florence Colombani, *op. cit.*, p. 19.
57 Paul Valéry, *Cahiers/Notebooks*. Translated and edited by Brian Stimpson, Paul Gifford, Robert Pickering ... [et al.] Based on the French *Cahiers* edited by Judith Robinson-Valéry. 5 vols. Peter Lang, New York, Frankfurt, 2000–2010. This quotation is in Stephen Romer's translation, in v. 5, pp. 526f.
58 Paul Valéry, *Cahiers, idem*. In his thirteenth tale, *The tale of the seven beggars,* Rabbi Nahman of Breslev exalts non-being, the sign of a stage superior to that of being. Only the blind man can truly see, the man with a stutter truly speak, etc.
59 Maurice Blanchot, "Mallarmé's Experience" in *The Space of Literature*, tr. Ann Smock, University of Nebraska Press, 1982, 37–47, p. 43.
60 Maurice Blanchot, "The Essential Solitude" in *The Space of Literature*, tr. Ann Smock, University of Nebraska Press, 1982, 19–34, pp. 20f.

Bibliography

Balzac, Honoré de

Balzac, Honoré de, *The Girl with the Golden Eyes and Other Stories*. A new translation by Peter Collier, Oxford University Press, Oxford, 2012.

Claudel, Paul

English

THEATRE

Claudel, Paul. *Tête-d'Or. A Play in Three Acts*, translated by John Strong, Newberry, Yale University Press, New Haven, 1919.

Claudel, Paul. *The city: A play*, translated by John Strong Newberry, Yale University Press, New Haven, 1920.

Claudel, Paul. *Three plays: The Hostage, Crusts, The Humiliation of the Father*, translated by John Heard, H. Fertig, New York, 1991.

Claudel, Paul. *Two dramas: Break of noon (Partage de midi), The tidings brought to Mary (L'annonce faite a Marie)*, translations and introductions [by] Wallace Fowlie, H. Regnery Co., Chicago, 1960.

Claudel, Paul. *The satin slipper; or, The worst is not the surest*, translated by the Rev. Fr. John O'Connor, with the collaboration of the author, Sheed & Ward, London, 1931.

Claudel, Paul. *The book of Christopher Columbus: A lyrical drama in two parts*, Yale University Press, New Haven, 1930.

PROSE

Claudel, Paul. *Knowing the East (Connaissance de l'Est)*; translated with an introduction by James Lawler, Princeton University Press, Princeton, N.J. c. 2004.

Claudel, Paul. *The eye listens (L'oeil ecoute)*, translated by Elsie Pell, Kennikat Press, Port Washington, N.Y., 1969.

Claudel, Paul. *Ways and crossways*, translated by John O'Connor with the collaboration of the author, Kennikat Press, Port Washington, N.Y., 1968.

Claudel, Paul. *Claudel on the theatre*, edited by Jacques Petit and Jean-Pierre Kempf, translated by Christine Trollope, University of Miami Press, Coral Gables, Fla., 1972.

POETRY

Claudel, Paul. *Five great odes (Cinq grandes odes)*, translated by Edward Lucie-Smith, Rapp & Carroll, London, 1967.

Claudel, Paul. *Poetic art (Art poetique)*, translated by Renee Spodheim, Kennikat Press, Port Washington, N.Y., 1969.

Claudel, Paul. *A hundred movements for a fan (Cent phrases pour eventails)*, translated and with an introduction by Andrew Harvey & Iain Watson, Quartet Books, London, 1992.

French

Claudel, Paul, *Oeuvres complètes*, Gallimard, Paris, 1950–1986 (29 volumes).

Claudel, Paul, *Théâtre I & II*, Gallimard, Paris, 1965–1967.

Claudel, Paul, *On répète Tête d'or* dans Michel Lioure, *Tête d'or de Paul Claudel*, Annales littéraires de l'université de Besançon, 291, Besançon, 1984

Claudel, Paul, *La Sagesse ou la Parabole du Festin*, dans *Théâtre II*, Gallimard, Paris, 1967.

Claudel, Paul, *Jeanne d'Arc au bûcher*, dans *Théâtre II*, Gallimard, Paris, 1969.

Claudel, Paul, *Histoire de Tobie et de Sara*, dans *Théâtre II*, Gallimard, Paris, 1969.

Claudel, Paul, *Supplément aux œuvres complètes* (I, II, III), Annales littéraires de l'Université de Besançon (1990–1994).

Claudel, Paul, *Le Poète et la Bible*, tome I, Gallimard, Paris, 1998.

Claudel, Paul, *Mémoires improvisés*, Gallimard, Paris, 1954.

Claudel, Paul, *Mes idées sur le Théâtre*, textes recueillis et présentés par Jacques Petit et Jean-Pierre Kempf, Gallimard, Paris, 1966.

Claudel, Paul, *Œuvres en prose*, Gallimard, Paris, 1965.

Claudel, Paul, *L'Evangile d'Isaïe*, Gallimard, Paris, 1951

ON CLAUDEL

Antoine, Gerald, *Claudel ou l'enfer du génie*, Robert Laffont, Paris, 2004.

De Lubac, Henri, et Bastaire, Jean, *Claudel et Péguy*, Aubier, Paris, 1974.

La Figure d'Israël, Cahiers Paul Claudel VII, Gallimard, Paris, 1968.

Lécroart, Pascal (ed.), *Claudel Politique*, Aréopage, 2009.

Lioure, Michel, *Tête d'or de Paul Claudel*, Annales littéraires de l'Université de Besançon, Besançon, 1984.

Moraly, Yehuda, *Claudel metteur en scène: La frontière entre les deux mondes*, Presses universitaires franc-comtoises, Besançon, 1998.

Petit, Jacques, *Bernanos, Bloy, Claudel, Péguy: quatre écrivains catholiques face à Israël*, Calmann-Lévy, Paris,1972.

Dort, Bernard

Dort, Bernard, *Théâtre public*, Seuil, Paris, 1967.

Dort, Bernard, *Théâtre réel*, Seuil, Paris, 1971.

Dort, Bernard, *Théâtre en jeu*, Seuil, Paris, 1979.

Dort, Bernard, *La représentation émancipée*, Actes Sud, Arles, 1988.

Dort, Bernard, *Le spectateur en dialogue*, P.O.L, Paris, 1995.

On Dort

Meyer-Plantureux, Chantal, *Bernard Dort, un intellectuel singulier*, Seuil, Paris, 2000.

Fellini, Federico
English

Fellini, Federico. *The Journey of G. Mastorna: The Film Fellini Didn't Make*, Berghahn, New York–Oxford, 2013.

French

Fellini, Federico ; Buzzati, Dino et Rondi, Brunello, *Le Voyage de G. Mastorna* traduit de l'italien par Françoise Pieri avec la collaboration de Michèle Berni Canani, Editions Sonatine, Paris, 2013.

Mejean, Jean-Max. *Fellinicittà*. Editions de La Transparence, Chatou, 2009.

Italian

Fellini, Federico, *Il viaggio di G. Mastorna,* Bompiani, Milano, 1995.

On Fellini

Aldouby, Hava. *Federico Fellini: Painting in Film, Painting on Film*, University of Toronto Press, Toronto, 2013.

Betti, Liliana, *Fellini,* Little, Brown and Company, Boston, 1976.

Bondanella, Peter. *The Films of Federico Fellini*, Princeton University Press, Princeton, 1992.

Federico Fellini: Contemporary Perspectives (edited by Frank Burke and Marguerite R. Waller), University of Toronto Press, Toronto, 2002.

Kezich, Tullio, *Federico Fellini: The Films,* Rizzoli International Publications, 2010.

Levergeois, Bertrand, *Fellini,* Éditions de l'Arsenal, Paris, 1994.

Stubbs, John C. *Federico Fellini as Auteur: Seven Aspects of His Films*, Southern Illinois University Press, Carbondale, 2006.

Waller, Marguerite, Marita Gubareva and Frank Burke (ed.), *A Companion to Federico Fellini*, Wiley Blackwell, Hoboken, NJ, 2020.

Zanelli, Dario, *L'inferno immaginario di Federico Fellini*, Guaraldi, 1995.

Zapponi, Bernadino, *Il mio Fellini*, Marsilio, Venezia, 1995.

Genet, Jean
English
Novels

Genet, Jean, *Our Lady of the Flowers (Notre-Dame des Fleurs)*, translated by Bernard Frechtman, introduction by Jean-Paul Sartre, Grove Press, New York, 1963.

Genet, Jean, *The thief's journal (Journal du voleur(*, foreword by Jean-Paul Sartre, translated by Bernard Frechtman, Grove Press, New York, 1987.

THEATRE

Genet, Jean, *Two plays: The maids. Death watch*, translated by Bernard Frechtman, introduction by Jean-Paul Sartre, Grove Press, New York, 1954.

Genet, Jean, *The balcony: A play in nine scenes (Le balcon)*, translated by Bernard Frechtman, Grove Press, New York, 1958.

Genet, Jean, *The blacks: a clown show (Les Negres, clownerie)*, translated by Bernard Frechtman, Faber, London, 1967.

Genet, Jean, *The screens: a play in seventeen scenes (Les Paravents)*, translated by Bernard Frechtman, Grove Press, New York, 1962.

ESSAYS

Genet, Jean, *Reflections on the theatre, and other writings*, translated by Richard Seaver, Faber, London, 1972.

Genet, Jean, *Rembrandt*, translated by Randolph Hough, Hanuman Books, Madras, NY, 1988.

Genet, Jean, *Prisoner of love (Le Captif amoureux)*, translated by Barbara Bray, introduction by Edmund White, Wesleyan University Press, Hanover, N.H., 1992.

Genet, Jean, *Fragments of the artwork (Fragments ... et autres textes(*, translated by Charlotte Mandell, Stanford University Press, Stanford, CA., 2003.

Genet, Jean, *The declared enemy: texts and interviews (L' Ennemi declare)*, edited by Albert Dichy, translated by Jeff Fort, Stanford University Press, Stanford, CA., 2004.

Genet, Jean, *The Criminal child: Selected essays (L'Enfant criminel)*, translated by Jeffrey Zuckerman and Charlotte Mandell, New York Review Books, New York, 2020.

French

Genet, Jean, *La Sentence*, suivi de *J'étais et Je n'étais pas*, Gallimard, Paris, 2010.
On Genet:

Bendhif-Syllas, Myriam, *Genet-Proust : Chemins croisés*, L'Harmattan, Paris, 2010.

Coe, Richard, *Jean-Genet: a checklist of his works in French, English and German*, Australian Journal of French Studies, vol VII, 1969.

Genet, a collection of critical essays, edited by Peter Brooks and Joseph Halpern, Prentice-Hall, Englewood Cliffs, N.J., 1979.

Lavery, Carl. *The Politics of Jean Genet late theatre*, Manchester University Press, Manchester, 2010.

Moraly, Jean-Bernard, *Genet, la vie écrite*, Éditions de la Différence, Paris, 1998.

Moraly, Jean-Bernard, *Le Maître fou: Genet théoricien du théâtre*, Nizet, Saint Genouph, 2009.

Moraly, Jean-Bernard, ed. *Les Nègres au Port de la Lune, Genet et les differences*, editions de la Difference, Paris, 1988.
Sartre, Jean-Paul, *Saint Genet: actor and martyr*, translated by Bernard Frechtman, G. Braziller, New York, 1963.
White, Edmund, *Genet: a biography*, Alfred A. Knopf, New York, 1993.

Kubrick, Stanley
Castle, Alison. *Stanley Kubrick's Napoleon: The Greatest Film Never Made*, Taschen, Cologne, 2009.

Mallarmé, Stéphane
English
Arnar, Anna Sigridur. *The Book as Instrument: Stéphane Mallarmé, the Artist's Book, and the Transformation of Print Culture*. University of Chicago Press, Chicago, 2011.
Cohn, Robert G. *Mallarmé's Masterwork*. De Gruyter Mouton, The Hague, Paris, 1966.

French
Benoit, Eric, *Mallarmé et le mystère du « Livre »*, Champion, Paris, 1998.
Scherer, Jacques. *Le Livre de Mallarmé*. Gallimard. Paris, 1957.

Monet, Claude
Clemenceau, Georges. *Claude Monet: The Water Lilies* (translated. by George Boras), Doubleday, Doran and Co., Garden City, NY, 1930.
King, Ross. *Mad Enchantment: Claude Monet and the Painting of the Water Lilies*. Bloomsbury. New York, 2017.
Water Lilies, Monet (edited by Charles F. Stuckey), HL Levin Assoc., NY, 1988.

Newton, Isaac
Goldish, Matt. *Judaism in the Theology of Sir Isaac Newton*. Kluwer Academic, Dordrecht, 1988.
Morrison, Tessa. *Isaac Newton's Temple of Solomon and his Reconstruction of Sacred Architecture*. Birkhauser, Basel, 2011.

Pirandello, Luigi
Pirandello, Luigi, *The mountain giants, and other plays*, translated by Marta Abba, Crown Publishers, New York, 1958.
Pirandello, Luigi, *Théâtre III*, Gallimard, Paris, 1985.

Schoenberg, Arnold
Worner, Karl Heinrich. *Schoenberg's Moses and Aaron*, translated by Paul Hamburger, St. Martin's Press, NY, 1963.
Leibowitz, René, *Schoenberg*, Seuil, Paris, 1969.

Vigny, Alfred de
English
Vigny, Alfred de, *Stello: A Session with Doctor Noir* (translated by Irving Massey), McGill University Press, Montreal, 1963.

Vigny, Alfred de, *An English translation of Alfred de Vigny's Daphne: La deuxieme consultation du Docteur Noir (Daphne: the second consultation of Doctor Noir)*, translated by Henry F. Majewski, Edwin Mellen Press, Lewiston, NY, c. 2010.

French
Vigny, Alfred de, *Œuvres complètes*, I et II, Gallimard, Paris, 1955–1960.

ON VIGNY
Bonnefoy, Georges, *La pensée religieuse et morale d'Alfred de Vigny*, Hachette, Paris, 1944.

Visconti, Luchino
English
Blom, Ivo Leopold. *Reframing Luchino Visconti: Film and art*, Sidestone Press, Leiden, 2017.

French
Colombani, Florence, *Proust-Visconti, une affinité élective,* Philippe Rey, Paris, 2006.

Correspondence and Diaries
Claudel, Paul, *Journal,* vols. I and II, Gallimard, Paris, 1968, 1969.

Correspondance Claudel-Barrault, presented and annotated by Michel Lioure, *Cahiers Paul Claudel X,* Gallimard, Paris, 1974.

Correspondance Claudel-Audrey Parr, presented and annotated by Michel Malicet and Michel Lioure, *Cahiers Paul Claudel XIII,* Gallimard, Paris, 1990.

Correspondance Genet-Frechtman (selected letters), in *Théâtre complet,* Gallimard, Paris 2002.

Renard, Jules, *Journal,* Gallimard, Paris, 1935.

General Bibliography
Books
Blanchot, Maurice, *The Space of Literature,* translated by Ann Smock, University of Nebraska Press, Lincoln, 1982

Blanchot, Maurice, *Le livre à venir*, Gallimard, Paris, 1959.

Blanchot, Maurice, *L'entretien infini*, Gallimard, Paris, 1969.

Buzzati, Dino, *Il sacrilegio*, in *I sette messaggeri*, Mondadori, Milano, 1984.

Chekhov, Anton, *The Seagull*, in *Plays*, translated with notes by Peter Carson, Penguin Classics, London, 2002.

Cocteau, Jean *Le Passé défini*, I–II–III, Gallimard, Paris, 1983, 1989.
Dante, Alighieri, *Œuvres complètes*, Gallimard, Paris, 1988.
Menasce, Jean de, *Quand Israël aime Dieu*, Plon, Paris, 1931.
Poe, Edgar Allan, *Never bet the devil your head*, in, *Complete Stories and Poems of Edgar Allan Poe*, Knopf Doubleday, New York, 1984.
Poulet, Robert, *Aveux spontanés*, Plon, Paris, 1963.
Proust, Marcel, *A la recherche du temps perdu*, Gallimard, Paris, 1991.
Serouya, Henri, *La Kabbale*, Grasset, Paris, 1947.
Valéry, Paul *Notebooks (Cahiers)*, translated and edited by Brian Stimpson, Paul Gifford, Robert Pickering, 5 vols. Peter Lang, New York, 2000–2010.
Weiswieller, Carole, *Jean Cocteau : les années Francine*, Seuil, Paris, 2003.
Yeschua, Silvio, *Valéry, le roman et l'œuvre à faire*, Minard, Paris, 1976.

Articles

Benson, Daniel, "L'absence positive : une rencontre entre Jacques Rancière et Maurice Blanchot"; Espace Maurice Blanchot, www.blanchot.fr.
Brunel, Pierre, « Tête d'or 1949 », *Revue des lettres modernes*, 1965, n°s 114–116.
Eades, Caroline, « L'Évocation des enfers : mythe et cinéma », dans *La mythologie et l'Odyssée*, textes réunis par André Hurst et Françoise Liloublan, Droz, Paris, 2002.
Faragi, C.J., "Leonardo's *Battle of Anghiari*", *Art bulletin*, n° 76, 1994.
Leshem Ramati, Ayval, "Newton and the Kabbalah: on the secrets of the Creation hidden in the Temple", *Parcours Judaïques* 10, Paris, 2006, pp. 97–130.
Lozano Sampredo, Tereza, "La narration d'une quête de l'idéal absolu : l'art et l'artiste dans *Le Chef d'œuvre inconnu* et *Une mort héroïque*", *Annales de Filologia Francesa*, n° 13, 2004–2005.
Zollner, "*La Battaglia di Anghiari* di Leonardo de Vinci fra mitologia e politica", Lettura Vinciana, n° 27, Florence, 1998.

Filmography, Iconography and Unpublished Texts

Filmography
Blanchard, Gilles, *Tête d'or* (2007).
Bromberg, Serge and Medrea, Ruxandra, *L'Enfer d'Henri-Georges Clouzot* (2009).
Carpio, Maite, *Il misterioso viaggio di Federico Fellini* (2003).

Fellini, Federico
La Strada (1954).
Le Notti di Cabiria (1957).
Dolce Vita (1960).
Otto e Mezzo (1963).
Toby Dammit in *Spirits of the Dead* (1968).
Fellini: a director's notebook (1969)
Fellini-Satyricon (1969).
Fellini's Casanova (1976).
Prova d'orchestra (1978).
E la nave va (1983).
Ginger e Fred (1985).
La Voce della luna (1990).

Fulton, Keith et Pepe, Luis, *Lost in La Mancha* (2002).
Malle, Louis, *My dinner with André* (1981).
Rouch, Jean, *Les Maîtres fous* (1955).

Iconography
Catalogue de l'exposition *Le Cycle des Nymphéas,* Société des musées nationaux, Paris.
Fellini, Federico, *The Book of Dreams*, Rizzoli International, New York, 2008.
Manara, Milo and Fellini, Federico, *Le Voyage de G. Mastorna dit Fernet*, Editions Casterman, Tournai, 1996.
Manara, Milo and Fellini, Federico, *Due viaggi con Federico Fellini: Viaggio a Tulum: Il viaggio di G. Mastorna detto Fernet*, Mondadori, Milano, 2001.

Unpublished texts

Fellini, Federico; Buzzati, Dino; Rondi, Brunello, *Il viaggio di G. Mastorna*, typed screenplay, 1966.

Genet, Jean
Lettres à Frechtman.
Lettre à Decimo.
Les Folles.
Peur de mourir.

Index

Fictional characters are listed within single quotes, with the name of the book/story/drama/film in brackets. In most cases the character is indexed under the first name e.g. 'Guido' (Fellini's *Otto e mezzo*).

'Aaron' (Schoenberg's *Moses und Aron*), 109, 110, 111
Abba, Marta, 4
Abrahami, Ouri, *plate 11*
Acco Festival, *plates 13–16*
'Adalgisa' (Bellini's *Norma*), 43
Aeschylus, 9, 32, 59
AGIS (Associazione Generale Italiana dello Spettacolo), 63
Agor, Yaacov, *plate 10*, *plate 11*, *plate 20*
'Albertine' (Proust's *À la recherche du temps perdu*), 112
'Aldina' (Fellini's *La Voce della Luna*), 97
Alexander the Great, 16, 18
Algerian War, 57
'Ali Habenichts' (Claudel's *Le Pain Dur*), 9–10, 128*n*
Almaz, Michael, *plate 9*
Almog, Aaron, *plate 10*, *plate 20*
Amalek, 17
'Amalia' (Fellini's *Ginger e Fred*), 96
Amrouche, Jean, 23
Anouilh, Jean, 46
antisemitism, 26–8
'Apollo' (Aeschylus's *Oresteia*), 59
Arafat, Yasser, 51
Aristophanes, 9, 59
Aristotle, 89
'Armandino' (Fellini's *Il viaggio di G. Mastorna*), 73, 83, 84, 87–8, 98
'Arthur' (Genet's *Le Balcon*), 53
Associazione Generale Italiana dello Spettacolo (AGIS), 63
Astaire, Fred, 96
'Athena' (Aeschylus's *Oresteia*), 32, 59

Ballets Russes, 13
Balzac, Honoré de, *Le Chef d'oeuvre inconnu*, 1–2, 122
'Baron de Charlus' (Proust's *À la recherche du temps perdu*), 112
Barrault, Jean-Louis, 8–9, 16, 19, 20, 21
Barsacq, André, *plate 2*
Barthélemy Saint-Hilaire, Jules, 108
Barthes, Roland, 114, 115, 116
'Bartholoméus I' (Ionesco's *L'Impromptu d'Alma*), 114
'Bartholoméus II' (Ionesco's *L'Impromptu d'Alma*), 114
La Bataille d'Alger, 57
Benigni, Roberto, 97
'Benjamin Elul of Alexandria' (Vigny's *Daphné*), 106
Benoit, Éric, 2
Bentaga, Abdallah, 34, 49
Berghahn Books, 64
Bergman, Ingmar, 93, 101
Bernhard, Ernst, 67, 69, 71, 73, 135*n*
Bernhardt, Sarah, 47
Betti, Liliana, 63, 66, 74, 77, 136*n*
Beutler, William, *plate 35*
Blanchard, Gilles, *plate 3*, *plate 4*, *plate 5*, *plate 6*
Blanchot, Maurice, 104, 116, 125
Bloch, Ann, 38, 131–2*n*
Bompiani publishing house, 6, 63
Bondanella, Peter, 6
Bondarchuk, Sergei, 113
Bonneval, Sabine de, 45–6
Boulanger, Georges Ernest, 17
Bourseiller, Antoine, 49, 132*n*
Brando, Marlon, 112
Brecht, Bertolt, 114, 116
Brethes, Romain, 66
Brod, Max, 139*n*
Bromberg, Serge, 113

Brown, Fredric, 69, 90, 95
Brunel, Pierre, 16, 21
Buloz, François, 108
Burgundy, Duke of, 89
Buzzati, Almeria, 135*n*
Buzzati, Dino
   Fellini interviews, 69
   Il sacrilegio, 63, 70, 90, 101, 135*n*
   illness and death of, 135*n*
   relations with Fellini, 71–2, 134*n*
   Il viaggio di G. Mastorna, 5, 63, 64, 67, 70, 71–2, 79, 91, 123, 135*n*

'Cabiria' (Fellini's *Notti di Cabiria*), 100
Caesar, Julius, 18
calligraphy, 50
Cambridge University, 120
Cannes Film Festival, 97
'the Cardinal' (Fellini's *Otto e mezzo*), 100
'Carla' (Fellini's *Otto e mezzo*), 100
Carpio, Maite, 6, 66, 136*n*, *plate 24*, *plate 31*
'Casanova' (Fellini's *Fellini's Casanova*), 102
'Cassius' (Claudel's *Tête d'Or* – first version 1889), 17
Castillejo, David, 120
Castle, Alison, 113
Cattarinich, Mimmo, *plate 21*, *plate 25*, *plate 26*, *plate 27*
Cau, Jean, 52
Cavazzoni, Ermanno
   fictionalised version of *Mastorna* screenplay, 6, 64, 79–80
   Mastorna's return to life, 91–2
   Il poema dei lunatici, 64, 97
   "Les Purgatoires du XXe siècle", 65–6
   La Voce della Luna, 97, 99
'Cébès' (Claudel's *Tête d'Or* – first version 1889), 16, 33
'Cébès' (Claudel's *Tête d'Or* – third version 1949), 21
Cecchi d'Amico, Suso, 122
Cerberus, 95
Cervantes, 114
Chabrol, Claude, 113
Chagall, Marc, 111
'Chantal' (Genet's *Le Balcon*), 53, *plate 10*
Chazot, Jacques, 46
Chekhov, Anton, *The Seagull*, 4
the Cherubim, 139*n*
Chouraqui, André, 8
Christianity, Claudel's works, 8, 11–12, 13–14, 15, 16, 21–6, 33, 104
Churchard, Graeme, *plate 34*
Ciment, Michel, 113

Cinecittà journal, 64
'Claire' (Genet's *Les Bonnes*), 57, 58
Claudel, Camille, 26
Claudel, Paul, *plate 1*
   Aeschylus's *Agamemnon*, 9
   Aeschylus's *Oresteia*, vi, 9, 32
   L'Annonce Faite A Marie, 30–1
   attitude towards Israel, 27–8, 29–30
   attitude towards Jews, 26–33
   Au milieu des vitraux de l'Apocalypse, 27–8
   biblical drama with music, 8, 12–16, 28, 128*n*
   biblical texts, 8, 12, 13, 14, 15, 17, 25, 28, 30
   Coûfontaine trilogy, 5, 8, 9–10, 128*n*
   Coûfontaine trilogy (fourth play), vi–vii, 5, 8, 9–12, 32–3, 119, 123
   Danse des Morts, 13, 15
   L'Endormie, 26
   "Entretiens avec André Chouraqui", 8
   L'Évangile d'Isaïe, 16, 20–1, 29, 30
   L'Histoire de Tobie et de Sara, 13, 15
   Incantations from *Les Choéphores*, 9
   Jeanne d'Arc au bûcher, 13, 15
   Journal, 5, 8, 11–12, 20, 21, 28
   Judaism and Christianity dialogue, 8, 11–12, 13–14, 15, 16, 21–6, 33, 104
   literary output, 62
   Mémoires improvisés, 11, 23
   Oeuvres complètes, 8
   On répète Tête d'Or (1949), 8–9, 16, 18, 19–26, 29–30, 92, 123, *plate 7*
   L'Otage, 8, 9, 33
   L'ours et la lune, 31
   Le Pain Dur, 8, 9–10, 27, *plate 2*
   Le Père humilié, 8, 10–11, 27, *plate 3*, *plate 4*
   Protée, 32, 131*n*
   Le Ravissement de Scapin, 20
   La Sagesse ou la Parabole du Festin, 13, 15, 23
   Le Soulier de satin, 31
   Soulier de satin, vi
   Tête d'Or (first version 1889), 16–19, 21, 22–3, 30
   Tête d'Or (second version 1895), 16, 18, 23
   Tête d'Or (third version 1949), 8–9, 16, 18, 19–26, 29–30, 92, 123, *plate 7*
   Tête d'Or (film), *plate 5*, *plate 6*
   vision experienced in Guadeloupe, 8, 11, 12, 123
Clemenceau, Georges, 118
Clouzot, Henri-Georges, 113, *plate 34*
Cocteau, Jean, 35, 44–5, 46, 56, 89, 130*n*

Colette, 130*n*
Colin, Rosica, 47, 132*n*
Colombani, Florence, 6, 66, 111, 112–13
Columbia production company, 113
Comédie-Française, 20, 45, 46, 135*n*, plates 28–30
Confucius, 89
Copeau, Jacques, 13
Coppola, Francis Ford, 114
Corriere della Sera newspaper, 69

D'Annunzio, Gabriele, 13, 112
Daëms, Marie, 46
Daglidis, Antonis, *plates 17–19*
Dalle, Béatrice, *plate 6*
Dante, *Divine Comedy*, vii, 67, 69–70, 71, 76, 86, 90, 91, 96
'Daumier' (Fellini's *Otto e mezzo*), 72, 92, 137*n*
'David, King' (Claudel's *Tête d'Or* – first version 1889), 16, 17
David, King of Israel, 17
Davis, Angela, 58
'De Cercis' (Fellini's *Il viaggio di G. Mastorna*), 73, 85, 98
De Laurentiis, Alfredo, 70
De Laurentiis, Dino
  The Bible, 69
  Brown's *What mad universe* rights, 69
  Carpio's documentary interviews, 66
  Dinocittà Studios, 68
  dispute with Fellini over *Mastorna*, 74–5
  Fellini's *La Dolce Vita*, 69
  Fellini's illness, 76
  Fellini's letters on *Mastorna*, 63, 65, 70, 71, 78, 79, 80, 81, 83, 84, 86, 87, 136*n*
  Fellini's *La Strada*, 69
  Mastorna contract signing with Fellini, 69
  Mastorna lead role, 76
  Mastorna screenplay text, 71
  as most celebrated producer of the times, 68
  reconciliation with Fellini over *Mastorna*, 75–6
  severing of ties with Fellini, 6, 77
De Laurentiis, Luigi, 70, 77
De Michele, Giorgio, 75
De Sica, Vittorio, 73
death
  and artistic creation, vii–viii
  Claudel's *L'Annonce Faite A Marie*, 30–1
  Claudel's *Tête d'Or* (third version 1949), 23, 123, 129*n*
  Fellini's diary, 74

Fellini's dream, 64–5, 80
Fellini's *Il viaggio di G. Mastorna*, 64–5, 85–6, 91–2, 101, 104, 122, 123
Genet's writings, 37, 38, 39–41, 44, 46, 47–8, 51, 52, 92
death instinct, and homosexuality, 37, 38, 40, 44, 46, 52, 92
Debussy, Claude, 13
'Mme Decarnin' (Genet's *Pompes Funèbres*), 55
Decimo
  Genet's *Les Folles*, 45, 46, 47
  Genet's *La Lettre à Decimo*, 36–7, 43, 54, 56
  Genet's "Le Prétexte", 39
  relationship with Genet, 36–7, 40, 43, 45, 46
  tuberculosis, 37, 43, 46
Deco, Eleftheria, *plates 17–19*
Deneuve, Catherine, 112
Derrida, Jacques, 61
di Venanzo, Gianni, 68, 73
Diaghilev, Serge, 13
Dietrich, Marlene, 111
Dinocittà Studios, 68, 70, 72, 97, 99, *plate 24*
Dionysus, 17, 59
Divine Comedy (Dante), vii, 67, 69–70, 71, 76, 86, 90, 91, 96
Dobbs, B.J.T., 120
'Docteur Noir' (Vigny's *Daphné*), 106, 107
'Docteur Noir' (Vigny's *Stello*), 107
Doelnitz, Marc, 45, 46
Dohrn, Wolf, 9
Donnay, Maurice, 27
Dort, Bernard, *plate 36*
  L'acteur, 116
  Autothéâtrographie, 114–16, 119, 122, 139*n*
  Journal, 115, 116
  Le Monde chronicles, 115
  La représentation emancipée, 114, 115
  Le spectateur, 115–16
  Le spectateur en dialogue, 114, 116
  Le Théâtre impossible, 116
  Théâtre public, 114, 116
Douer, Shoshana, *plate 9*
Dreyer, Carl Theodor, 104, 114
Dreyfus Affair, 26, 27
Drumont, Édouard, 26, 27
'Duchesse de Guermantes' (Proust's *À la recherche du temps perdu*), 112
Dumas, Alexandre, 46
Durand-Ruel, Paul, 117
Duvignaud, Jean, 58

Index

Éditions Sonatine, 6, 64, 70, 78
'Edmea Tetoua' (Fellini's *E la nave va*), 92
Eger, Raymond, 93
Einstein, Albert, 120
'Encolpius' (Fellini's *Fellini Satyricon*), 101
'Erinyes' (Aeschylus's *Oresteia*), 32
Etruscans, viii–ix
The Eumenides (Aeschylus), 32, 59
Eurydice, 125
Ezekiel (Biblical prophet), 13, 32, 119, 130*n*
Ezekiel's Temple, 121

Feld, Tziporah, *plate 9*
Fellini, Federico, *plate 21*
   abandonment of *Mastorna*, 5–6, 63, 74–5
   Agenze matrimoniale, 62
   awards ceremonies, 137*n*
   Il Bidone, 62
   Christianity theme, 68, 100, 101, 102
   cinematographic output, 62–3
   Città' delle donne, 99–100, 102
   clairvoyance interest, 68, 69
   clairvoyant predictions about *Mastorna*, 122
   I Clowns, 92, 101
   creative crises, viii, 63, 67, 68, 93, 94, 101, 114, 138*n*
   The Decameron, 69, 77
   diary, 63, 74
   La Dolce Vita, viii, 63, 67, 68, 69, 70, 100, 101, 103, 137*n*
   dreams, 64–5, 73, 80
   E la nave va, 92, 102, 103
   existence after death, vii–ix, 65, 74, 85–6, 91–2, 101, 104, 122, 123
   Fellini: a Director's notebook, 6, 66, 93
   Fellini Satyricon, vii, 66, 69, 77, 93, 101, 102, 103, 134*n*
   Fellini's Casanova, 102
   Ginger e Fred, 93, 96, 98, 102, 103
   Giulietta degli spiriti, 63, 67, 68, 72, 74, 100, 101, 102
   I Vitelonni, 62
   illness (1976), 76
   interviews, 64, 69
   Intervista, 97, 102
   Luci del varietà, 62, 134*n*
   The Merovingian Chronicles, 71, 77
   Notti di Cabiria, viii, 63, 67, 68, 100, 102
   Orlando Furioso, 69, 71, 74, 77
   Otto e mezzo, viii, 2, 5, 63, 67, 68, 70, 72, 73, 75, 79, 92, 93, 100, 102, 103, 113, 137*n*
   periods of creative sterility, 104

Prova d'Orchestra, 92, 99, 103
Roma, 94, 99, 101, 102, 103
   and the sacred, 100–2, 119
Lo sceicco bianco, 62
   self-portrait as Mastorna, *plate 31*
   spiritualism, 68–9, 101
La Strada, 62, 67, 68, 69, 76, 100, 101, 137*n*
Le Tentazioni del dottore Antonio, 63
Toby Dammit, 93–6, 98, 134*n*, *plate 21*, *plate 25*, *plate 26*, *plate 27*
Il viaggio di Anita, 102
Il viaggio di G. Mastorna ditto Fernet, 77–8, 135*n*, *plate 22*, *plate 23*
Il viaggio a Tulum, 102
La Voce della Luna, 64, 92, 93, 97–100, 103
   see also Il viaggio di G. Mastorna (Fellini)
Fénelon, François, 89
Films Marceau, 93, 94
Flaiano, Ennio, 2, 67, 70, 71, 134*n*
Fontenelle, M. de (Bernard Le Bovier), 89
France
   antisemitism, 26–8
   Dreyfus Affair, 26, 27
France-Culture radio channel, 6, 66, 111
Frechtman, Bernard
   correspondence with Genet, 5, 40, 47, 59, 133*n*
   Genet's dream project, 52
   La Lettre à Decimo, 37
   replaced by Gallimard, 49
   Rouch's *Les Maîtres fous*, 58
'Fred' (Fellini's *Ginger e Fred*), 103
Freud, Sigmund, 24
Fulgor production company, 75
Fulton, Keith, 113–14

Gallimard publishing house, 49
Garabit viaduct, *plate 34*
Garbo, Greta, 111, 112
Garmati, Michel, 45
Geffroy, Gustave, 117
'Gelsomina' (Fellini's *La Strada*), 100
Gemara, 50
Genet, Jean, *plate 8*
   'adame Miroir, 34, 40, 61
   artistic crisis, 34–5, 36, 38–9, 76, 114, 138*n*
   L'Atelier d'Alberto Giacometti, 42
   attitude towards Israel, 51–2
   Le Bagne, 35, 40, 48
   Le Balcon, vii, 34, 35, 38, 44, 52–4, 55–6, 57, 59, 60, *plate 10*, *plate 11*, *plate 20*
   Les Bonnes, vii, 38, 55, 56, 57, 58, 60, *plate 9*

Genet, Jean *(continued)*
  Le Captif amoureux, 38, 50, 51, 58, 60, 122, 133*n*
  concept of God, 49, 132*n*
  correspondence with Frechtman, 5, 40, 47, 59, 133*n*
  death theme in writings, 37, 38, 39–41, 44, 46, 47–8, 51, 52, 92
  'discontinuity' notion, 42, 54
  'dream project', 5, 45, 47–8, 49, 52, 55–61, 104
  Elle, 35
  L'enfant criminel, 34, 40, 61
  L'étrange mot d'. . ., 42, 54, 60–1, 92
  financial accounts, 133*n*
  Les Folles, 44–7, 51
  Fragments, 5, 38–45, 52, 53, 54, 56, 57, 58
  "Fragments d'un discours", 38, 42
  "Fragments d'un second discours", 38, 54
  Le Funambule, 34, 42, 54, 60
  Greece trip (1956), 59
  Greek drama, 59
  homosexuality, 38, 61
  homosexuality and the death instinct, 37, 38, 44, 46, 52, 92
  immortality of the soul, 51
  J'étais et je n'étais pas, 50–2, 137*n*
  Journal du Voleur, 34
  Judaeo-Christian morality, 50
  letter to Sartre, 37, 38, 46
  letters to Ann Bloch, 38, 131–2*n*
  La Lettre à Decimo, 36–7, 43, 54, 56
  literary output, 62
  Madeleine Gobeil interview, 34–5
  Les Maîtres fous film, 58–9
  Les maîtresses de Lenin, 58
  mirror effects, 36, 40, 43–4, 52, 53, 54, 55
  morality, 37, 38, 39, 44, 49, 50, 51, 52, 56–7, 60, 104
  La Mort, vii, 5, 35–6, 45, 47–8, 52, 56, 60, 119, 122, 123
  nature of homosexuality, 37, 38, 40–2, 44, 45, 46, 47, 52, 56, 92
  Les Nègres, vii, 35, 37, 38, 56, 57–8, 59, 60, plates 13–16
  Oeuvres complètes, 44, 56
  Les Paravents, vii, 35, 44, 47, 48, 54, 56–7, 58, 59, 60, 89–90, plates 17–19
  periods of creative sterility, 104
  Peur de mourir, 48–9, 51
  Pompes Funèbres, 55
  "Le Prétexte", 38–40
  Proust's influence on, vii, 36
  Querelle de Brest, 55–6

  Sartre's *Saint Genet, comédien et martyr*, 34–6, 37, 38, 44, 55
  Sartre's theory of homosexuality, 37, 38
  La Sentence, 49–51
  suicidal thoughts, 35, 39–40
  theatre within theatre effects, 44
  theoretical texts, 54–5
  time as sacred, 49
  'treatise on the beautiful', 57–8, 60
  'treatise on the good', 52, 56–7, 60
  Weisweiller parties, 45
'Georges de Coûfontaine' (Claudel's *L'Otage*), 9
' Georges, the Police Chief' (Genet's *Le Balcon*), 44, 52, 54, 56, 57, *plate 10*
Gherardi, Piero, 67, 68
Gide, André, 13
'Gilberte' (Proust's *À la recherche du temps perdu*), 112
Gili, Jean, 66
Gilliam, Terry, 113–14, 138*n*
'Giorgio' (Fellini's *Otto e mezzo*), 100
'Giulietta' (Fellini's *Giulietta degli spiriti*), 68, 101, 102
Gluck, Christoph Willibald, 89
Gobeil, Madeleine, 34–5
Godard, Jean-Luc, 71
Goldish, Matt, 120
Golovinski, Mathieu, 89
'Gonnella' (Fellini's *La Voce della Luna*), 97, 98
Gramont, Elizabeth de, 13
Gregory, André, 2, 114, 122
Il Grifo journal, 77, 78
Grimaldi, Antonio, 77
Grotowski, Jerzy, 114
Guerra, Tonino, 6, 77, 79, 96, 134*n*, 136*n*
'Guido' (Fellini's *Otto e mezzo*), 2, 63, 72, 75, 79, 100, 103
'Guido Zeta' (Fellini's *Il viaggio di G. Mastorna*), 79, 93
Guillemot, Maurice, 117
'Gunther' (Wagner's Ring cycle), 128*n*
'Gustav von Aschenbach' (Visconti's *Death in Venice*), 112
Gyp, 27

Habima Theatre, *plate 9*
Halevy, Moshe, 12
Hals, Frans, 60
Haouka movement, 59
Harlan, Jan, 113, 138*n*
Harlan, Veit, 138*n*
Hart, Roger, 45

Index

Harvard University, 120
Hasidism, 28
'Head of the Revolutionaries' (Genet's *Le Balcon*), 56, *plate 10*
Heijermans, Herman, 12
Hellerau Festival Theatre, 9
Hepburn, Audrey, 111
Herzl, Theodor, 111
Hirsch, Robert, 45, 46
Hitler, Adolf, 17, 18, 19
Holocaust, 16
Holy Trinity, 119
homosexuality
   and the death instinct, 37, 38, 40, 44, 46, 52, 92
   Genet's writings, 37, 38, 40–2, 44, 45, 46, 47, 52, 56, 92
   Sartre's theory, 37, 38
Honegger, Arthur, 8, 13, 23, 129*n*
Huillet, Danièle, 109

Ibert, Jacques, 13
Ibn Ezra, 20
'Iole' (Fellini's *Il viaggio di G. Mastorna*), 86, 99–100
Ionesco, Eugène, 53, 114
'Irma' (Genet's *Le Balcon*), 53–4, 55–6, 57, 58, 60
Isaiah (Biblical prophet), 27–8, 130*n*
Italian Society of Authors, 78
Italnoliggio, 75
'Ivo Salvini' (Fellini's *La Voce della Luna*), 97, 98
Izraeli, Razia, *plate 10*

'Jacques Hury' (Claudel's *L'Annonce Faite A Marie*), 31
Jerusalem, National Library of Israel, 119, 120
Jesus Christ, (Claudel's *Tête d'Or* – third version 1949), 21, 22
Jewish calligraphy, 50
'Jewish waiter' (Claudel's *Tête d'Or* – third version 1949), 23–5, 26, 29
Jewish women, in literature, 27
Joan of Arc, 13, 30
Joly, Maurice, 89
'Joseph Jechaïah' (Vigny's *Daphné*), 106
Jouhandeau, Marcel, 45
Judaism, Claudel's works, 8, 11–12, 13–14, 15, 16, 21–6, 33, 104
'the Judge' (Genet's *Le Balcon*), *plate 11*
'Judith Fushiani' (Donnay's *Le Retour de Jerusalem*), 27

Julian the Apostate, 105–6, 107, 108

Kabballah, 28
Kafka, Franz, 139*n*
Kant, Immanuel, 66
Kezich, Tullio
   Fellini biography, 6, 63, 64, 66, 78
   Il viaggio di G. Mastorna screenplay, 6, 63, 79, 84, 136*n*
Khan Theatre, Jerusalem, *plate 10*
Kidron, Ephraim, *plate 9*
Konorti, Shabtai, *plate 20*
Kostantinidis, Damianos, *plates 17–19*
Krasheninnikov, Nikolay Alexandrovich, 12
Kubrick, Stanley, 111–12, 113, 138*n*, *plate 35*
Kurosawa, Akira, 93

La Fontaine, Jean de, 45
Lawrence, T.E., *The Seven Pillars of Wisdom*, 36, 131*n*
Lazare, Bernard, 27
Le Poulain, Jean, 45, 46
Lécroart, Pascal, 128*n*
Leibowitz, René, 109, 110
Leone, Sergio, 77
Leshem Ramati, Ayval, 121
La Libre Parole newspaper, 26
Lioure, Michel, 16, 19, 128–9*n*
'Louis' (Claudel's *Le Pain Dur*), 10
Louis, Duke of Burgundy, 89
'Luisa' (Fellini's *Il viaggio di G. Mastorna*), 79, 83
Luke, Gospel of, 13
Lurianic Kabbalah, 121
Lynch, David, 111
'Mme Lysiane' (Genet's *Querelle de Brest*), 55–6

La Machine à écrire (Cocteau), 45
MacQueen, Steve, 73
'Madame' (Genet's *Les Bonnes*), 55, 57
'Maître Frenhofer' (Balzac's *Le Chef d'oeuvre inconnu*), 1–2, 122
Les Maîtres fous (Rouch), 58–9
Malka, Moshe, *plates 13–16*
Mallarmé, Stéphane
   Hérodiade, 44
   Livre, 2–4, 5, 48, 105, 116, 122, 123
   ultimate work of art as impossible, 125
   Un coup de dés jamais n'abolira le hasard, 36, 131*n*
Malle, Louis
   Marlene Dietrich story, 111
   My Dinner with André, 2, 114, 122

Malle, Louis *(continued)*
    Toby Dammit, 93
Manara, Milo
    France-Culture interview, 6, 66
    Il viaggio di G. Mastorna graphic novel, 6, 62, 77–8, 79, 93, 135*n*, 136*n*, *plate 22*
Manganaro, Jean-Paul, 66
Mangano, Silvana, 69
Mankiewicz, Joseph L., 111
Manuel, Frank E., 120
'Marcello' (Fellini's *La Dolce Vita*), 63, 100
Marchand, Léopold, 130*n*
Marlowe, Christopher, 16
Martin, Saint, 108
Marty, Éric, 51
Masina, Giulietta, 69, 76, 96, 135*n*
'Mastorna' (Fellini's *Il viaggio di G. Mastorna*), viii, 73, 74, 76, 78, 79, 80, 81–90, 91, 95–6, *plate 24*
Mastroianni, Marcello, 66, 73, 96, 111, *plate 24*
Matthew, Gospel of, 13
'Maurice' (Fellini's *Otto e mezzo*), 92, 137*n*
'Max Aruns' (Schoenberg's *Der Biblische Weg*), 111
'Maya' (Fellini's *Otto e mezzo*), 92
Mayer, Andreas, 47, 132*n*
Medrea, Ruxandra, 113
Menasce, Jean de, 28
Menelik, King of Shewa, 17
Meyer-Plantureux, Chantal, 115
Michal (biblical character), 17
'Michel' (Donnay's *Le Retour de Jerusalem*), 27
Michelangelo, *plate 3*
Michelson, Annette, 58
Milhaud, Darius, 8, 9, 13, 15, 28, 128*n*
Mina, 73
Mishnah, 50
Molière, 89
Le Monde, 115
Monet, Claude
    Bassins aux Nymphéas, 117
    "Les Nymphéas, séries de paysages d'eau" exhibition, 118
    Nymphéas project, 116–18, 122, *plates 37–38*
Monicelli, Mario, 67
Monroe, Marilyn, 111
Monteverdi, Claudio, 89
Morrison, Tessa, 121
Moscow International Film Festival, 67
Moser, Thomas, 109

'Moses' (Schoenberg's *Moses und Aron*), 109, 110, 111
Mozart, Wolfgang Amadeus, 60

Nadar, Félix, *plate 32*
Nahman of Breslev, Rabbi, 140*n*
Nahmanides, 20
'Napoleon' (Claudel's *L'Otage*), 9
Napoleon I, Emperor of the French, 18
National Library of Israel, Jerusalem, 119, 120
Nazism, 16, 19, 28
Newman, Paul, 73
Newton, Sir Isaac
    The Chronology of Ancient Kingdoms Amended, 119
    A dissertation upon the Sacred Cubit of the Jews and the Cubits of the Several Nations, 120
    Observations upon the Prophecies of Daniel and The Apocalypse of St John, 119
    theological writings, 119–21, *plate 39*, *plate 40*
Nichols, Mike, 6
Nicholson, Jack, 111
Nickler, Reto, 109
Nietzsche, Friedrich, 49
Nijinsky, Vaslaw, 13
non-being, 140*n*
Norma opera, 43
Notariani, Pietro, 99

'Odette' (Proust's *À la recherche du temps perdu*), 128*n*
Offenbach, Jacques, 9
Ohel Theatre, 12, 13
Olivier, Laurence, 73, 91
'Ommu' (Genet's *Les Paravents*), 44, 57, 58
Orangerie galleries, 118
'Orestes' (Aeschylus's *Oresteia*), 59
'Orian' (Claudel's fourth play to his Coûfontaine trilogy), 8
'Orian' (Claudel's *Le Père humilié*), 10–11, *plate 4*
'Oriane de Guermantes' (Visconti's *Death in Venice*), 112
Ormesson, Wladimir, comte d', 29
Orpheus, 89, 93, 125
'Orso' (Claudel's *Le Père humilié*), 10
Osiris, Wanda, 73
Oxford University, 120

Pacino, Al, 111
Paris Match, 21, 129*n*

Paris Opera, 8, 13
Parr, Audrey, 8, 15, 128*n*
Pasolini, Pier Paolo, 64–5
Péguy, Charles, 26–7
Penini, Avi, *plate 20*
'Pensée' (Claudel's fourth play to his Coûfontaine trilogy), 8, 11–12, 31, 33
'Pensée' (Claudel's *Le Pain Dur*), 10, 128*n*
'Pensée' (Claudel's *Le Père humilié*), 10, 27, 128*n*, *plate 4*
Pepe, Luis, 113–14
Peretz, Isaac Leib, 12
Perret, Jacques, 20
Perryman, Marcus, 6
Pezzola, Pasqualina, 69
Pinelli, Tullio, 67, 70, 71, 97, 134*n*
'Pipo' (Fellini's *Ginger e Fred*), 96, 98
Pirandello, Luigi, *The Mountain Giants*, 4–5, 109
Pirandello, Stefano, 4–5
Pizzi, Pier Luigi, 66, 68, 72, 74, 94
Plato, 89, 92
Playboy, 34–5
Pluto, 125
Poe, Edgar Allan, 93–4
Poirot-Delpech, Bertrand, *plate 8*
' Police Chief' (Genet's *Le Balcon*), 44, 52, 54, 56, 57, *plate 10*
'Pollione' (Bellini's *Norma*), 43
Pontecorvo, Gillo, 57
Pontet, Vincent, *plates 28–30*
Pontina studios, 99
'the Pope' (Claudel's fourth play to his Coûfontaine trilogy), 8
'the Pope' (Claudel's *L'Otage*), 9, 10
'the Pope' (Claudel's *Le Père humilié*), 11
'Porbus, François' (Balzac's *Le Chef d'oeuvre inconnu*), 1–2
Portsmouth, Duke of, 120
Poulet, Robert, 45, 52
'Poussin, Nicolas' (Balzac's *Le Chef d'oeuvre inconnu*), 1–2
Preuves journal, 59
'Princess' (Claudel's *Tête d'Or* – first version 1889), 16–17, 22–3
'Princess' (Claudel's *Tête d'Or* – second version 1895), 23
'Princess' (Claudel's *Tête d'Or* – third version 1949), 19, 21, 22, 23, 24, 25, 26
Protocols of the Elders of Zion, 89
'Prouhèze' (Claudel's *Le Soulier de satin*), 31
Proust, Marcel
  À la recherche du temps perdu, vii, 2, 100, 112–13, 122, 128*n*
  influence on Genet, vii, 36
  Le Temps retrouvé, 2
Proverbs, Book of, 8, 13–15, 17, 23, 30

'the Queen' (Genet's *Le Balcon*), 53
'Querelle' (Genet's *Querelle de Brest*), 56
Quignon, Louise, *plate 4*

Racine, Jean, 138*n*
Rampling, Charlotte, 112
Ravel, Maurice, 13
Raz, Jacob, *plate 10*
Rebatet, Lucien, 128*n*
Reform Judaism, 111
Reggiani, Serge, 113
Régnier, Henri de, 4
Rembrandt, 48–9, 54, 56, 60
Rémond, Marie, 135*n*, *plates 28–30*
Renard, Jules, 26
Renoir, Jean, *La Règle du jeu*, 128*n*
Richter, Hans, 75
Rizzoli, Angelo, 67, 68
Rochefort, Marquis de, 26
'Rodrigue' (Claudel's *Le Soulier de satin*), 31
'Roger, Head of the Revolutionaries' (Genet's *Le Balcon*), 56, *plate 10*
Rogers, Ginger, 96
Rol, Gustavo, 69, 73–4, 78, 122, 135*n*, 136*n*
Rondi, Brunello
  Ginger e Fred, 96
  relations with Fellini, 64
  Il viaggio di G. Mastorna, 5, 63, 64, 67, 70–1, 72, 79, 91
Rondi, Umberto, 6, 79
Rotunno, Giuseppe, 66, 68, 72
Rouch, Jean, 58
Rozen, Aliza, *plate 20*
Rubinstein, Ida
  background, 13
  Claudel's biblical drama with music, 8, 14, 15, 16
  Claudel's *Jeanne d'Arc au bûcher*, 13
  Claudel's letters, 128*n*
  Claudel's *La Sagesse*, 13, 23
  leaves France (1940), 15

'Lieutenant Sablon' (Genet's *Querelle de Brest*), 56
'Saïd' (Genet's *Les Paravents*), 44, 57
Saint Victor, Paul de, 32
'Saint-Loup, Gilberte de' (Proust's *À la recherche du temps perdu*), 2, 128*n*
Salerno, Enrico Mario, 76

'Salvini' (Fellini's *La Voce della Luna*), 97, 98
Samostrata, Lucian, 89
Samuel, Book of, 17
'Sandra' (Visconti's *Sandra*), 112
'Saraghina' (Fellini's *Otto e mezzo*), 100, 101–2
'Sarah' (Claudel's fourth play to his Coûfontaine trilogy), 8, 11, 31, 33
Sartre, Jean-Paul
  Genet's dream project, 52
  Genet's letter, 37, 38, 46
  Saint Genet, comédien et martyr, 5, 34–6, 37, 38, 44, 55
  theory of homosexuality, 37, 38
Saul, King of Israel, 17
'Savini' (Cavazzoni's *Il poema dei lunatici*), 97
Schoenberg, Arnold, *plate 33*
  Der Biblische Weg, 111
  Die Jakobsleiter, 110
  Judaism, 110–11
  Moses und Aron, 109–11
  Pierrot lunaire, 110
  Protestantism, 110, 111
Schulsinger, Joseph, 28
Sega, Ercole, 66–7, 76
Sénémaud, Lucien, 39, 40
Serouya, Henri, 20
Servius Tullius, King of Rome, viii
Shakespeare, William, 60
Shawn, Wallace, 114
Shuster, Yaffa, *plates 13–16*
'Sichel' (Claudel's *Le Pain Dur*), 9–10, 27, 128*n*
'Siegfried' (Wagner's Ring cycle), 16, 18
Silman, Yehuda Kaddish, 12
'Simon Agnel' (Claudel's *Tête d'Or* – first version 1889), 16–17, 18–19, 22
'Simon Bar Yona' (Claudel's *Tête d'Or* – third version 1949), 20, 21–2, 23–6, 29, 92
Socrates, 89
'Solange' (Genet's *Les Bonnes*), 57, 58
Solomon's Temple, 119–21, *plate 40*
Sonatine Publishers, 6, 64, 70, 78
'Sophie Von Essenbeck' (Visconti's *The Damned*), 112
Stamp, Terence, 94
'Stello' (Vigny's *Daphné*), 106, 107
Stéphane, Nicole, 112
Sternfeld, Moshe, *plate 10*
Stourdzé, Sam, 66
Straub, Jean-Marie, 109

Stravinsky, Igor, 13
'Swann, Madame' (Proust's *À la recherche du temps perdu*), 112
'Swann' (Proust's *À la recherche du temps perdu*), 128*n*
'Sygne' (Claudel's *L'Otage*), 9, 10, 33
Szpirglas, Philippe, *plates 13–16*

Tabernacle, 119–20, *plate 39*
Talmud, 50
Tamburlaine, 16
Tassone, Aldo, 6, 64, 65, 66
Temple of Ezekiel, 121
Temple of Solomon, 119–21, *plate 40*
Les Temps Modernes journal, 5, 37, 38, 45
'Tête d'Or' (Claudel's *Tête d'Or* – first version 1889), 16, 17, 18–19
'Tête d'Or' (Claudel's *Tête d'Or* – third version 1949), 23, 26
Théâtre de L'Atelier, *plate 2*
Théâtre des Champs-Elysées, 11
Théâtre du Vieux Colombier, 11
Théâtre National de Bretagne, *plate 3*
Third Temple, 119
Tiresias, 58
'Toby Dammit' (Fellini's *Toby Dammit*), 93–6, 98
Tognazzi, Ugo, 76
Tosi, Pierre, 112
Toto the clown, 73, 137*n*
Toulouse-Lautrec, Mapie de, 46
La Traviata (opera), 43
'Trigorin' (Chekhov's *The Seagull*), 4
'Turelure' (Claudel's *L'Otage*), 9, 10, 128*n*
'Turelure' (Claudel's *Le Pain Dur*), 9–10, 128*n*

Vadim, Roger, 93
Valentino, Rudolph, 73
Valéry, Paul
  Cahiers, 123–4
  Eupalinos ou l'Architecte, 36, 131*n*
  Mallarmé's *Livre*, 4
  Sémiramis, 13
  ultimate work of art as impossible, 125
Verlaine, Paul, 3–4
Il viaggio di G. Mastorna (Fellini)
  abandonment of filming by Fellini, 5–6, 63, 74–5
  The accident, 80
  The airport, 87–8
  The ancestors, 86
  The awards ceremony, 84–5, 91, 95–6, 102

Buzzati/Rondi texts, 5, 63, 64, 67, 70, 71–2, 79, 91, 123, 135*n*
Cavazzoni's fictionalized text, 6, 64, 79–80
The cemetery, 86
departure, 88
English text, 78–9
existence after death, vii–ix, 65, 85–6, 91–2, 101, 104, 122, 123
farewell to parents, 87
Fellini: a Director's notebook, 6, 66, 93
Fellini's diary, 63
Fellini's letters to De Laurentiis, 63, 65, 70, 71, 78, 79, 80, 81, 83, 84, 86, 87, 136*n*
Finale, 89
France-Culture radio channel, 6, 111
Guerra screenplay, 6, 77, 79, 96, 134*n*, 136*n*
The identity photo, 86–7
The immortality of the body, 85–6
indifference philosophy, 87, 91, 99, 123
influence on *Ginger e Fred*, 93, 96, 98
influence on *Toby Dammit*, 93–6, 98
influence on *La Voce della Luna*, 93, 97–100
journey structure, 102
La Cicciona's kitchen, 79, 84, 99
The little Chinese girl pilot, 88
Make-up, 84
Mastorna's room, 81
mentions in the rest of Fellini's work, vii–viii, 93–100
Milo Manara's graphic version, 6, 62, 77–8, 79, 93, 135*n*, 136*n*, *plate 22*
mirror of the world, 102, 122
The motel, 80
The night in the customs officers' hut, 88
The nightclub, 79, 81, 83
The orgy of the dead, 83–4
origins, 66–7
The pariahs of the city of the dead, 83
play directed by Marie Rémond, *plates 28–30*
rejection of religion, 101, 102–3
and the sacred, 101, 119
screenplay published by Kezich, 6, 63, 79, 84, 136*n*
screenplay versions, 78–93
The station, 82
The station master's office, 83
as a 'totalising' artwork, 102
The valley in the mountains, 88
Zanelli's *L'inferno immaginario di Federico Fellini*, 6, 63–4, 65, 66, 70, 79, 134*n*

Zapponi screenplay, 6, 77, 79, 93, 134*n*, 136*n*
Vigny, Alfred de, 105–9, *plate 32*
Christianity, 106, 108
Daphné: La deuxieme consultation du Docteur Noir, 105–6, 107–9, 119
Journal, 105–6, 108
Stello: la première consultation du Docteur Noir, 105–6, 107, 108
Les Stoïciens, 108
Villagio, Paolo, 97
'Violaine' (Claudel's *L'Annonce Faite A Marie*), 30–1
Visconti, Luchino, 68, 111–14
cinematographer, 68
Conversation Piece, 112
The Damned, 112
Death in Venice, 112
The Innocent, 112
The Leopard, 112
Ludwig, 112
Proust's *À la recherche du temps perdu*, 112–13, 122
Sandra, 112
Vitez, Antoine, *plate 36*
Voltaire, 52

Wagner, Richard, 18, 110, 128*n*
'waiter' (Claudel's *Tête d'Or* – third version 1949), 23–5, 26, 29
'Warda' (Genet's *Les Paravents*), 58, 60
Weisweiller, Carole, 45–6
Weisweiller, Francine, 45–6
Westfall, Richard, 120
White, Edmund, 36
Wibot, Roger, 45
Wilde, Oscar, 83
Wilder, Billy, 137*n*
Wisdom (Book of Proverbs), 8, 13–15, 17, 23, 30
World Congress of Jews, 28
Worms, Gérard, 46
Worms, Jeannine, 46

Yahuda, Abraham Shalom, 120, 121
Yale University, 120

'Zampanò' (Fellini's *La Strada*), 100
Zanelli, Dario
Fellini's dispute with De Laurentiis, 74
Fellini's founding of Fulgor, 75
Fellini's *Giulietta degli spiriti*, 67
Fellini's letters on *Mastorna*, 6, 65, 79
Fellini's *Otto e mezzo*, 73

Zanelli, Dario *(continued)*
   friendship with Fellini, 63
   L'inferno immaginario di Federico Fellini,
      6, 63–4, 65, 66, 70, 79, 134n

Zapponi, Bernadino, 6, 77, 79, 93, 134n, 136n

Zweig, Stefan, 12